AI-Enabled Apps with .NET MAUI

How to Build Cross-Platform .NET MAUI Apps with the Latest AI Capabilities

Codrina Merigo

Apress®

AI-Enabled Apps with .NET MAUI: How to Build Cross-Platform .NET MAUI Apps with the Latest AI Capabilities

Codrina Merigo
Boffalora d'Adda, Lodi, Italy

ISBN-13 (pbk): 979-8-8688-1816-5   ISBN-13 (electronic): 979-8-8688-1817-2
https://doi.org/10.1007/979-8-8688-1817-2

Copyright © 2026 by Codrina Merigo

Managing Director, Apress Media LLC: Welmoed Spahr
Acquisitions Editor: Ryan Byrnes
Development Editor: Laura Berendson
Editorial Assistant: Gryffin Winkler

Cover designed by eStudioCalamar

Cover image designed by sergeycauselove on freepik (freepik.com)

Distributed to the book trade worldwide by Springer Science+Business Media New York, 1 New York Plaza, New York, NY 10004. Phone 1-800-SPRINGER, fax (201) 348-4505, e-mail orders-ny@springer-sbm.com, or visit www.springeronline.com. Apress Media, LLC is a Delaware LLC and the sole member (owner) is Springer Science + Business Media Finance Inc (SSBM Finance Inc). SSBM Finance Inc is a **Delaware** corporation.

For information on translations, please e-mail booktranslations@springernature.com; for reprint, paperback, or audio rights, please e-mail bookpermissions@springernature.com.

Apress titles may be purchased in bulk for academic, corporate, or promotional use. eBook versions and licenses are also available for most titles. For more information, reference our Print and eBook Bulk Sales web page at http://www.apress.com/bulk-sales.

Any source code or other supplementary material referenced by the author in this book is available to readers on GitHub. For more detailed information, please visit https://www.apress.com/gp/services/source-code.

If disposing of this product, please recycle the paper

To my sibling, Amy, my favorite artist.

You've always encouraged me to keep going, to believe, and to be bold. I hope you never stop chasing what inspires you, because you are meant for great things.

Table of Contents

About the Author

Codrina Merigo is an international speaker, mentor, and coding coach with a long-standing passion for mobile apps and AI. With 13 years of experience in web development with Xamarin.Forms and MAUI, she currently works as a digital product manager, managing mobile apps that have recently migrated to MAUI. Codrina is especially passionate about UX and UI. She speaks at 10–12 conferences per year about MAUI and AI and is a mentor with the .NET Foundation.

About the Technical Reviewer

Shaun Lawrence is an experienced software engineer who has been specializing in building mobile and desktop applications for the past 20 years. He is a recognized Microsoft MVP in Development Technologies for his work helping the community learn and build with Xamarin.Forms and .NET MAUI. His recent discovery of the value he can add by sharing his experience with others has thrust him on to the path of wanting to find any way possible to continue it.

Shaun actively maintains several open source projects within the .NET community. A key project for the scope of this book is the .NET MAUI Community Toolkit where he predominantly focuses on building good quality documentation for developers to consume. Shaun lives in the UK with his wife, two children, and their dog.

Acknowledgments

First, I would like to express my sincere gratitude to Ryan and the entire team at Apress for this incredible opportunity and for their support throughout this journey.

I am also deeply grateful to Shaun, the technical editor who reviewed this book and provided invaluable feedback. Your exceptional attention to detail guided me through every chapter and greatly enhanced the quality of this book.

I would like to thank the teams at Microsoft and .NET MAUI for their ongoing inspiration and for fueling my passion for technology every day.

Finally, I want to thank my family–my partner Daniel, my sister Amy, my mother Petronela, and my father Massimo. Your encouragement gave me the courage to take on this challenge and persevere. I am deeply grateful for all the support, from cooking meals to bringing me coffee or water while I was immersed in writing.

A special shout-out to my cousin Andreea and my longtime friend Alina for their tremendous encouragement and motivation along the way.

CHAPTER 1

Introduction to .NET MAUI

Introduction

In this first chapter, you will get an overview of .NET and .NET MAUI. We will see also the benefits of .NET MAUI and the platforms we can target with this framework. Then we will start preparing our development environment to be ready with the examples we will build together in the following chapters.

Before we dive into the technical details, I just wanted to share with you how I got here. Let us go back 14–15 years when I was just a university student. I studied at the University of Milan, a tiny department in a city 40 kilometers from Milan called Crema. When I had to choose my study path, I had IT in mind, but they also have a cybersecurity path. It sounded remarkably interesting, as the IT systems were growing and spreading, and I already had a pretty good IT knowledge. I felt that by learning cybersecurity, I could gain more skills and learn how to protect people's privacy and even prevent cybercrimes. The course around IT law was one of my favorites!

I had studied ICT in high school too, but my first encounter with programming was back in 2001 when I learned Borland C++ in middle school and simply loved it! During my university time, I discovered that Microsoft offices near Milan offer courses for students who want to learn more about Microsoft technologies. At that time, the Windows Phone operating system had just launched. We had Windows Phone 7 by the time I went into the Microsoft offices. There, the evangelists were showing the secrets behind this new operating system by offering laboratories for students who wanted to learn more. In this way, I got to discover Silverlight, XAML, and C#. I also managed to create simple apps for the Windows Phone. I still remember my very first applicaion, a simple application that randomly generated six numbers between 1 and 90 (the inspiration came from an Italian lottery game). Seeing the app in action on an actual device was an actual adrenaline rush for me. I also remember the thrill when I received

C. Merigo, *AI-Enabled Apps with .NET MAUI*, https://doi.org/10.1007/979-8-8688-1817-2_1

the email that my application had been published to the Windows Phone Store. That email is pinned on my mailbox, and I am happy to share that with you after all these years! You can see the e-mail content in Figure 1-1.

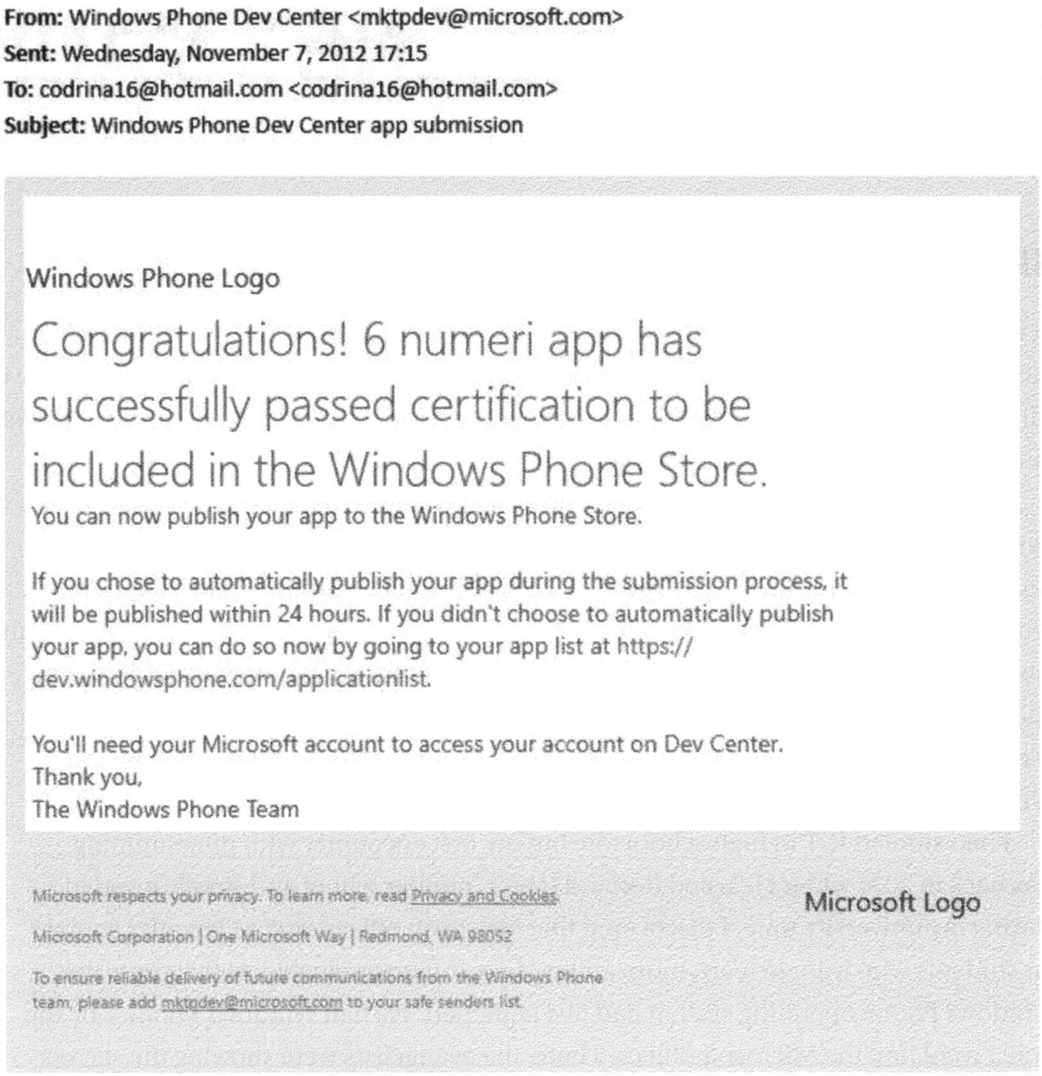

From: Windows Phone Dev Center <mktpdev@microsoft.com>
Sent: Wednesday, November 7, 2012 17:15
To: codrina16@hotmail.com <codrina16@hotmail.com>
Subject: Windows Phone Dev Center app submission

Windows Phone Logo

Congratulations! 6 numeri app has successfully passed certification to be included in the Windows Phone Store.

You can now publish your app to the Windows Phone Store.

If you chose to automatically publish your app during the submission process, it will be published within 24 hours. If you didn't choose to automatically publish your app, you can do so now by going to your app list at https://dev.windowsphone.com/applicationlist.

You'll need your Microsoft account to access your account on Dev Center.
Thank you,
The Windows Phone Team

Microsoft respects your privacy. To learn more, read Privacy and Cookies.

Microsoft Corporation | One Microsoft Way | Redmond, WA 98052

To ensure reliable delivery of future communications from the Windows Phone team, please add mktpdev@microsoft.com to your safe senders list.

Microsoft Logo

Figure 1-1. *Email from Windows Store capture*

As I continued my studies and started to work with Microsoft technologies, my passion for mobile development grew even more. I was a .NET and web developer when I had the opportunity to become a Xamarin developer in a medical company, thanks to a great Microsoft MVP and friend, Alessandro Del Sole. I will forever be grateful to him as he introduced me to Xamarin and Xamarin.Forms. As different mobile operating systems were available around the world and as a very curious person, it felt natural to dive into cross-platform development and understand how an app can target all available platforms. As you might remember, Windows Phone has been discontinued, and the new focus is Android and iOS. With our .NET background, Xamarin was the natural choice when we started building a consumer app in the medical field. Now, the application we started to work on more than seven years ago has been migrated to .NET MAUI, and it is helping people around the world!

Since I started university and discovered the Microsoft community here in Italy, I went to so many conferences and met amazing speakers. I was so inspired by that community and admired their work, and wished I could, one day, have the same positive impact on others.

As I was diving into Xamarin.Forms, I also got into the first challenges, one of them being UI testing. As I managed to learn how to write UI tests, I also thought that other developers could benefit from my experience, so I decided to propose my very first technical session at a big European conference to share my experience. I was selected for the first edition of XamExpertDay (today known as MauiDay). The same session has been selected to be part of .NET Conf: Focus on Xamarin 2020. I have received feedback from people around the world who had the same issues as me in the beginning. Helping others is the best feeling ever. I finally started to feel more connected with the community, and it motivated me to continue presenting my sessions at conferences all over the world, meeting so many great people and trying to make a difference. Now, blending my two passions, cross-platform development and AI, into this book is another way for me to stay connected and feels amazing. We will see more about AI and how I got there in the next chapters, so let's focus on .NET.

.NET

.NET is a free, cross-platform, open source development platform for building diverse types of applications. With .NET, you can use multiple languages, editors, and libraries to build for web, mobile, desktop, games, IoT, and more. Or my personal favorite definition: it is the platform for building anything!

You can write .NET apps in C#, F#, or Visual Basic.

- C# is a simple, modern, object-oriented, and type-safe programming language.

- F# is a programming language that makes it easy to write succinct, robust, and performant code.

- Visual Basic is an approachable language with a simple syntax for building type-safe, object-oriented apps.

I am for sure a C# girl, but for MAUI, I go XAML first–what does this even mean? Stay tuned as we will see this in the following chapters!

.NET MAUI

Moving on with .NET MAUI, the acronym for .NET Multi-platform App UI and the successor of Xamarin.Forms, .NET MAUI is a cross-platform open source framework that helps developers to create, build, and package mobile and desktop applications written in C# and XAML. It allows to target mobile, including tablets, for Android and iOS, and desktop, Windows, or macOS, all from one single codebase. It can also target Tizen TVs and screens provided by Samsung.

Note   You can find it on GitHub at *https://github.com/dotnet/maui*.

You will just need to write code once, which will be able to run everywhere thanks to a single API. You will focus on writing your application and .NET MAUI will take care of the platform-specific layer. You will have a single project, which will share code, tests, and business logic across the platform.

Additional options for sharing code between web and client include .NET MAUI Blazor, which allows you to integrate web-based technologies directly within a .NET MAUI application. This book will not cover the Blazor part, but I am sure you will be able to easily extend the examples.

In .NET MAUI, accessing platform-specific features is easier than you might think, and there are a few handy ways to do it. For quick differences between platforms, you can use conditional compilation like *#if ANDROID* or *#if IOS* right in your shared code. If you want to keep things cleaner and more organized, partial classes let you split platform-specific implementations into their own files inside the *Platforms* folder. For a more scalable setup, especially if your app grows, it's a good idea to use interfaces and dependency injection—this way you can register the right implementation for each platform without cluttering your shared logic. And if you ever need full control, .NET

MAUI gives you direct access to the native APIs as .NET for Android, .NET for iOS, .NET for macOS (Mac Catalyst), or the Windows UI Library (WinUI) 3. In Figure 1-2, you can see a simplified diagram of where we are.

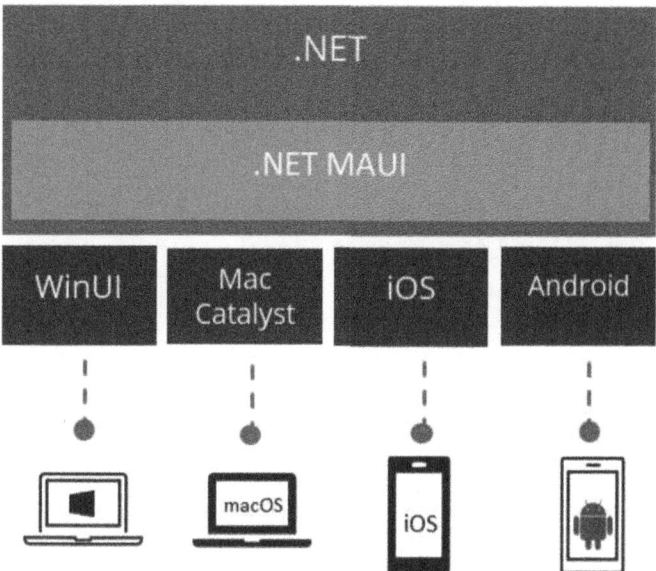

Figure 1-2. *.NET MAUI-supported platforms*

.NET MAUI Focus

.NET MAUI provides direct access to over 60 device platform features through C#, including isolated storage, sensors, geolocation, and more. With a single codebase, and project, you can target multiple devices while managing cross-platform resources like images, icons, and splash screens (the first screen you see when your application is up and running). On Windows, .NET MAUI integrates with WinUI, enabling apps to leverage the latest native features on supported versions of Windows 10 and 11.

The result of your project will be a native application. If you are familiar with mobile app packages, you have surely heard about .aab for Android and .ipa for iOS; these will be exactly our outputs. In Figure 1-3, you can see a simplified view of the different architectures on the supported platforms.

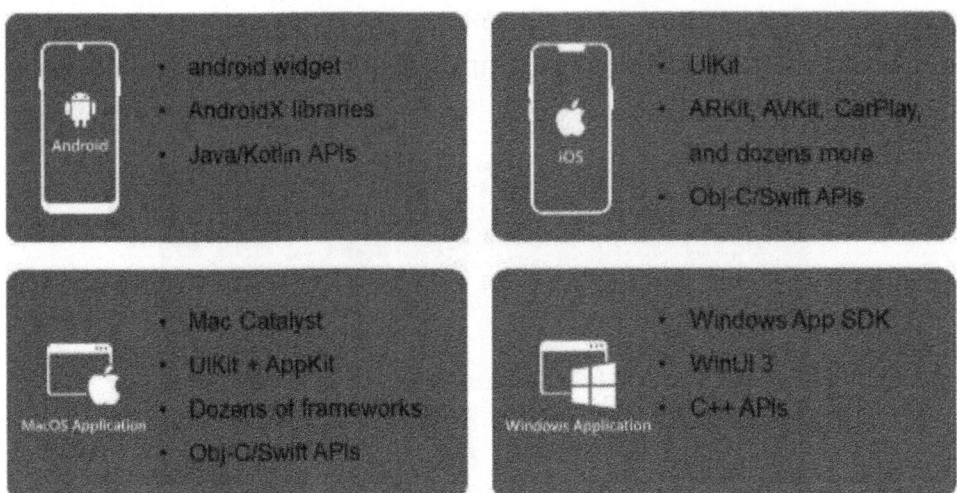

Figure 1-3. *Native applications components*

This also simply means that if you do not have particular UI requirements, your controls will translate to the specific implementation on the targeted platform. When you use controls that look totally different on the platform, you will get the operating system rendering of the component. For example, you can see in Figure 1-4 how a slider is translated on iOS or Android.

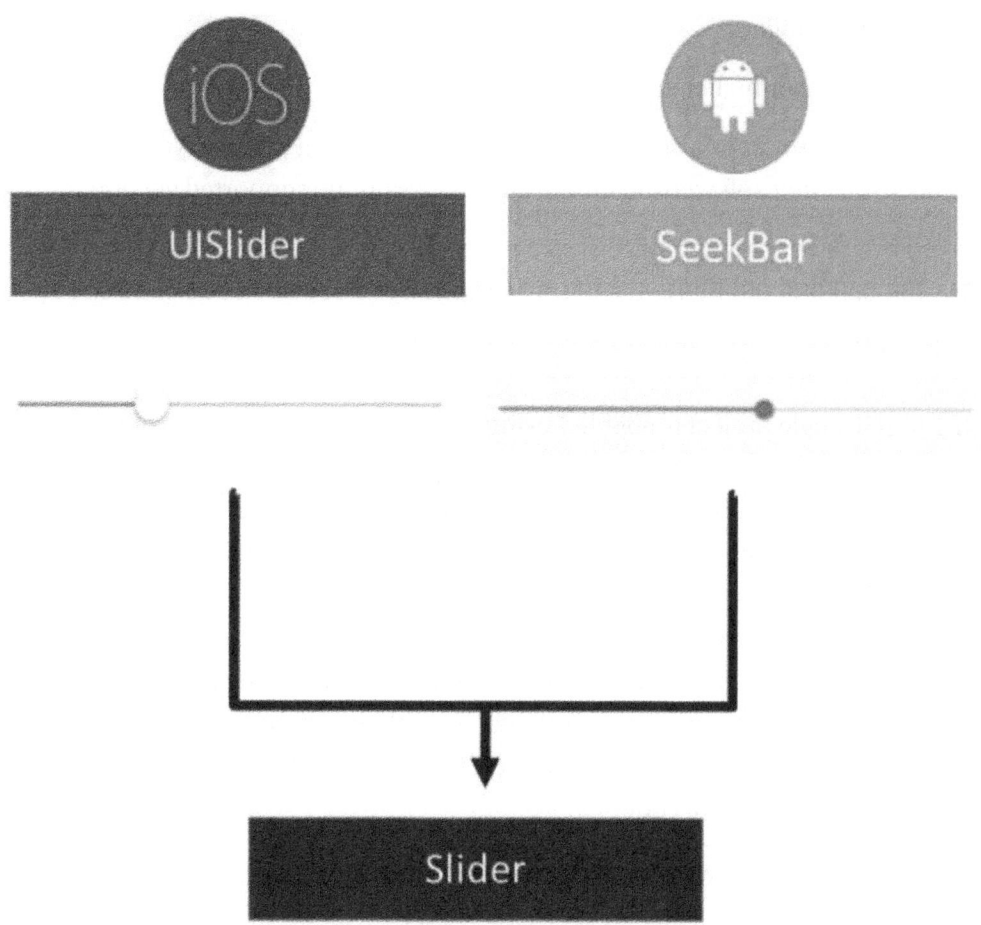

Figure 1-4. *Sample image for a slider component*

.NET Multi-platform App UI (.NET MAUI) apps can be developed for the following platforms:

- Android 5.0 (API 21) or higher

- iOS 12.2 or higher

- macOS 12 or higher, using Mac Catalyst

- Windows 11 and Windows 10 version 1809 or higher, using Windows UI Library (WinUI) 3

.NET MAUI Blazor apps have the following additional platform requirements:

- Android 7.0 (API 24) or higher

- iOS 14 or higher

- macOS 12 or higher, using Mac Catalyst

.NET MAUI Blazor apps also require an updated platform-specific WebView control. Please check the Microsoft website for the latest news on the supported version.

Note   You can find out more at `https://learn.microsoft.com/dotnet/maui/supported-platforms?view=net-maui-9.0`.

.NET MAUI single project is enabled using multitargeting and the use of SDK-style projects. To be able to create your app, additional packages will need to be installed. Windows app SDK is required for windows; for android development, the Android SDK and JDK are required and a Networked Mac, with the latest version of Xcode installed, is needed for iOS development.

Even though UI is emphasized within the acronym, we can go beyond it; with simple access to APIs, we can in fact access services and features belonging to each platform. We can perform different app actions and interact with the clipboard, device sensors, file system, or the network. We can handle notifications or for desktop apps create a second window with literally a line of code!

```
var SecondWindow = new Window { Page = new NewPage1 {  } };
Application.Current.OpenWindow(secondWindow);
```

Looks really nice! I didn't want to scare you from Chapter 1 with code blocks, but it is really that simple! So, let's move on and prepare our environment to see .NET MAUI in action.

Prepare Your Development Environment

To be able to follow all the examples in this book, you will need to have the latest version of Visual Studio installed. You can also use Visual Studio Code. If you prefer Visual Studio Code, remember to install the .NET MAUI Extension (the C# and C# Dev Kit extensions will automatically be installed as dependencies).

Note   You can find more info on the system requirements for installing Visual Studio at `https://learn.microsoft.com/visualstudio/ releases/2022/system-requirements`.

Within this book, I will be using Visual Studio Professional 2022 on a Windows PC with the Android SDK installed. The Visual Studio Community version can also be used to follow along with the examples. When you sign into Visual Studio Community, you get access to a broad set of free developer tools, including Azure credits, and more as part of Visual Studio Dev Essentials.

Please refer to the license terms on `https://visualstudio.microsoft.com/ license-terms/vs2022-ga-community/`.

You will also require an Azure account, an OpenAI account, and a Google Gemini account. Unfortunately, a free account in OpenAI is no longer available, but with a simple "*Pay as you go*" account, currently priced at $5 + taxes, you can test and get to see *ChatGPT* in action.

Visual Studio Setup

If you want to install Visual Studio, during the installation remember to flag the .NET Multi-platform App UI development box to get started.

If you already have Visual Studio, open your Visual Studio Installer as shown in Figure 1-6, click *Modify* and select the .NET Multi-platform App UI development box as in Figure 1-5.

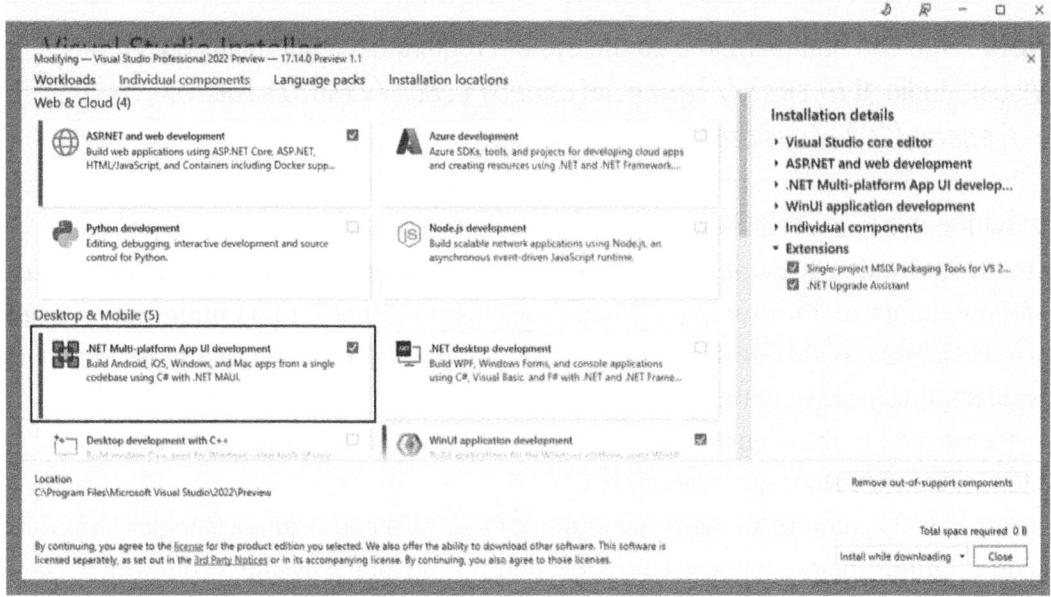

Figure 1-5. *Visual Studio installation window*

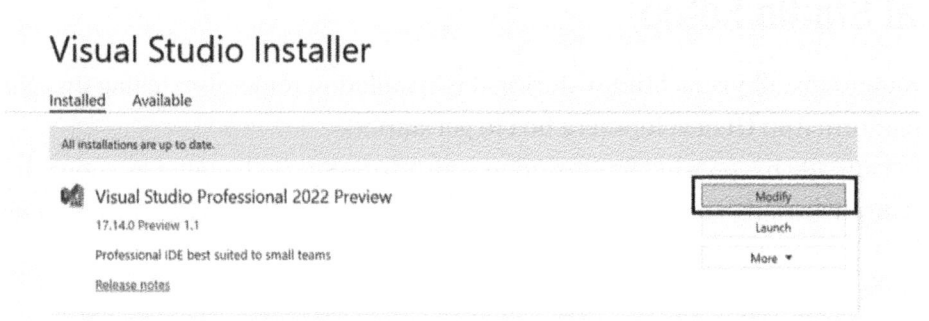

Figure 1-6. *Modify Visual Studio installation*

Create Your .NET MAUI Application

Now we finally come to the fun part–let's create our .NET MAUI application that we will use as the base for all our examples in this book. After you have installed the workload, just click the "Create new project" option as shown in Figure 1-7.

Figure 1-7. *Visual Studio–Create new project*

.NET MAUI App should be there as soon as you search for ".NET MAUI", as in Figure 1-8. Select the first option .NET MAUI App, name your project, and select the latest framework version.

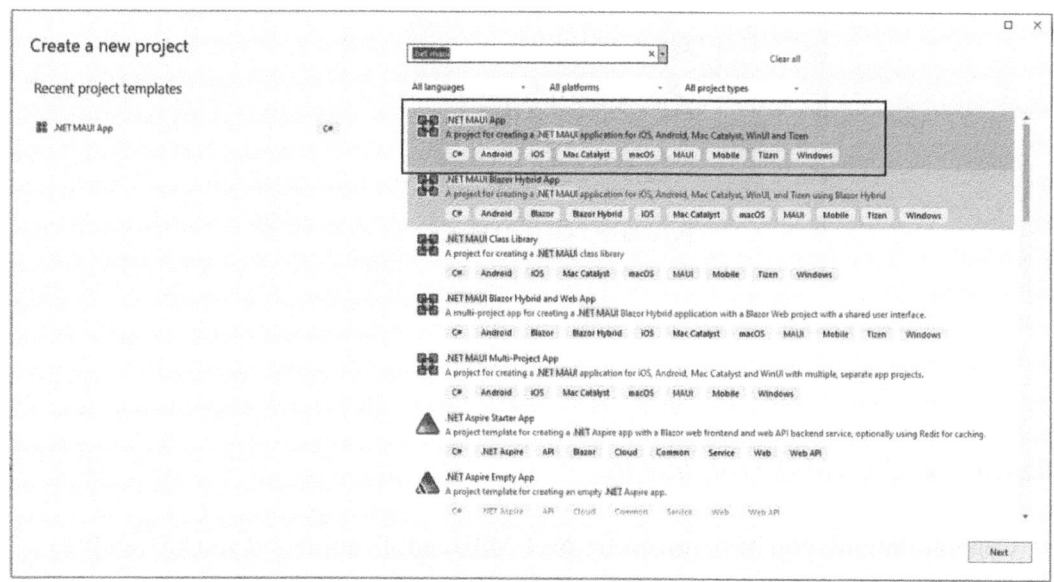

Figure 1-8. *Visual Studio–.NET MAUI project*

Visual Studio will then do the magic for you, and you will see your app ready to be used within all of the platforms that we have seen in the intro chapter–Android, iOS, Mac Catalyst, Tizen, and Windows. In Figure 1-9 you can see the newly created solution contents.

11

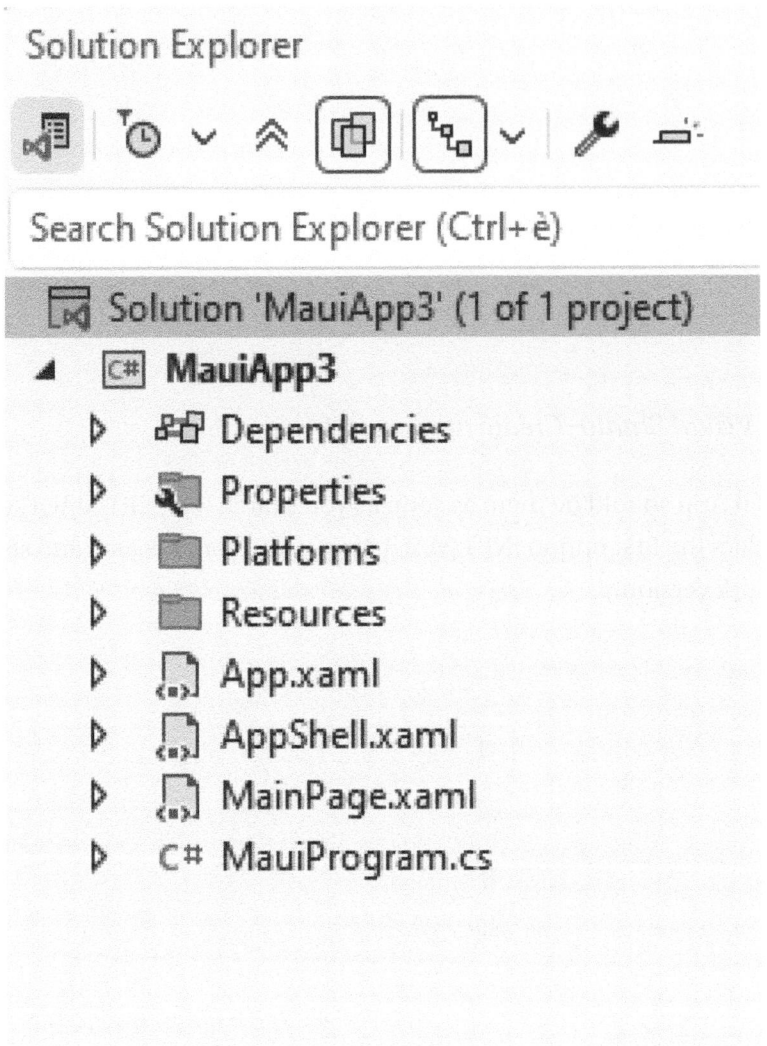

Figure 1-9. *.NET MAUI solution tree*

Congratulations, you have now your .NET MAUI application and you are ready to follow all the examples in this book! We will see the solution files in detail later on, but first let's get an overview of AI to be ready to create our AI-enabled apps!

Summary

In this first chapter, I shared my personal story of how I began my mobile development journey and went down the memory lane of the path that got me here. Along the way, you have also learned what .NET MAUI is–Microsoft's powerful cross-platform framework for building native apps for Android, iOS, macOS, and Windows using a single codebase. We have also seen the steps on how to prepare your development environment using Visual Studio, ensuring you are ready to follow the examples from the next chapters. You have also created your (maybe) very first .NET MAUI application–first of many more!

Now, as we look ahead to the next chapter, we'll begin exploring the exciting world of artificial intelligence (AI). You'll get familiar with key concepts and terminology in the AI landscape and understand the different types of AI services available today. We'll focus especially on Azure AI–Microsoft's cloud-based platform that brings powerful AI capabilities into your applications. We will get an idea of how AI works behind the scenes, and the next chapter will set the foundation for your AI journey.

CHAPTER 2

Introduction to AI

Introduction

In this chapter, you will get an introduction about artificial intelligence (AI) and learn some basic definitions about AI. You will also get an overview of the most common AI services with a focus on Azure AI.

These days, as you visit different websites, you might be greeted by a pop-up, usually in the right bottom corner of the page. This pop-up invites you to do an action or offers to help you navigating the website or the services that the website is offering. These chat boxes are called "chatterbot"—a term later shortened to "chatbot"—and are designed to simulate a human interaction. You can find them in different channels too, like in social media or communication platforms. As a Xamarin.Forms developer, I was curious about how to integrate a chatbot into a mobile application, so I created a dedicated session to explore it and presented it at some conferences. The implementation was relatively straightforward, but what truly surprised me was learning about the origins of chatbots. The very first one, named Eliza, was developed in 1966 by Joseph Weizenbaum. Eliza was a pioneering chatbot designed to simulate a conversation with a psychotherapist. It used open-ended questions inspired by Carl Rogers' conversational techniques to encourage users to open. Even though AI and chatbots are far more advanced and widespread today, the desire to converse with computers is something that has fascinated us since the early days of computing. This was my first in-depth encounter with some form of AI, more than five years ago, and now I feel that AI is part of our daily life.

© Codrina Merigo 2026
C. Merigo, *AI-Enabled Apps with .NET MAUI*, https://doi.org/10.1007/979-8-8688-1817-2_2

AI Is Everywhere

While creating your .NET MAUI application in Visual Studio, maybe you already ran into AI. GitHub Copilot was there for me as you can see in Figure 2-1 and how Microsoft defines it–the AI companion or, as I see it, another chatbot waiting for your input. You can try to use GitHub Copilot within the examples of the book, but you don't necessarily have to. Remember that it uses *"the power of AI to help you"* as it's in its tagline.

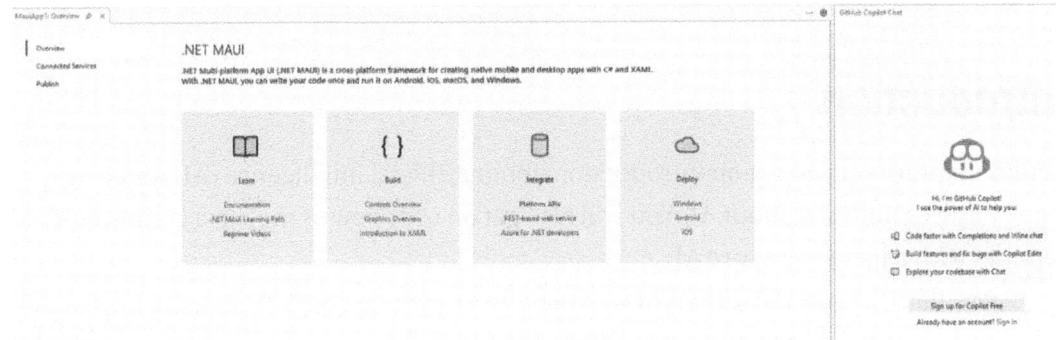

Figure 2-1. *GitHub Copilot*

AI is indeed everywhere, now even on your chat applications, websites, or the Microsoft Office tools, but what is AI, artificial intelligence? **AI** is a subfield within computer science, specifically data science, associated with constructing machines that can simulate human intelligence. This is especially useful for solving complex problems using massive amounts of data with high accuracy and minimum costs. In the following diagram, in Figure 2-2, you can see a simplified version of the areas within data science.

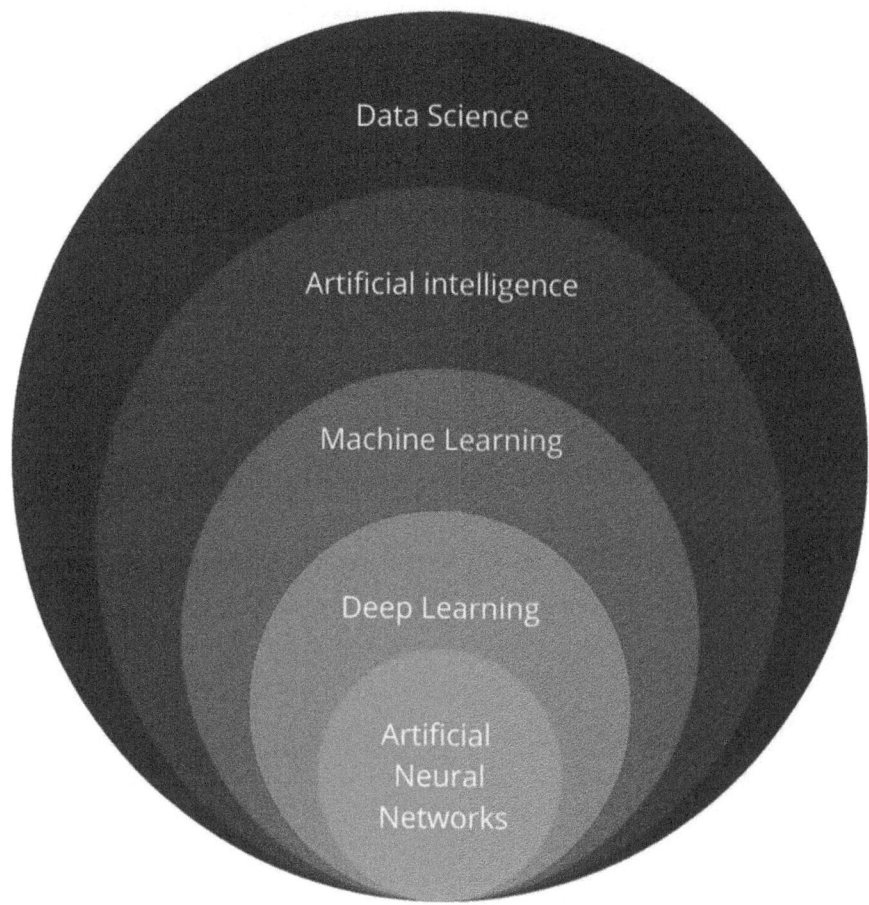

Figure 2-2. *Simplified diagram*

Data science is the field of study that combines programming, statistics, and domain knowledge to extract meaningful insights and knowledge from data. It involves collecting, analyzing, and interpreting substantial amounts of information to help organizations make data-driven decisions or discover hidden patterns.

Machine learning is a specialized branch of artificial intelligence (AI) that empowers systems to automatically learn and evolve through experience, without the need for explicit programming. Instead of relying on a predetermined set of instructions, ML algorithms process vast amounts of data, identify complex patterns, and continuously refine their understanding. This allows them to make increasingly accurate decisions or predictions over time. Through iterative learning, these systems adapt to the latest information, improving their performance and expanding their capabilities as they encounter more data.

Deep learning is a subset of machine learning that uses neural networks with many layers to automatically learn from substantial amounts of data. It is especially powerful for tasks such as image recognition, speech processing, and natural language understanding. Deep learning models can learn complex patterns on their own, requiring less manual feature engineering. They are typically trained on large datasets and use significant computational power.

Artificial neural networks are models inspired by the human brain, consisting of layers of interconnected "neurons" that process and transform data. They learn patterns by adjusting the connections between neurons during training. ANNs are used for tasks like image recognition, speech processing, and natural language understanding, making them a core part of deep learning.

However, to make it simple after all these definitions, AI is a **simulation** of human intelligence performed by computer systems and, as such, it might be just an illusion. Keep in mind that, so far, AI does not really "understand" what is being asked, at least not in the way we would. Instead, it recognizes the structure of the query, usually referred to as *prompt*, and produces a response based on what they have learned through machine learning. The answers may seem correct most of the time, but upon further review, it becomes apparent that they are not. You can try this out by asking an AI how it feels about something, and you will see that AI thinks it can actually *feel* it.

AI Models

An AI model is a program or algorithm that uses a set of data which enables it to recognize certain patterns. This allows it, when provided with enough information, to reach a conclusion or make a prediction.

After you have identified your problem to be solved with AI, you will need to perform **five** simple steps. First, gather your database on the problem that you want to solve. Second, clean, prepare, and manipulate your data in order for it to be consistent. Then you will need to train your model. In some AI frameworks, you will need at least five samples of data. The learning part in machine learning is achieved by training the model on the sample datasets. Probabilistic trends and correlations are applied there. Since the learning process can be supervised or semisupervised, data scientists must label the data thoughtfully to optimize the results. If there is a proper feature extraction, supervised learning needs a lower quantity of training data than unsupervised learning. Once your model is trained, you will need to test it as the fourth step and check that everything works as expected. Last and fifth step, you will need to improve, adopt, or extend your model based on your needs. Once your model is trained and tested, you can start using it.

Within the examples of this book, we will rely on already trained and tested models provided by Microsoft, Google, and OpenAI. So, you do not need to be a data scientist, be a machine learning expert, or have data science knowledge to work with these AI models. With some basic flows, which will be covered in the next chapter, you can even add your own AI to a .NET MAUI application if you already have one.

A trending type of artificial intelligence is generative artificial intelligence or gen AI. This is a type of AI that can create new content such as images, stories, videos, music, or even slides. It can act as another content creator or a thought partner for you. Maybe the most famous one is now ChatGPT. We will be looking more into ChatGPT and how to integrate it into our example app in the next chapters.

Overview of AI Services (Azure AI, Google AI, OpenAI)

As AI is everywhere, so are the AI services. It's even likely that, as you read this book, new AI services are being distributed. Most of the cloud providers offer their own services, and big tech companies or open source AI services are already available for us developers to integrate in our projects.

Based on the offerings, we can find prebuilt machine learning models ready to use or custom models that we can personalize based on our requirements. Usually, these services offer, in addition to the models, API for developers, testing UIs and even SDKs. Microsoft with Azure AI, Google with Gemini, or OpenAI–now also in partnership with Microsoft–offer a variety of services. Of course, other providers like Amazon, IBM, Meta, Oracle, etc., offer their own similar services.

We will be focusing on Azure AI, Google Gemini, and OpenAI; all these are online AI services. By the end of this book, we will also see an example with offline AI offering with EDGE.

Azure AI

"Empower all developers to become AI developers"–this is exactly what Azure AI defines itself and it offers plenty of models (more than 1700) and services for developers to get started on the Azure cloud platform. A nice overview of the artificial intelligence and machine learning of Azure can be found at `https://azurecharts.com/overview/aiml` and a snapshot is in Figure 2-3. We will be using mainly Speech + Language and Vision services also known as Cognitive Services.

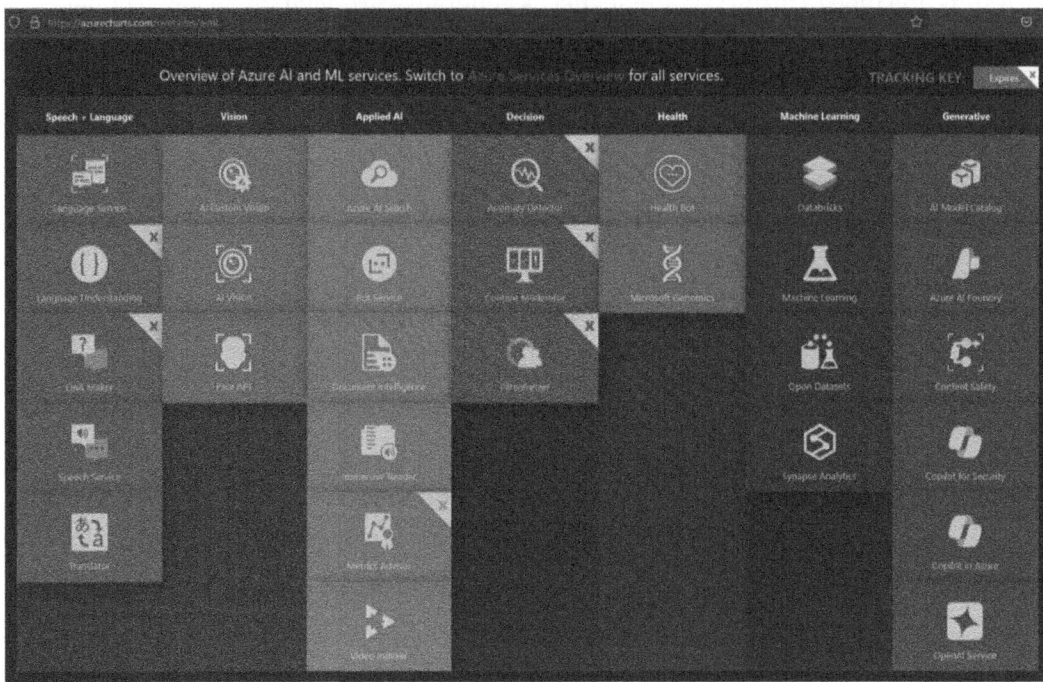

Figure 2-3. *Overview of Azure AI + ML from* `https://azurecharts.com/overview/aim`

Azure AI Foundry is the new place for Azure AI that offers everything you need to start your AI journey. You can start there by trying the demo versions of lots of pretrained models and find what solves your problem. You can easily create a new project, test or customize your models, assess and improve them, and make them ready for your application. In the model catalog, you will find models curated by Azure AI, but also provided by some partners, Azure OpenAI models exclusively available on Azure, and

Hugging Face models. My favorite part is the demo and playground where you can test the models and see the "magic" happening instantly. The same magic that we will integrate into a .NET MAUI application.

Google AI

"Making AI helpful for everyone" is Google's promise for everyone, and we will look at it with a developer eye to understand Google's capabilities through the Gemini ecosystem. Gemini offers more than AI models, but we will use the most famous Google feature: search. Google AI is all about pushing the boundaries of what artificial intelligence can do. They focus on machine learning, helping computers learn from data on their own, and natural language processing, which makes it easier for AI to understand and generate human-sounding language. They're also working on computer vision, teaching machines to "see" and interpret images, and robotics, where AI helps improve how robots function. They also dive into AI ethics research to make sure that AI is developed and used responsibly.

OpenAI

In contrast with Azure or Gemini, which are parts of bigger companies, OpenAI is a focused AI research and deployment company, and its mission is *"to ensure that artificial general intelligence—AI systems that are generally smarter than humans—benefits all of humanity."* Their most famous product so far is ChatGPT, but they also launched Sora as of the end of 2024, a model that can create video from text.

Note   You can try Sora at *https://openai.com/sora/*.

ChatGPT is an example of a model, perhaps the most well-known one, that interacts with the user in a conversational way and has a sibling model, called **InstructGPT**, · which is trained to follow an instruction in a prompt and provide a detailed response. Recently, ChatGPT got its own interface in a canvas that makes it easier to interact with it. GPT is an acronym for *generative pretrained transformer*. That might sound like a sci-fi movie, but it's nothing more than a framework for the uprising generative artificial intelligence, the type of AI that can generate text, images, videos, slides, maps, or other form of data you might need. It is based on deep learning and has the capability to generate novel human-like content that is catchy for users which might be the reason why it is so popular now. It has quickly become the go-to assistant for lots of different businesses and people these days, but as stated on the chat interface, it is crucial to "check important info."

Summary

In this chapter, we've taken our first steps into the world of artificial intelligence. You have learned what AI is, starting with some basic definitions, and getting a feeling for the different types of AI services that are available. We also walked through the AI services we will be using throughout this book.

Coming up in the next chapter, you will learn how to call REST APIs right from your. NET MAUI app, connect to AI APIs, and handle their responses. We will also explore how to integrate AI-generated content into your apps and cover some best practices for your projects to help you build smarter and more intelligent applications.

CHAPTER 3

Integrating AI Capabilities in .NET MAUI

Introduction

In this chapter, you will get an overview of how to use the APIs provided by the AI services and how to better use them in .NET MAUI. We will also go over some best practices and tips to save time when implementing them in .NET.

We will see some basic definitions again that will help you work with the APIs. You will start getting more code blocks to play around with artificial intelligence and see it finally in action. Keep in mind coding best practices. I will be using some commenting too and basic error handling. I will try my best to use descriptive names, but as you will see, I am not the best creative person when it comes to naming variables or creating UI. If you find a variable named temp, don't be scared; it is not temperature, tempura, or temple–it is just *temporary* that got *permanent*. We won't be adding unit tests or even UI tests to the application that we build but I would strongly encourage you to do so in your production apps. Remember that GitHub Copilot Chat can help you along the way with creating the testing classes directly from Visual Studio. I can recommend you to be specific in your asks to Copilot and what you really want to test and review everything to ensure accuracy before pushing that commit to the main branch!

How to Call REST APIs in .NET MAUI

In our application, we will interact with the different AI services by sending a request and processing a response. All these services usually provide REST (REpresentational State Transfer) API and HTTP verbs. They are using the same HTTP verbs that web browsers use to interact with a server by retrieving web pages.

© Codrina Merigo 2026
C. Merigo, *AI-Enabled Apps with .NET MAUI*, https://doi.org/10.1007/979-8-8688-1817-2_3

The verbs are

- **GET**: As the name implies, retrieve data from the web service.

- **POST**: Send the request to create a new item of data on the web service.

- **PUT**: Not so obvious, but it is to update an item of data on the web service.

- **PATCH**: Maybe not so common, but it is used to update an item of data on the web service by describing a set of instructions about how the item should be modified.

- **DELETE**: Just delete an item of data on the web service.

In a .NET MAUI app, you can easily connect to a REST API using the **HttpClient** class. This class, built-in .NET I, helps you send HTTP requests and receive responses from a web service. Since API calls can take time, I can recommend to run them asynchronously to keep your app responsive. Whether you're fetching data, sending information, or handling API responses, HttpClient makes it simple to interact with web services in your app.

REST-based web services primarily use JSON (JavaScript Object Notation) to transmit data, as it is a lightweight and efficient data-interchange format and a media type. So, the services we will be using have mainly three parts:

- Base URI (Uniform Resource Identifier)

- HTTP methods like the ones above

- JSON media type

In our .NET MAUI app, we will need a *HttpClient object* declared at the class level, which we will be using all over our application. We can create an *ApiService* and define our GET, POST, PUT, PATCH, and DELETE methods as shown in Listing 3-1.

Listing 3-1. Service implementation

```
using System.Text;
using System.Net.Http.Json;
using System.Text.Json;
```

```csharp
namespace MauiApp.Services
{
    public class ApiService
    {
        private readonly HttpClient _httpClient;

        public ApiService()
        {
            _httpClient = new HttpClient();
        }

    //GET
        public async Task<string> GetDataAsync()
        {
            string url = "myApi";
            try
            {
                var response = await _httpClient.GetStringAsync(url);
                return response;
            }
            catch (Exception ex)
            {
                return $"Error: {ex.Message}";
            }
        }
        //POST
        public async Task<string> PostDataAsync(object data)
        {
            string url = "myApi";
            try
            {
                var response = await _httpClient.
                PostAsJsonAsync(url, data);
                return await response.Content.ReadAsStringAsync();
            }
```

```csharp
    catch (Exception ex)
    {
        return $"Error: {ex.Message}";
    }
}

//DELETE
//pass the id of the item we want to delete
public async Task<bool> DeleteItemAsync(int id)
{
    string url = $"myApi";

    try
    {
        HttpResponseMessage response = await _httpClient.
        DeleteAsync(url);

        if (response.IsSuccessStatusCode)
        {
            Console.WriteLine($"Item {id} deleted successfully.");
            return true;
        }
        else
        {
            Console.WriteLine($"Failed to delete item {id}. Status
            Code: {response.StatusCode}");
            return false;
        }
    }
    catch (Exception ex)
    {
        Console.WriteLine($"Error deleting item {id}: {ex.
        Message}");
        return false;
    }
}
```

```
//PUT
    public async Task<bool> UpdateItemAsync(int id, object updatedItem)
    {
        string url = $"myApi";

        try
        {
            HttpResponseMessage response = await _httpClient.
            PutAsJsonAsync(url, updatedItem);

            return response.IsSuccessStatusCode;
        }
        catch (Exception ex)
        {
            Console.WriteLine($"Error updating item {id}: {ex.
            Message}");
            return false;
        }
    }

    //PATCH
    public async Task<bool> PatchItemAsync(int id, object
    partialUpdate)
    {
        string url = $"myApi";

        try
        {
            string json = JsonSerializer.Serialize(partialUpdate);
            var content = new StringContent(json, Encoding.UTF8,
            "application/json");

            HttpResponseMessage response = await _httpClient.
            PatchAsync(url, content);

            return response.IsSuccessStatusCode;
        }
        catch (Exception ex)
```

```
        {
                Console.WriteLine($"Error updating item {id}: {ex.Message}");
                return false;
        }
    }
  }
}
```

The response we get from *HttpResponseMessage.IsSuccessStatusCode* indicates if our request succeeded or not. Most common response codes are in Table 3-1.

Table 3-1. *Response Status Codes*

Code	Message	Meaning
200	OK	Everything went ok
201	CREATED	A new resource has been created before the response was sent, used for PUT or DELETE
204	NO CONTENT	Successfully processed request and the response is intentionally blank, used for PUT or DELETE
400	BAD REQUEST	The request is not understood by the server
404	NOT FOUND	The requested resource does not exist on the server
409	CONFLICT	The request could not be carried out because of a conflict on the server

Understand How to Use AI APIs, Handle Authentication, and How to Handle Responses

AI services offers AI APIs ready to use, but we will usually need to call an endpoint, authenticate, and provide a location, from some APIs.

Authentication is usually handled with secret keys made available by the services providers. We will be integrating Azure AI, Google AI, and OpenAI services. Make sure you have created accounts with these providers to be able to follow the examples we will tackle in the next chapter.

How to Process AI-Generated Content

While preparing the examples, the natural approach was to use the `async/await` pattern while writing C# code. In this way, we are running the task in the background without using the main thread of our application. This pattern is particularly useful when creating the UI, especially in a mobile app written with .NET MAUI. We will then have our `Task` or `Task<T>` and then we will have a result to process.

As we are requesting some kind of response from an AI service, the users are waiting for a response; we can keep them entertained by showing a progress indicator. So, in our XAML page, we will use the `Activity indicator`. The native one is just fine, but you can always get creative, design your own, and give it a name. `IsRunning` and `isVisible` properties will be false by default, and I will add here my favorite `Color`, red as shown in Listing 3-2.

Listing 3-2. ActivityIndicator code

```
<ActivityIndicator x:Name="LoadingIndicator"
                   IsRunning="False"
                   IsVisible="False"
                   Color="Red"/>
```

In our code behind page, we can handle visibility and progress based on when the response is ready to be displayed to the user as shown in Listing 3-3.

Listing 3-3. Handle LoadingIndicator Visibility

```
// Show the ActivityIndicator
LoadingIndicator.IsVisible = true;
LoadingIndicator.IsRunning = true;

// Call your AI API

// Hide the ActivityIndicator
LoadingIndicator.IsRunning = false;
LoadingIndicator.IsVisible = false;
```

We can also use Background processing or offline mode and retrieve cached response. Of course, we can implement logging, retries, and error messages based on the API we are calling and the related REST API responses.

As you have seen in the console apps we have created to integrate the various API services, we have the key usually as strings, just for testing purposes. As we will create apps in .NET MAUI, we can use the SecureStorage to store our secret keys as they are simple key/value pairs as shown in Listing 3-4.

Listing 3-4. Set SecureStorage value

```
using Microsoft.Maui.Storage;
await SecureStorage.Default.SetAsync("AiSvCKey ", "MY_API_KEY");
```

And then we can easily retrieve the key when we need to use it as shown in Listing 3-5.

Listing 3-5. Read Secure Storage value

```
string apiKey = SecureStorage.GetAsync("AiSvCKey ").Result;
```

To get our responses from the AI services, we can also use SDK or the respective client library. For example, Azure Cognitive Services offer their SDK for different services. A complete list can be found at https://learn.microsoft.com/en-us/dotnet/api/overview/azure/cognitive-services?view=azure-dotnet. You just have to install the desired client library for .NET with NuGet and use your Azure endpoint and API key we created previously.

As you can see in the following example, once we have created our client, we can call the AI service we want, like DetectLanguage, and process the response as shown in Listing 3-6.

Listing 3-6. Class implementatio for the API

```
Uri endpoint = new("<endpoint>");
AzureKeyCredential credential = new("<apiKey>");
TextAnalyticsClient client = new(endpoint, credential);

string text ="ciao.";

try
{
    Response<DetectedLanguage> response = client.DetectLanguage(text);
    DetectedLanguage language = response.Value;

    Console.WriteLine($"Detected language is {language.Name} with a
    confidence score of {language.ConfidenceScore}.");
}
```

```
catch (RequestFailedException exception)
{
    Console.WriteLine($"Error Code: {exception.ErrorCode}");
    Console.WriteLine($"Message: {exception.Message}");
}
```

Most of the time, the AI service response will be in a JSON (JavaScript Object Notation) format. Maybe you have already worked with this format, and you already are familiar with the value:key format and brackets.

There are some simple rules to remember about JSON:

- Strings need to be in quotes.

- Your keys should be in quotes.

- Integers, Booleans, and null values should not have quotes.

- The last field or item in a list has NO ENDING COMMA.

- An array (or list) of data must be in [brackets].

- Your JSON should start and end with {curly braces}.

We will receive a JSON string, as shown in Listing 3-7, and we have to deserialize it. Some services require a JSON as an input, as we saw in the language detection example:

Listing 3-7. JSON Structure

```
{
  "documents": [
    {
      "id": 1,
      "text": "ciao"
    }
  ]
}
```

We can use Newtonsoft.Json for JSON serialization/deserialization. You can install Newtonsoft.Json via NuGet. From Visual Studio, go to Tools ➤ NuGet Package Manager ➤ Manage NuGet Packages for Solution as shown in Figure 3-1. Search for Newtonsoft. Json and install it.

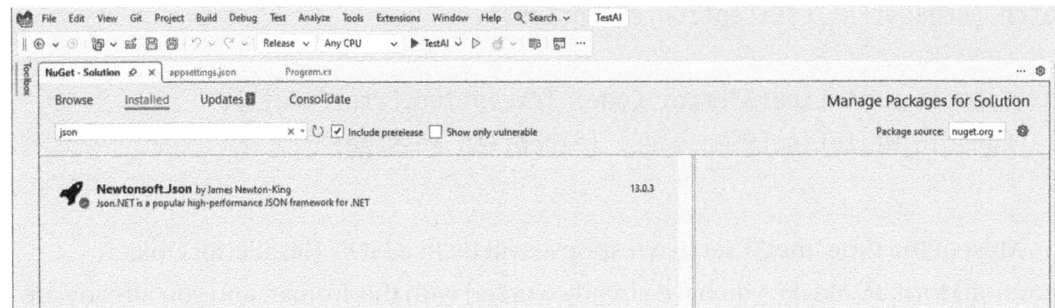

Figure 3-1. *Install Newtonsoft.Json from NuGet*

Note   You can find out more at `https://www.nuget.org/packages/`
`Newtonsoft.Json/13.0.3#show-readme-container`.

You can also install Newtonsoft.Json from the CLI by typing `dotnet add package`
`Newtonsoft.Json`.

The JSON response from the `DetectLanguage` API can be found in Listing 3-8.

Listing 3-8. JSON response

```json
{
  "documents": [
    {
      "id": "1",
      "warnings": [],
      "detectedLanguage": {
        "name": "Italian",
        "iso6391Name": "it",
        "confidenceScore": 1.0
      }
    }
  ],
  "errors": [],
  "modelVersion": "2024-11-01"
}
```

We will then use Newtonsoft.Json to create a model that maps the response, for each property, in c#. We will map to objects using the *[JsonProperty]* attributes as shown in Listing 3-9.

Listing 3-9. JSON Property mapping

```
public class LanguageDetectionResponse
{
    [JsonProperty("documents")]
    public List<DetectedDocument>? Documents { get; set; }

    [JsonProperty("errors")]
    public List<object>? Errors { get; set; }
}

public class DetectedDocument
{
    [JsonProperty("id")]
    public string? Id { get; set; }

    [JsonProperty("warnings ")]
    public List<object>? Wzarning { get; set; }

    [JsonProperty("detectedLanguages")]
    public List<DetectedLanguage>? DetectedLanguages { get; set; }
}

public class DetectedLanguage
{
    [JsonProperty("name")]
    public string? Name { get; set; }

    [JsonProperty("iso6391Name")]
    public string? IsoCode { get; set; }

    [JsonProperty("confidenceScore")]
    public double Confidence { get; set; }
}
```

Then this is how calling our API will look like, with minimal error handling, just for the example purposes. We can have a `ResultLabel` somewhere in our XAML page where we will bind the response from the API into the *Text* property as shown in Listing 3-10.

Listing 3-10. ResultLabel.Text logic

```
string inputText = "Ciao"; // Example input
var result = await AzureLanguageService.DetectLanguageAsync(inputText);

    if (result?.Documents != null && result.Documents.Count > 0)
    {
        var detectedLang = result.Documents[0].DetectedLanguages?[0];

        if (detectedLang != null)
        {
            ResultLabel.Text = $"Detected: {detectedLang.Name} ({detectedLang.
            IsoCode}) \nConfidence: {detectedLang.Confidence:P}";
        }
    }
    else
    {
        ResultLabel.Text = "Language detection failed.";
    }
```

Before using an AI service, we shall take some time to understand how the response is created and how the content is generated. We can also check the response, do some clean up, and filter keywords or inappropriate words that we don't want our user to read. We can use, for example, another AI service, the Azure Content Moderator (`https://learn.microsoft.com/en-us/azure/ai-services/content-moderator/overview`) or Azure AI Content Safety (`https://learn.microsoft.com/en-us/azure/ai-services/content-safety/overview`), to do this. We will delve into a more comprehensive overview of the safety features of AI in Chapter 14.

How to Integrate Azure AI

To integrate Azure AI in our application, first, we will need to create our AI resource. For that, head to the Azure Portal at https://portal.azure.com/ and sign in with your account that has an Azure subscription. As mentioned in Chapter 1, you can sign up for a free resource, a student free one, or a *"Pay as you go"* resource.

Second, search for AI services inside the search bar and create a new resource as shown in Figure 3-2.

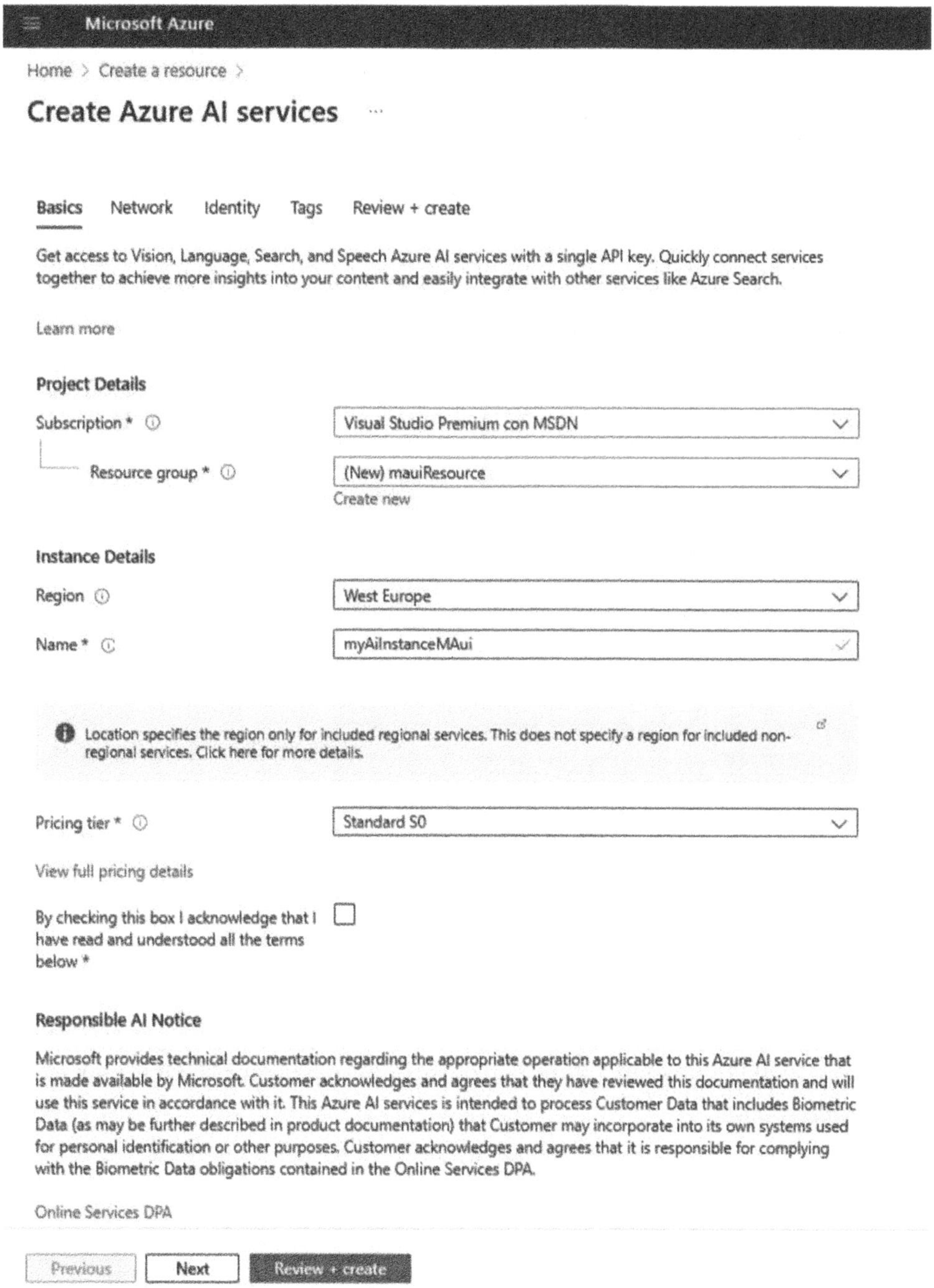

Figure 3-2. *Create Azure AI services*

You will need to fill in the following information:

- **Subscription**: Select your Azure subscription.

- **Resource Group**: Choose an existing resource group or create a new one.

- **Region**: Select an available region that fits your needs, I am in Italy, so I go with West Europe.

- **Name**: Enter a distinctive name for your resource. This is unique so to be creative here!

- **Pricing Tier**: Select *Standard S0* for the pricing tier.

After the acknowledgment checkbox, click *Review + create* and your resource will be shortly created for you and ready to be used.

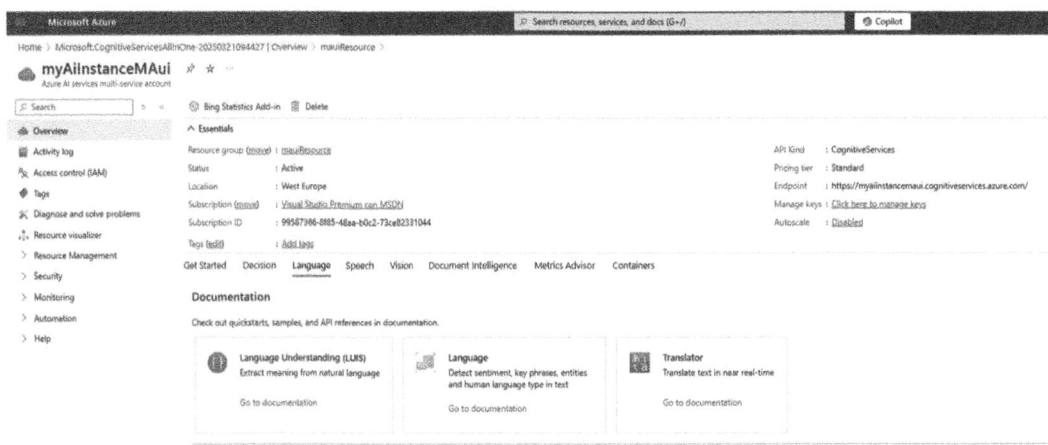

Figure 3-3. *Resource overview screen*

Navigate to your newly created resource by clicking the "Go to resource" button. The resource screen is shown in Figure 3-3. In this new page, on the left menu, expand *Resource management*.

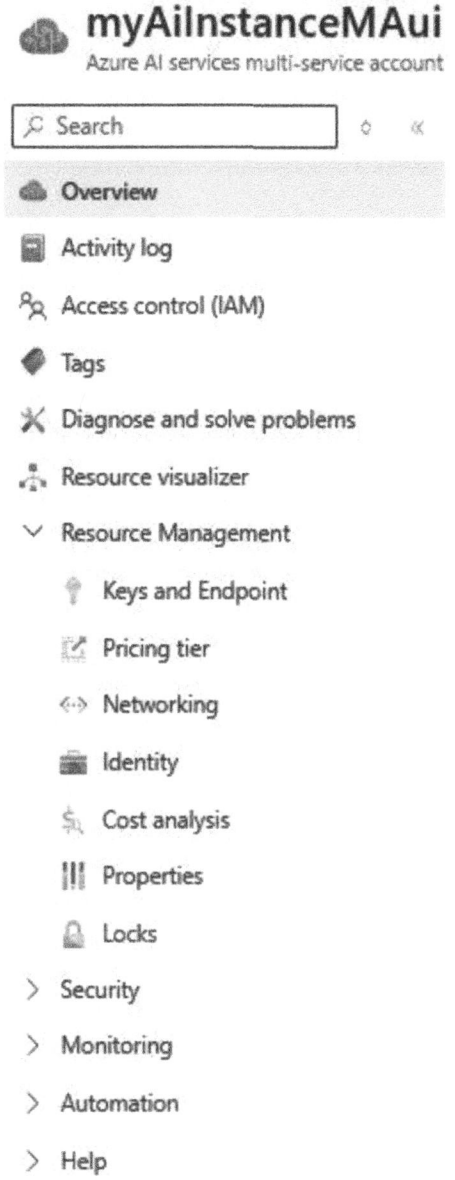

Figure 3-4. *AI service instance menu*

In this section, shown in Figure 3-4, you will find the info you need to use the APIs in your application. By clicking Keys and Endpoint, you will find the info we need to call our REST APIs. This is shown in Figure 3-5. Here you will find your keys, the Location/Region info, and more importantly our Endpoint for the AI services, also known as Cognitive Services. You will have two different keys, but you can use either of them for your API Calls. One common practice is to use one for development and another for production.

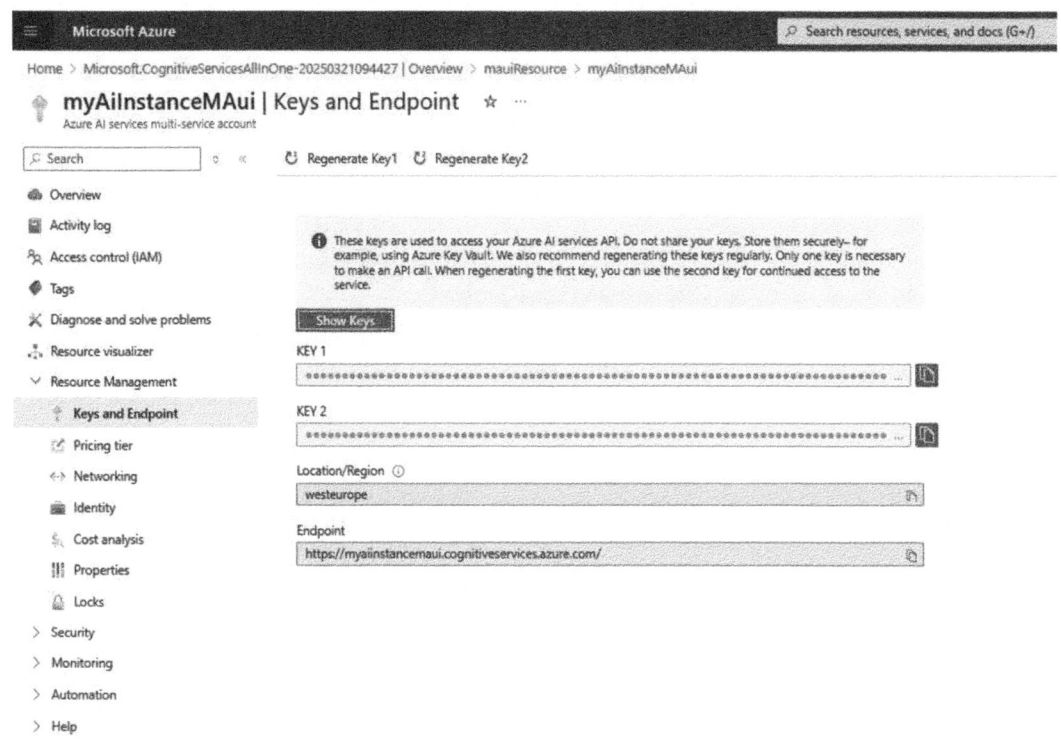

Figure 3-5. *Keys and endpoint*

To quickly test our AI service, create a simple client application, so that you get used to the pattern of provisioning and using the AI services.

Open Visual Studio, select the *Console App* project type and create a new one as shown in Figure 3-6. Give your project a creative name and select the latest framework version.

Figure 3-6. *Create a new console app in Visual Studio*

In this testing application, we will call a simple API, named *Language detection* (https://learn.microsoft.com/en-us/azure/ai-services/language-service/language-detection/overview). In Figure 3-7 is shown the Overview page for the AI services.

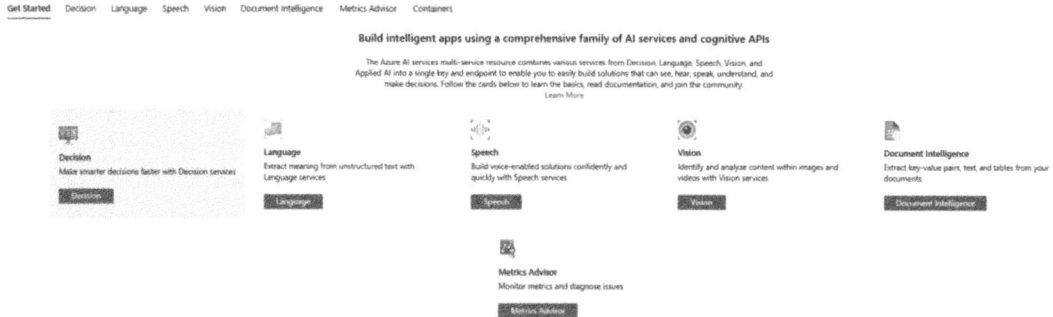

Figure 3-7. *AI services overview*

To test the API, you can go to https://language.cognitive.azure.com/tryout/detectLanguage and you will find a nice UI to understand the structure of the API.

You can use the samples, and then click Run to see the result as shown in Figure 3-8.

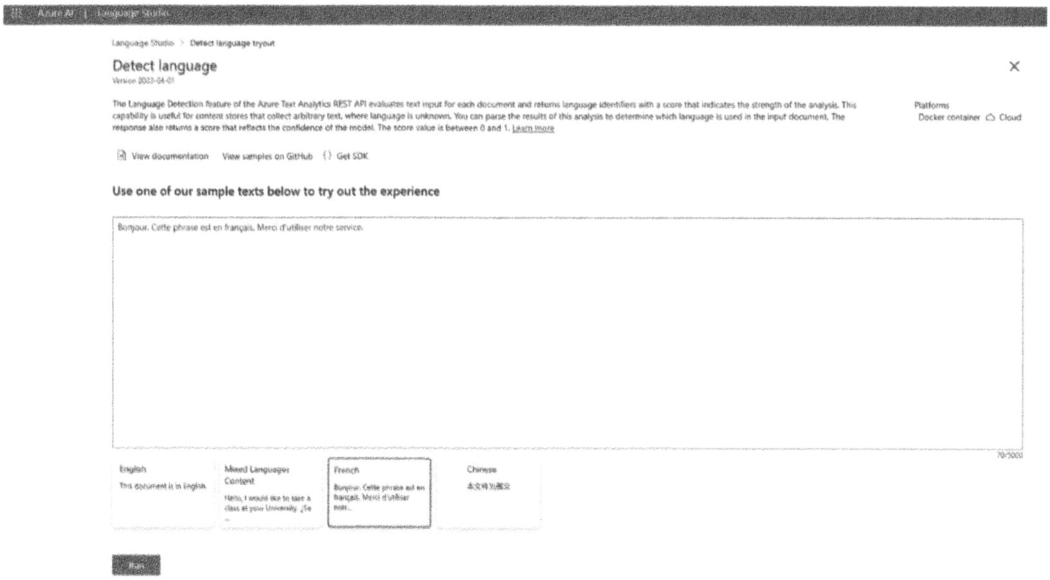

Figure 3-8. *Language Studio "Detect language" tryout screen*

The results will be provided for you with a simple UI, as shown in Figure 3-9, or in JSON format as shown in Figure 3-10.

Run

Examine the results

Result   JSON

Language detected

French

Confidence: 100.00%

Original text

Bonjour. Cette phrase est en français. Merci d'utiliser notre service.

Figure 3-9. *Result screen*

Result   **JSON**

```json
{
    "documents": [
        {
            "id": "id__10954",
            "detectedLanguage": {
                "name": "French",
                "iso6391Name": "fr",
                "confidenceScore": 1
            },
            "warnings": []
        }
    ],
    "errors": []
}
```

Figure 3-10. *JSON screen*

In our test app, we will use the JSON format to display the information in the console application.

Let's start by creating a new console application–then we will add two variables that will store your endpoint and key values as shown in Listing 3-11.

Listing 3-11. Variable set for the API

```
private static string AiSvcEndpoint;
private static string AiSvCKey;

AiSvcEndpoint ="YOUR_ENDPOINT";
AiSvCKey ="YOUR_API_KEY";
```

Inside the async main method, we will provide the application with some text, until a keyword is detecting, for example, "exit" as shown in Listing 3-12.

Listing 3-12. Console application logic

```
static async Task Main()
{// Get user input (until they enter "exit")
string userText = "";
while (userText.ToLower() != "exit")
{
    Console.WriteLine("Enter some text ('exit' to stop)");
    userText = Console.ReadLine();
    if (userText.ToLower() != "exit")
    {
        // Call function to detect language
        await GetLanguage(userText);
    }
}

}
```

Listing 3-12 Console application logic Then we will call our Language detection API and we will pass the text that the user has entered.

The Language detection API returns several pieces of information: one predominant language for each document you submit, along with its ISO 639-1 name, a human-readable name, the confidence score, a script name, and a script code according to ISO 15924 standard. ISO name and standards are provided by the International Organization for Standardization.

To call the API, we will need to send a request body in a JSON format that will be displayed in our console application. We will have a simple key-value structure with an id and a text as shown in Listing 3-13.

Listing 3-13. JSON Format for the API

```json
{
  "documents": [
    {
      "id": 1,
      "text": "ciao"
    }
  ]
}
```

We will then call the Language API and handle the response, another JSON key-value structure. The detected language response will contain the name, iso6931 name, and a confidence score as shown in Listing 3-14.

Listing 3-14. Response API JSON format

```json
{
  "documents": [
    {
      "id": "1",
      "warnings": [],
      "detectedLanguage": {
        "name": "Italian",
        "iso6391Name": "it",
        "confidenceScore": 1.0
      }
    }
  ],
  "errors": [],
  "modelVersion": "2024-11-01"
}

Language: Italian}
```

If there are errors, we will see them inside the errors array. We can also check the *modelVersion* date. We simply can extract the language name and prompt that to the user. The full *GetLanguage* function will look like in Listing 3-15:

Listing 3-15. GetLanguage implementation

```
static async Task GetLanguage(string text)
{
    // Construct the JSON request body
    try
    {
        JObject jsonBody = new JObject(
            // Create a collection of documents (we'll only use one, but
                you could have more)
            new JProperty("documents",
            new JArray(
                new JObject(
                    // Each document needs a unique ID and some text
                    new JProperty("id", 1),
                    new JProperty("text", text)
            )))));

        // Encode as UTF-8
        UTF8Encoding utf8 = new UTF8Encoding(true, true);
        byte[] encodedBytes = utf8.GetBytes(jsonBody.ToString());

        // Let's take a look at the JSON we'll send to the service
        Console.WriteLine(utf8.GetString(encodedBytes, 0, encodedBytes.
        Length));

        // Make an HTTP request to the REST interface
        var client = new HttpClient();
        var queryString = HttpUtility.ParseQueryString(string.Empty);

        // Add the authentication key to the header
        client.DefaultRequestHeaders.Add("Ocp-Apim-Subscription-Key",
        AiSvCKey);
```

```csharp
// Use the endpoint to access the Text Analytics language API
var uri = AiSvcEndpoint + "text/analytics/v3.1/languages?" +
queryString;

// Send the request and get the response
HttpResponseMessage response;
using (var content = new ByteArrayContent(encodedBytes))
{
    content.Headers.ContentType = new MediaTypeHeaderValue("applica
    tion/json");
    response = await client.PostAsync(uri, content);
}

// If the call was successful, get the response
if (response.StatusCode == System.Net.HttpStatusCode.OK)
{
    // Display the JSON response in full (just so we can see it)
    string responseContent = await response.Content.
    ReadAsStringAsync();
    JObject results = JObject.Parse(responseContent);
    Console.WriteLine(results.ToString());

    // Extract the detected language name for each document
    foreach (JObject document in results["documents"])
    {
        Console.WriteLine("\nLanguage: " + (string)
        document["detectedLanguage"]["name"]);
    }
}
else
{
    // Something went wrong, write the whole response
    Console.WriteLine(response.ToString());
}
}
```

```
    catch(Exception ex)
    {
        Console.WriteLine(ex.Message);
    }

}
```

After adding the Newtonsoft.Json NuGet package and the headings from Listing 3-16, the app is ready to be built.

Listing 3-16. Heading for the console application logic

```
using System.Net.Http.Headers;
using System.Text;
using System.Web;
using Newtonsoft.Json.Linq;
```

You can now build and *Run* your console application and maybe use the same UI string that we had in the portal for French. You can see the run screen in Figure 3-11.

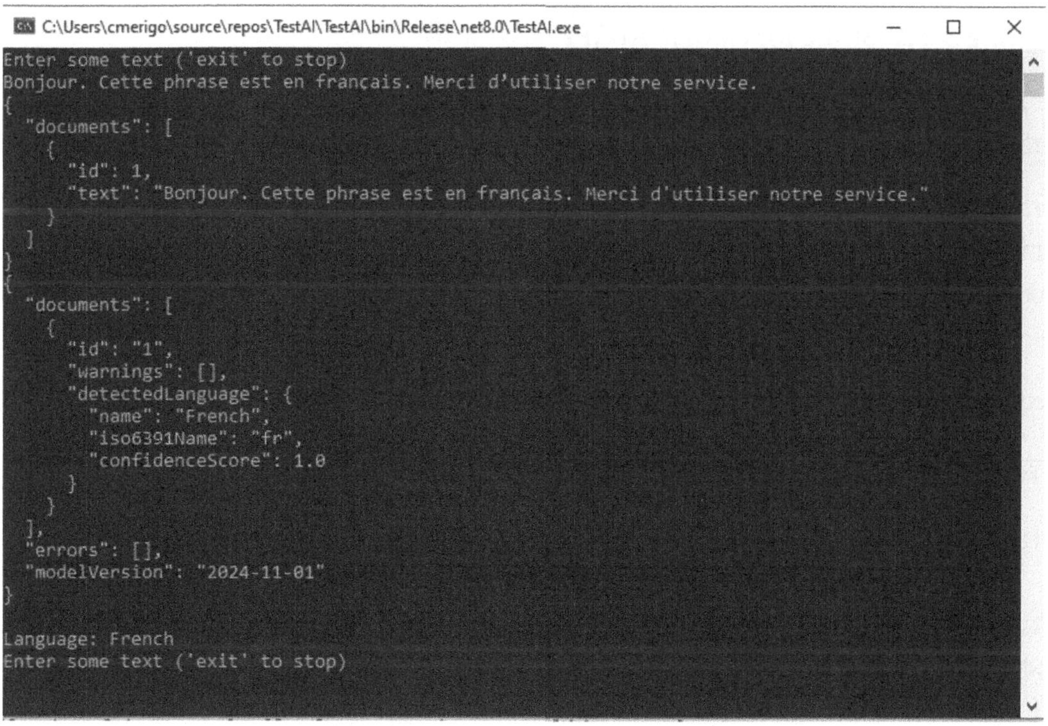

Figure 3-11. *Console application run screen for testing the language detect API*

Congratulations, you have just called a simple API from a console app! Now we are ready to follow the examples in the book and get more from the different services.

How to Integrate Google AI

Create or use your existing google account to start integrating Google Gemini.

First, we will need to understand how Google Gemini REST APIs are structured. We can find the specifications at `https://ai.google.dev/gemini-api/docs/quickstart?lang=rest`. As there is no .NET option, we can look at the REST example.

Our endpoint will be something like `https://generativelanguage.googleapis.com/v1beta/models/gemini-1.5-flash:generateContent?key=$YOUR_API_KEY`.

Then we will need to generate our API keys so we will go to `https://aistudio.google.com/app/apikey` and create our Google API key. For the test, create a new console application.We will be calling the *generateContent* API and we will ask our user to enter a request and let AI respond.

We will start by creating two variables that will store your endpoint and key values as shown in Listing 3-17.

Listing 3-17. String for Google AI API

```
private static string AiSvcEndpoint;
private static string AiSvCKey;

private static string AiSvCKey ="YOUR_API_KEY";
private static string AiSvcEndpoint = $"https://generativelanguage.googleapis.com/v1beta/models/gemini-2.0-flash:generateContent?key={AiSvCKey}";
```

Inside the async main method, we will provide the application some text, usually a request, until a keyword is detected, for example, "exit" as shown in Listing 3-18.

Listing 3-18. Console application code

```
static async Task Main()
{
string userText = "";
 while (userText.ToLower() != "exit")
 {
     Console.WriteLine("Enter your request ('exit' to stop)");
```

```
    userText = Console.ReadLine();
    if (userText.ToLower() != "exit")
    {
        // Call function to generate text
       string response=  await GenerateText(userText);
        Console.WriteLine("\n Google AI Response:");
        Console.WriteLine(response);
    }

 }
}
```

Based on the API specifications, we will need to create a *JSON request* with the format from Listing 3-19.

Listing 3-19. JSON Request format

```
 '{
  "contents": [{
    "parts":[{"text": "USER_ENTERED_TEXT"}]
    }]
    }'
```

And then we will display the response to the user. The *GenerateFunction* will look something like in Listing 3-20.

Listing 3-20. Final implementation

```
static async Task<string> GenerateText(string prompt)
{
    using HttpClient client = new HttpClient();

    var requestBody = new
    {
        contents = new[]
        {
            new { parts = new[] { new { text = prompt } } }
        }
    };
```

```
string jsonRequest = JsonSerializer.Serialize(requestBody);
var content = new StringContent(jsonRequest, Encoding.UTF8,
"application/json");

HttpResponseMessage response = await client.PostAsync(AiSvcEndpoint 1,
content);

if (response.IsSuccessStatusCode)
{
    string jsonResponse = await response.Content.ReadAsStringAsync();
    using JsonDocument doc = JsonDocument.Parse(jsonResponse);
    return doc.RootElement
            .GetProperty("candidates")[0]
            .GetProperty("content")
            .GetProperty("parts")[0]
            .GetProperty("text")
            .GetString();
}
else
{
    return $"Error: {response.StatusCode} - {await response.Content.
    ReadAsStringAsync()}";
}
}
```

After adding the Newtonsoft.Json NuGet package and the headings from Listing 3-21, the app is ready to be built.

Listing 3-21. Headers for the console application

```
using System.Net.Http.Headers;
using System.Text;
using System.Text.Json;
```

You can now build and *Run* your console application and "*ask*" something to the API. You can see the output of the console application in Figure 3-12.

```
C:\Users\cmerigo\source\repos\TestGoogleAI\TestGoogleAI\bin\Debug\net8.0\TestGoogleAI.exe          —    □    ×

?? AI Response:
That's a tough one, as "most famous" can be measured in different ways (popularity, cultural
 impact, etc.). However, **pizza** is arguably the most famous Italian food worldwide.

Here's why:

*   **Global Ubiquity:** Pizza restaurants and variations of pizza are found in nearly every
 country in the world.
*   **Versatility:** Pizza can be customized with countless toppings and crust styles, makin
g it appealing to diverse palates.
*   **Cultural Icon:** It's often associated with casual dining, family gatherings, and a ge
neral sense of comfort and enjoyment.
*   **Ease of Production:** While authentic Neapolitan pizza requires skill, simpler version
s are easy to make at home or in commercial settings.

While other Italian dishes like pasta (especially spaghetti), lasagna, and risotto are incre
dibly popular, pizza's global reach and adaptability give it the edge in terms of worldwide
fame.
Enter your request ('exit' to stop)
```

Figure 3-12. *Console application output screen for Google API*

How to Integrate OpenAI

OpenAI offers their APIs platform at https://platform.openai.com/; they don't have
a .NET example, but looking at the *curl* example format, we can see that we will have
an endpoint and we will need an API key. You can see the developer platform page in
Figure 3-13.

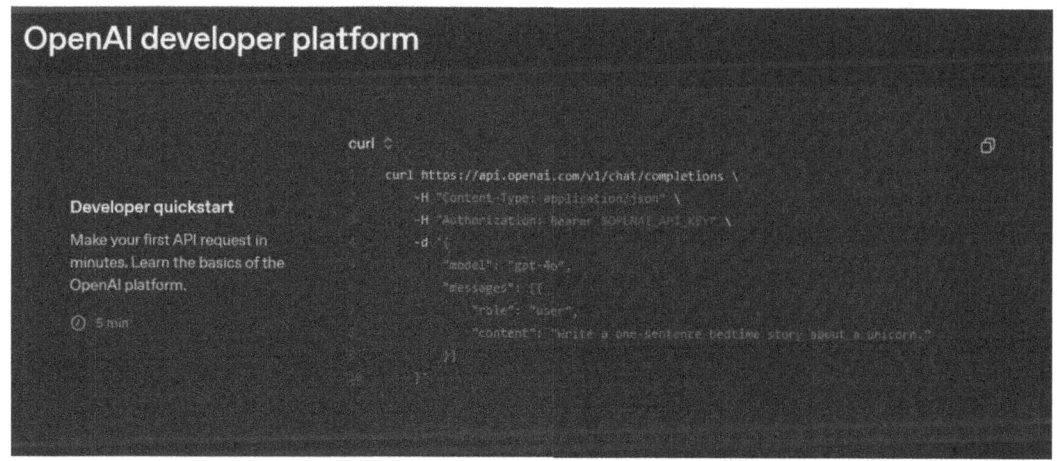

Figure 3-13. *OpenAI developer website*

We will need to log in to OpenAI and generate our key. Although they used to be included, currently free APIs are no longer provided, so you need to add a billing method to your OpenAI account. You can start with just $5 and see ChatGPT in action.

We will use the *completions* API to generate text output like you are using ChatGPT and the model will be *gpt-4o*.

We will start by creating a new console application. We will then create two variables that will store your endpoint and key values as shown in Listing 3-22.

Listing 3-22. Constant strings for the API AI

```
private static string AiSvcEndpoint;
private static string AiSvCKey;

private static string AiSvCKey = "YOUR_API_KEY";
private static string AiSvcEndpoint="https://api.openai.com/v1/chat/
completions";
```

Inside the async main method, we will provide the application some text, usually a request, until a keyword is detected, for example, "exit" as shown in Listing 3-23.

Listing 3-23. Console application implementation

```
static async Task Main()
{
string userText = "";
while (userText.ToLower() != "exit")
{
    Console.WriteLine("Enter your request ('exit' to stop)");
    userText = Console.ReadLine();
    if (userText.ToLower() != "exit")
    {
        // Call function to generate text
        string response = await GenerateText(userText);
        Console.WriteLine("\n Open AI Response:");
        Console.WriteLine(response);
    }
}
}
```

Based on the API specifications, we will need to create a *JSON request* with the format from Listing 3-24 and indicate a *max_tokens* number, for example, 100.

Listing 3-24. JSON request format

```
var
{
    model = "gpt-4o",
    messages = new[]
    {
    new { role = "user", content = prompt }
},
    max_tokens = 100
};
```

And then we will display the response to the user. The *GenerateText* function can be found in Listing 3-25.

Listing 3-25. GenerateText implementation

```
static async Task<string> GenerateText(string prompt)
{
    using HttpClient client = new HttpClient();
    client.DefaultRequestHeaders.Add("Authorization", $"Bearer
    {AiSvCKey}");

    var requestBody = new
    {
        model = "gpt-4o",
        messages = new[]
        {
        new { role = "user", content = prompt }
    },
        max_tokens = 100
    };
```

```
string jsonRequest = JsonSerializer.Serialize(requestBody);
var content = new StringContent(jsonRequest, Encoding.UTF8,
"application/json");

HttpResponseMessage response = await client.PostAsync(AiSvcEndpoint,
content);

if (response.IsSuccessStatusCode)
{
    string jsonResponse = await response.Content.ReadAsStringAsync();
    using JsonDocument doc = JsonDocument.Parse(jsonResponse);
    return doc.RootElement
                .GetProperty("choices")[0]
                .GetProperty("message")
                .GetProperty("content")
                .GetString();
}
else
{
    return $"Error: {response.StatusCode} - {await response.Content.
    ReadAsStringAsync()}";
}
}
```

After adding the Newtonsoft.Json NuGet package and the headings from Listing 3-26, the app is ready to be built.

Listing 3-26. Headers for the application

```
using System.Text;
using System.Text.Json;
```

You can now build and *Run* your console application and *"ask"* something to the API. You can see the output of the console application in Figure 3-14.

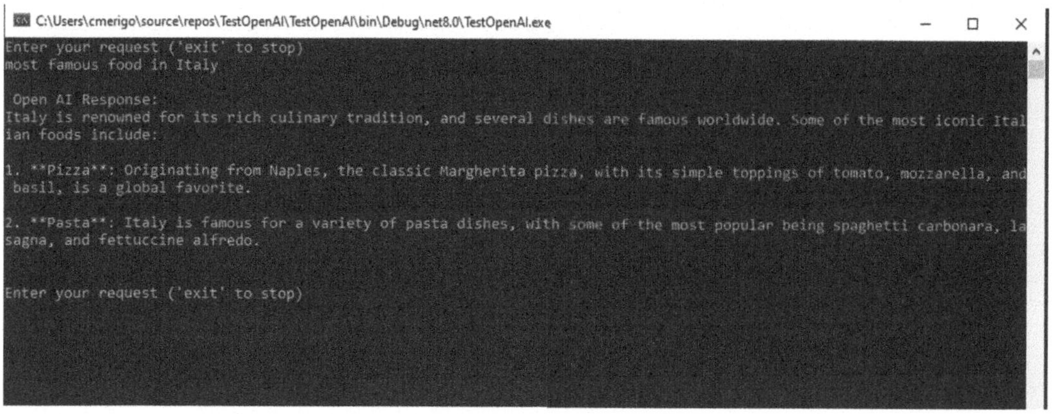

Figure 3-14. *Console app output for OpenAI API*

As an Italian, I can still debate for a long time on the responses, but you need to remember that AI is merely an illusion. You can challenge the APIs all the time and understand which one is better for you and your needs.

Summary

In this chapter, you learned how to call REST APIs from a .NET MAUI application and how to work with AI REST APIs, including managing AI API and API keys and handling responses. This is essential for connecting our app to the external services we will be using. We also explored how to integrate services from Azure AI, Google AI, and OpenAI and even took a detour to try to discover the best Italian food, hoping you are not getting hungry now!

In the next chapter, we will focus on the hands-on development of an example application. You'll get a clear overview of what the examples will do and how it will help reinforce everything you've learned so far. We'll then dive into Azure AI Text Analytics, one of the simplest services for working with language in your apps. You'll learn how to integrate sentiment analysis, allowing your app to understand and respond to the emotional tone of written text.

CHAPTER 4

Sentiment Analysis

Introduction

In this chapter, you will get an overview of how to use the sentiment analysis feature offered by the Azure AI Language service. Azure AI Language is a cloud-based service that provides natural language processing (NLP) features for understanding and analyzing text. NLP can be simply defined as a collection of algorithms, models, and tools that let you process text or speech as structured data so your application can extract meaning, run logic, and produce language-aware outputs. Thanks to NLP, machines can understand, interpret, and generate human language. This service combines linguistics with computer science and machine learning to process and analyze text and speech data. The Azure AI Language service provides a variety of features, and in the previous chapters, we explored language detection as one of them.

In this chapter, you will learn about the sentiment analysis feature offered by Azure AI Language, how to configure it in the Azure Portal, and how to integrate this feature into a .NET MAUI application.

Linguistics and Feelings

Now back to some more definitions–but don't worry, we won't have a quiz at the end of the book!

Linguistics is the science that studies language, and it's different from the language knowledge itself. We can all use a phone without knowing how the hardware works; a speaker can use a language without knowing its underlying structure. Linguists, on the other hand, can understand the internal structure of a language without actually speaking it.

© Codrina Merigo 2026
C. Merigo, *AI-Enabled Apps with .NET MAUI*, https://doi.org/10.1007/979-8-8688-1817-2_4

Recent definitions of linguistics now include

- **Phonetics**: The study of how speech sounds are produced and perceived

- **Phonology**: The study of sound patterns and changes

- **Morphology**: The study of word structure

- **Syntax**: The study of sentence structure

- **Semantics**: The study of linguistic meaning

- **Pragmatics**: The study of how language is used in context

- **Historical Linguistics**: The study of language changes

- **Sociolinguistics**: The study of the relation between language and society

- **Computational Linguistics**: The study that explores how computers can process human language

- **Psycholinguistics**: The study of how humans acquire and use language

Who would have thought that language, while so complex, could also feel so magical?

As you can imagine, *computational linguistics* uses algorithms and methods to model, analyze, and simulate human language. While formal linguistics gives us the "what" and "why" of language, computational linguistics focuses on the "how" applying technology to put linguistic theory into practice. Computational linguistics provides all the theoretical foundation and linguistics structures for NLP, while NLP applies this knowledge to build usable language processing systems and applications like sentiment analysis.

Some time ago, there was this song called "*I've got a feeling*" by the English band The Beatles. That tune has been singing in my head since the first time I ran into sentiment analysis. We humans, we all have feelings, but in the Internet world, how can we express that? How can we understand which feeling some comments we might receive on social media have? We have only string of text, some emojis, and maybe some punctuation.

The sentiment analysis feature from Azure AI Language comes in handy as it provides sentiment labels (such as "negative," "neutral," and "positive") based on the highest confidence score found by the service at a sentence and document level. This feature also returns confidence scores between 0 and 1 for each document and sentences within it for positive, neutral, and negative sentiment. With this service, we can understand how our users are feeling.

You can find the full list of supported languages here: `https://learn.microsoft.com/azure/ai-services/language-service/sentiment-opinion-mining/language-support`.

This service is great for analyzing reviews or comments, to monitor brand reputation and adjust strategies accordingly. It gives insights into user or customer opinions and emotions and helps with tailoring offerings. The model, though, might not recognize sarcasm, humor, or irony, as more context might be needed to understand the feeling (like facial expression, tone of voice of the author of the comment). Most industries benefit from this feature; you can mainly think of ecommerce websites, media, or travel services that use sentiment analysis to personalize products, content, and offers by detecting sentiment spikes. Politics or finance can also benefit from this service by simply analyzing social media, news, or trends easily. You can also apply sentiment analysis in healthcare to improve patient care by carefully analyzing their feedback or assessing the effectiveness of health campaigns.

Azure AI Language Service

As we have seen in the introduction, Azure AI Language is a cloud service that provides robust natural language processing (NLP) capabilities for understanding and analyzing text data. Developers can leverage this service to build intelligent applications by integrating its features using comprehensive client libraries, direct REST APIs, or by utilizing the convenient, web-based Language Studio for rapid prototyping and deployment. In this chapter, we will be using the sentiment analysis feature. There are different features that we can use; you can learn more about the services and which should you use at `https://docs.azure.com/ai-services/language-service/overview#which-language-service-feature-should-i-use`.

Azure AI Language service includes a rich collection of prebuilt examples designed to help you explore the services hands-on. These guided scenarios let you experiment with key capabilities directly in the browser, without writing any code or configuring resources. It's an easy, intuitive way to understand how the service behaves in real use cases, and it is a feature I personally really appreciate. Just click Run and see the magic!

To understand how the sentiment analysis feature of the Language service works, test it, and see it in action, you can go to `https://language.cognitive.azure.com/tryout/sentiment`. You can see an extract of the page in Figure 4-1.

Use one of our sample texts below to try out the experience

I bought a size S and it fit perfectly. I found the zipper a little bit difficult to get up & down due to the side rushing. The color and material are beautiful in person. Amazingly comfortable!

194/5000

Product Review (short)	Service Review (long)	Customer Complaint Email	Social Media Post	Employee survey feedback
I bought a size S and it fit perfectly. I found the zipper a...	Long waits..BUT FOR GOOD REASON. Some awesome Italian food ...	Hello, My name is Mateo Gomez and I visited Contoso...	I can describe my experience of this game in two words: "TEC...	The cafeteria food is getting worse by the day. $15 for a pl...

Run

Figure 4-1. *Language test service*

On this page, you can try all the *Analyze sentiment and opinion* services. You can also find some samples. Select one of the samples provided and click *Run* to see the results.

You will see the overall sentiment, with its score and the sentence analysis as shown in Figure 4-2.

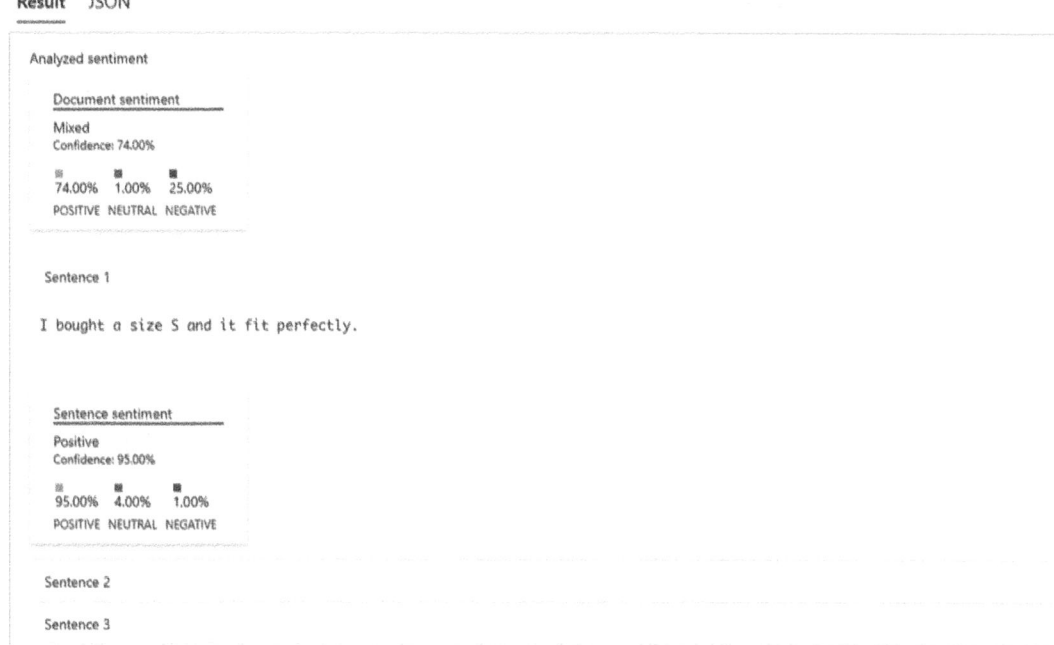

Result   JSON

Figure 4-2. *Sentiment analysis results*

If you switch to the JSON view, you will get the full API response, with the *documents* array containing the *sentiment* property and the *confidenceScores*. You will also see the *sentiment* and *confidenceScore* for each sentence as in Listing 4-1.

Listing 4-1. JSON results

```
{
    "documents": [
        {
            "id": "id__475",
            "sentiment": "mixed",
            "confidenceScores": {
                "positive": 0.74,
                "neutral": 0.01,
                "negative": 0.25
            },
```

```
            "sentences": [
                {
                    "sentiment": "positive",
                    "confidenceScores": {
                        "positive": 0.95,
                        "neutral": 0.04,
                        "negative": 0.01
                    },
                    "offset": 0,
                    "length": 40,
                    "text": "I bought a size S and it fit perfectly. "
                },
                {

                    "sentiment": "negative",
                    "confidenceScores": {
                        "positive": 0,
                        "neutral": 0,
                        "negative": 0.99
                    },
                    "offset": 40,
                    "length": 84,
                    "text": "I found the zipper a little bit difficult to
                    get up & down due to the side rushing. "
                },
                {

                    "sentiment": "positive",
                    "confidenceScores": {
                        "positive": 0.99,
                        "neutral": 0,
                        "negative": 0
                    },
```

```
                    "offset": 124,
                    "length": 48,
                    "text": "The color and material are beautiful in
                    person. "
                },
                {
                    "sentiment": "positive",
                    "confidenceScores": {
                        "positive": 0.99,
                        "neutral": 0,
                        "negative": 0
                    },
                    "offset": 172,
                    "length": 22,
                    "text": "Amazingly comfortable!"
                }
            ]
        }
    ],
    "errors": []
}
```

Create the Service

Once you have seen and tested the service, you will be ready to create your own instance of the sentiment analysis AI service in the Azure portal. Log in to https://portal. azure.com/ and click Create a resource. Then, search for the *Language service* Azure service provided by Microsoft as shown in Figure 4-3.

Once you click on the service, you will get an overview of the features available and the possibility to add custom ones as shown in Figure 4-4.

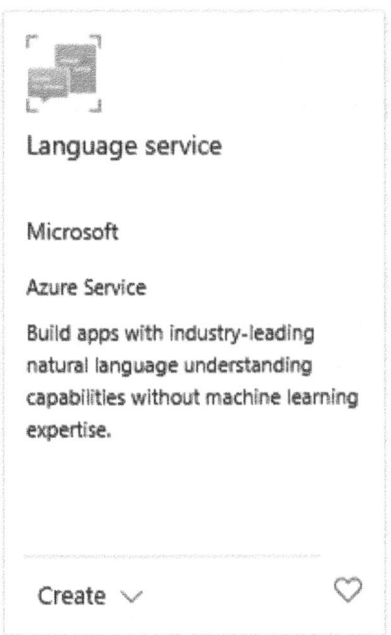

Figure 4-3. *Language service card on Azure*

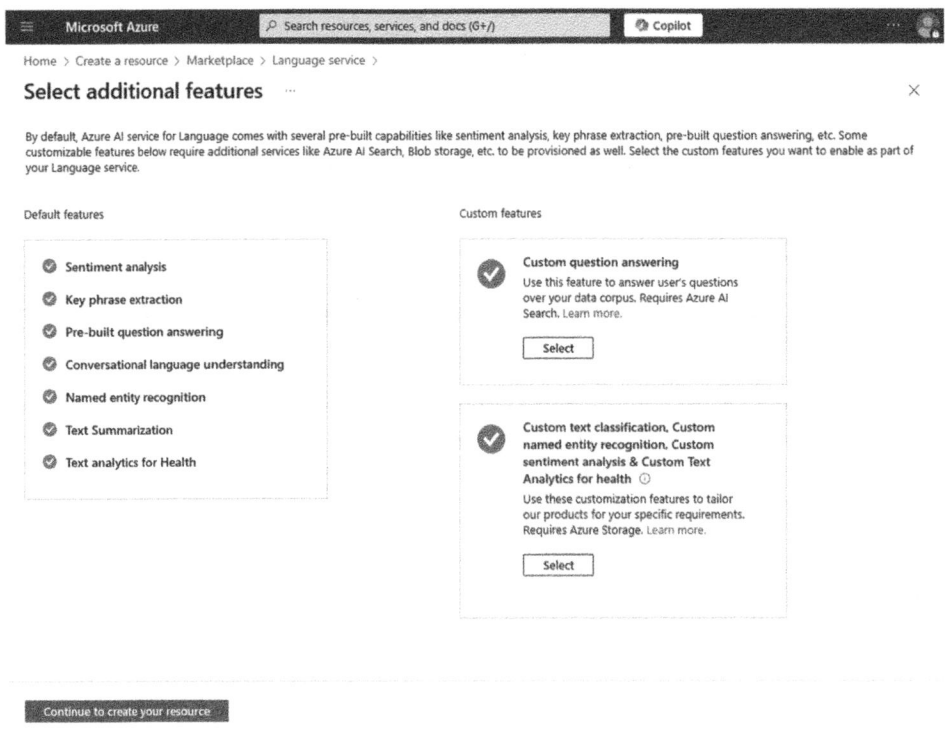

Figure 4-4. *Summary of Language service*

In the new page, as shown in Figure 4-5, select your subscription, use, or create a new resource group and give your service a name. You will also need to acknowledge the terms of the Responsible AI Notice so go and give it a read. We will explore more on responsible use of AI in Chapter 13.

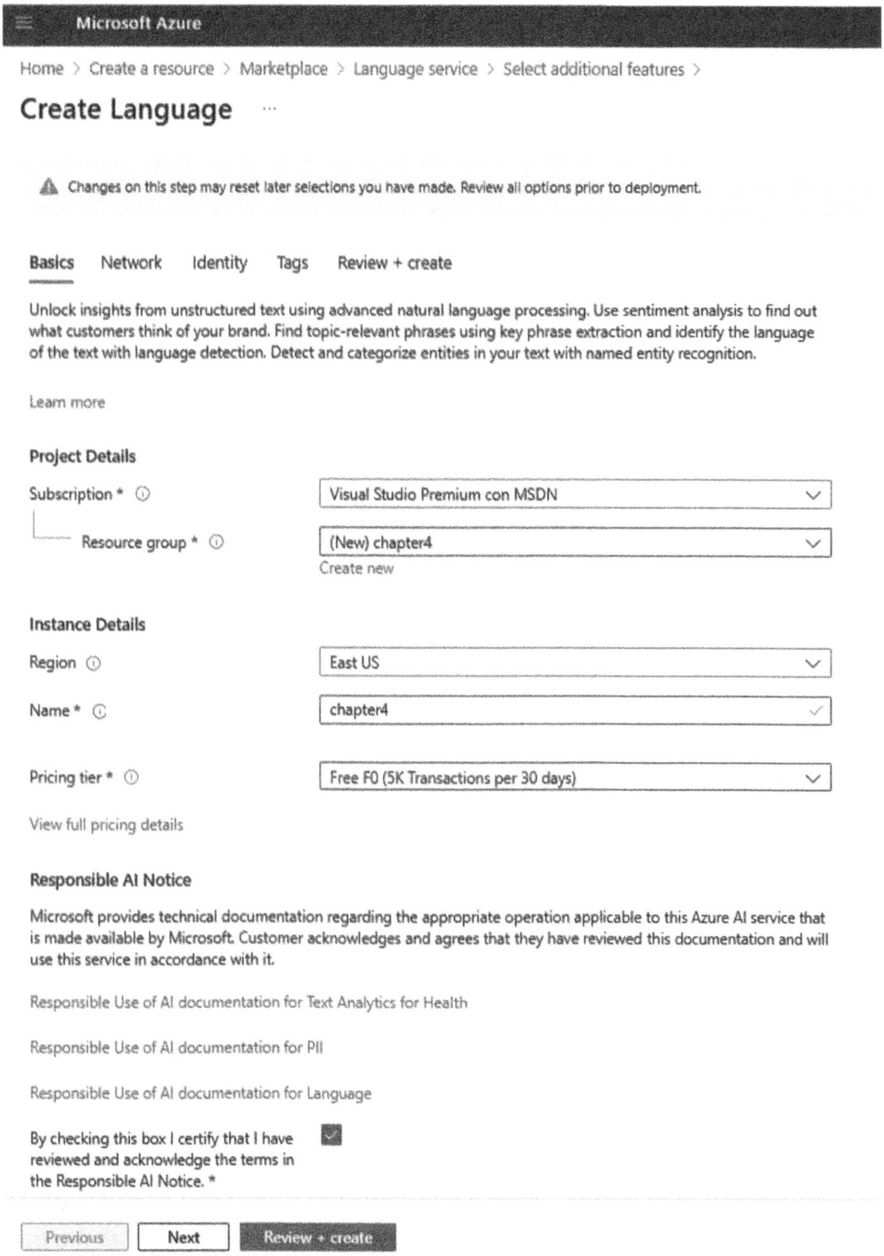

Figure 4-5. *Language service resource creation*

Once your resource has been created, open your resource and expand `Resource Management.` as shown in Figure 4-6. By *selecting Keys and Endpoint,* you can see your keys and endpoint. We will need this information in our project to be able to call the sentiment analysis API service.

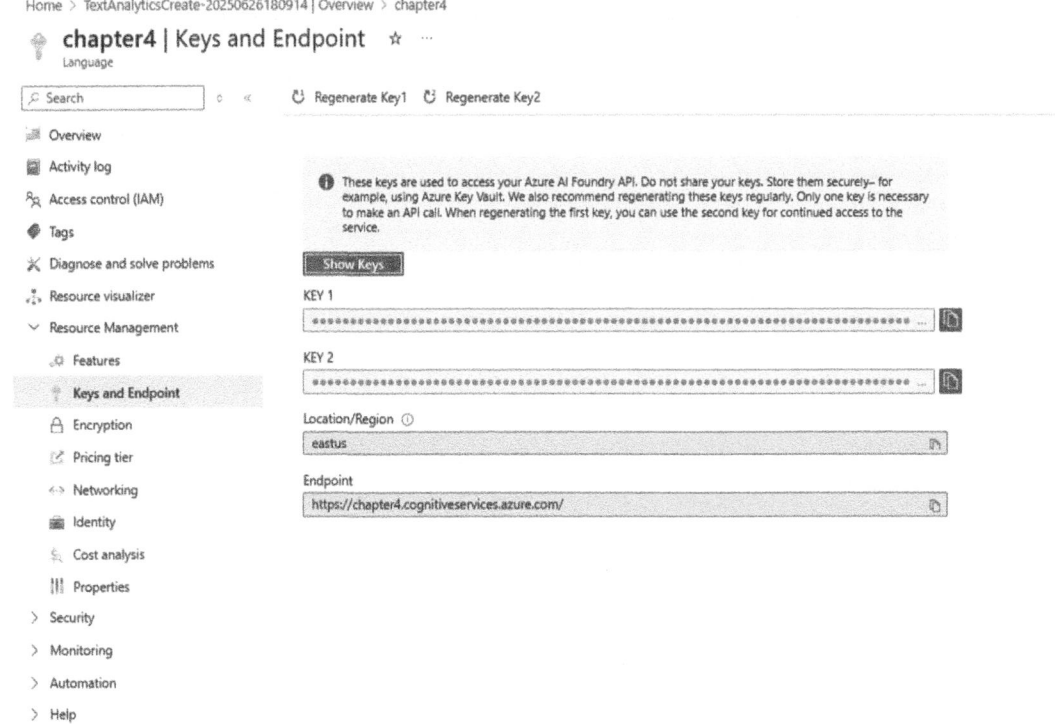

Figure 4-6. *Language service resource management keys and endpoint*

You can replace the keys and endpoint you will find inside the *Services* folder of the chapter solution with your own key and endpoint. Usually, one key is used for development and one for production.

Use the Service in Your App

Now that our cognitive service for Language is up and running, we can start using it in a .NET MAUI application. But, first, let me introduce you to the app we will be building together in the upcoming chapters. The idea is to create a personal AI assistant, like a digital version of a Swiss army knife that will come handy in different scenarios. To create the app, imagine you have reviews, comments, or just some written text and you want to understand the feeling behind those sentences. Our AI assistant will implement sentiment analysis and will provide us with the resulting sentiment in just a few seconds.

Let's start by creating a new .NET MAUI project in our preferred IDE or code editor. I will be using Visual Studio, but you can also use Visual Studio Code, as you prefer. If you already have Visual Studio installed, remember to check that "**.NET Multi-platform App UI development**" workload has been added to the installation. For Visual Studio Code, make sure you have added the .NET MAUI workload by using the `run dotnet workload install maui` commands. Please check Chapter 1 to review how to prepare your development environment and to create your .NET MAUI application.

You can create a new project for every example of the book, to keep them separated and unify our examples at the end to create our assistant.

After we have our .NET MAUI project, we will implement a simple XAML page that will contain an *Editor* control, so we can enter multiple line of text, and a simple *Button* to call our API. Once you hit the button, the result will be displayed in a pop-up. Let's start with the XAML page. You can modify the existing `MainPage.xaml`. The resulting page is shown in *Listing 4-2*.

Listing 4-2. Input page for sentiment analysis

```xml
<?xml version="1.0" encoding="utf-8" ?>
<ContentPage xmlns="http://schemas.microsoft.com/dotnet/2021/maui"
             xmlns:x="http://schemas.microsoft.com/winfx/2009/xaml"
             x:Class="Chapter4.MainPage">

    <VerticalStackLayout
    Padding="20"
    Spacing="20">

        <Label Text="Sentiment Analyzer"
            FontSize="24"
            HorizontalOptions="Center" />

        <Editor x:Name="InputEditor"
            Placeholder="Enter text here..."
            AutoSize="TextChanges"
            HeightRequest="250"
            SemanticProperties.Description="Entry box for your text"/>
```

```
    <Button Text="Analyze Sentiment"
        Clicked="OnAnalyze_Clicked"
        TextColor="White"
        CornerRadius="12"/>
  </VerticalStackLayout>
```

```
</ContentPage>
```

We will get the OnAnalyze_Clicked method in a second; now it's time to create the API we will be using in a service class. Create a new folder called Services. Inside the newly created folder, create a new class called SentimentService.cs. We will need to get out endpoint and our API key and store them into two variables. We will call our endpoint and pass the key from the Ocp-Apim-Subscription-Key header. The request body will be formed based on the request JSON. From the service, we will need to get the sentiment and the confidence as shown in the result JSON tab. You can find the SentimentService class implementation in Listing 4-3.

Listing 4-3. SentimentService.cs class

```
using System.Net.Http;
using System.Text.Json;
using System.Text;

namespace Chapter4.Services;

public class SentimentService
{
    private readonly string _endpoint = "https://YOUR-ENDPOINT.
cognitiveservices.azure.com/";
    private readonly string _apiKey = "YOUR-KEY";

    private readonly HttpClient _httpClient;

    public SentimentService()
    {
        _httpClient = new HttpClient();
    }
```

```csharp
public async Task<(string sentiment, double confidence)>
AnalyzeAsync(string text)
{
    var requestBody = new
    {
        documents = new[]
        {
            new {
                    id = "1",
                    language = "en",
                    text = text
            }
        }
    };

    string json = JsonSerializer.Serialize(requestBody);
    var content = new StringContent(json, Encoding.UTF8,
    "application/json");

    _httpClient.DefaultRequestHeaders.Clear();
    _httpClient.DefaultRequestHeaders.Add("Ocp-Apim-Subscription-Key",
    _apiKey);

    string url = $"{_endpoint}text/analytics/v3.1/sentiment";

    var response = await _httpClient.PostAsync(url, content);
    response.EnsureSuccessStatusCode();

    string responseJson = await response.Content.ReadAsStringAsync();

    using var doc = JsonDocument.Parse(responseJson);

    var root = doc.RootElement.GetProperty("documents")[0];

    string sentiment = root.GetProperty("sentiment").GetString() ??
    "unknown";

    var confidence = root.GetProperty("confidenceScores")
    .GetProperty(sentiment).GetDouble();
```

```
        return (sentiment, confidence);
        //return ("positive", 83);
    }
}
```

Once we have our sentiment and the confidence score from the API, we can map it as follows, and we can multiply the confidence score by 100 to return a percentage, formatting it to F2, F for fixation point and 2 for 2 decimal points. We can also bind a simple emoji, based on the sentiment itself.

After we have our response, we can display that in a simple Alert. We will add this logic inside MainPage.xaml.cs as shown in *Listing 4-4*.

Listing 4-4. MainPage.xaml.cs code

```
using Chapter4.Services;

namespace Chapter4
{
    public partial class MainPage : ContentPage
    {
        private readonly SentimentService _sentimentService;

        public MainPage()
        {
            InitializeComponent();
            _sentimentService = new SentimentService();
        }

        private async void OnAnalyze_Clicked(object sender, EventArgs e)
        {
            string text = InputEditor.Text;

            if (string.IsNullOrWhiteSpace(text))
            {
                await DisplayAlert("Error", "Please enter some
                text.", "OK");
                return;
            }
```

```
try
{
    var (sentiment, confidence) = await _sentimentService.
    AnalyzeAsync(text);

    // Map overall sentiment to emoji
    string emoji = sentiment.ToLower() switch
    {
        "positive" => ":)",
        "neutral" => ":|",
        "negative" => ":(",
        _ => "?"
    };

    string message = $"Sentiment: {sentiment.ToUpper()}
    {emoji}\n Confidence: {(confidence * 100):F2}%";

    await DisplayAlert("Sentiment Result", message, "OK");
}
catch (Exception ex)
{
    await DisplayAlert("Error", ex.Message, "OK");
}

    }

    }
}
```

We can test our service and page by building and deploying the project. We can select to run it on our Windows machine directly, and you can see the result in *Figure 4-7.*

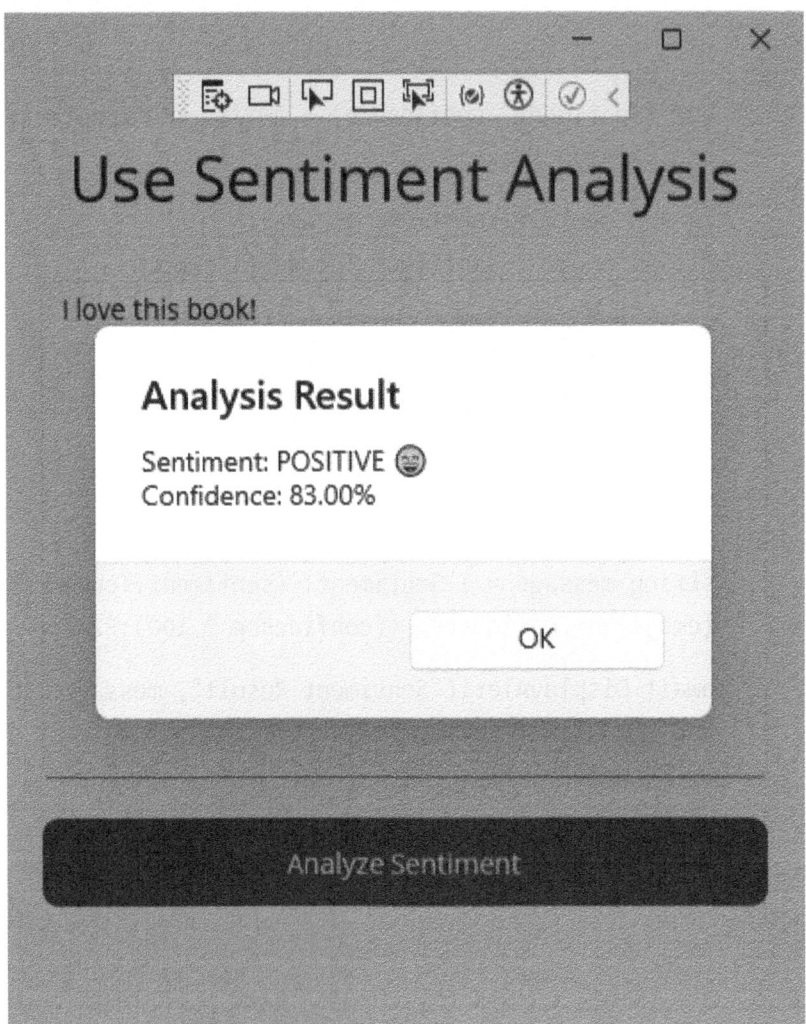

Figure 4-7. *Sentiment analysis application*

For Android development, it is crucial to have at least one Android emulator installed via the Android SDK Manager, or to use a physical Android device with Developer Mode and USB Debugging enabled. For macOS, you can target the application using Mac Catalyst, which requires a Mac with Xcode installed, and run it directly from Visual Studio to see a native Mac application. To run it on iOS, you will need to install iOS simulators via Xcode or connect a physical iPhone/iPad. You can find more information on deployment and testing at https://learn.microsoft.com/dotnet/maui/deployment.

Once the development environment is ready, you can run your app directly from Visual Studio by selecting an emulator or device and pressing Run (F5); Visual Studio will build, deploy, and launch the app automatically.

Our AI Assistant

Sentiment analysis based on the input test is just the first AI capability our assistant will integrate.

Next, I just want to share with you some notes on the app you can build by linking together all the samples in this chapter and in the upcoming chapters. The app needs an Internet connection to use the online AI services that are integrated. All the scenarios can be enhanced by using a database and a back-end service to store all the responses from the AI services.

For testing purposes, we will temporarily display the response information inside a pop-up or inside the page. Using simple CRUD operations, we can add a database to our app and give our AI assistant also a "memory."

You can use all the information from your assistant to train your GPT model as we will see in the next chapters and make your assistant even more tailored to your needs.

Your new AI assistant will start to take shape, one chapter and one project at a time. I would love to hear and see how you will enhance it!

Summary

In this chapter, we have looked deeper into Azure AI Language service. We had a deep dive into linguistics and learned how to use the service. We also had the first introduction to the app we will be building together in the next chapters and learned how to integrate the service into our application.

In the next chapter, we will focus on adding different chatbots to our assistant. We will start with a simple chatbot, then we will integrate ChatGPT and Gemini. By the end of the chapter, we will see how we can adapt the UI of the chatbot to our app themes and create a custom one.

CHAPTER 5

AI-Powered Chatbots

Introduction

In this chapter, you will start integrating chatbots into the AI assistant app. We will start by getting an overview of chatbots. We will continue by creating a simple chatbot using Azure AI Bot Service, a custom version of ChatGPT using OpenAI with Azure and a Gemini chatbot using Google AI Studio. By the end of the chapter, we will see different ways to style our chatbots and adapt them to our MAUI application.

Chatbots

As mentioned in Chapter 2, Eliza was the very first chatbot and it was developed back in 1966 by Joseph Weizenbaum. It felt incredible that users can have a conversation with a machine, and now more than 50 years later, we can find chatbots on different websites. They just pop around the page you are navigating and are there for you. From a developer point of view, bots are applications that can be found in various channels (websites, mobile apps, chat applications, etc.). Bots should have a pleasing user experience, and they should be intelligent.

When focusing on user experience (UX), there is a specific branch, called conversational user experience (CUX). CUX is an interaction mode that is based on natural language processing (NLP).

Chatbots use NLP to interact with the user in a "human" way, so it's important to develop a conversational experience more than just focusing on a simple dialogue. Usually, chatbots have a name and a built-in personality so that responses can contain emotional nuances and ensure that the users feel also understood, not only heard. Sometimes, chatbot can be used as the entry point for support systems so it's even

© Codrina Merigo 2026
C. Merigo, *AI-Enabled Apps with .NET MAUI*, https://doi.org/10.1007/979-8-8688-1817-2_5

more important to create a feeling of empathy and a relationship of trust with the user engaging in a conversation. We can integrate sentiment analysis in chatbots to help them better frame their messages.

Prompts

In the context of chatbots, we often speak about prompts, which are the foundation of interaction between humans and AI. They are the messages users type to communicate their questions, needs, or commands. Whether simple or complex, prompts guide the chatbot in understanding what the user wants and how to respond appropriately. As AI is just an illusion, it is very important to not give anything for granted when creating your prompts to be sent to a chatbot. The better the prompt, the better the reply. Understanding how prompts work makes chatting with AI smoother, more helpful, and a lot more fun—and let's be honest, sometimes writing a good prompt feels easier than naming a variable in your code!

Prompts aren't just about starting a conversation, they're also how we steer the chatbot in the right direction. They help set the topic, tone, and the kind of answer we're after (because sometimes we want Shakespeare, and other times, we just need a list of ingredients for a recipe). The more specific and clear we are, the better the chatbot can do its job, like giving good directions to someone who's never driven before. Want a summary? A translation? A poem about pizza? A well-crafted prompt makes it happen. A few tricks help a lot: tell the chatbot who it should be ("*Act as a cook*"), give it examples, use symbols or brackets to highlight the key stuff, and don't forget to set limits or formats if needed. You can also provide context and describe the audience that will receive the generated content. The more you guide it, the less likely it is to go rogue and write you a Shakespearean sonnet when you ask for a recipe—unless you're into that, of course. Asking for a poem or something that rhymes is a great way to detect chatbots in conversations when you are not sure if you are interacting with a chatbot. Give it a try and tell me after!

Integrate an Azure Chatbot

We will start with a simple Azure bot. Log in to the Azure portal, select the AI + machine learning category, and create a new Azure bot. Give your bot a handle (unique identifier), select the subscription and resource group, check all the options, and click Review + create. Review the information and click Review + create as shown in Figure 5-1.

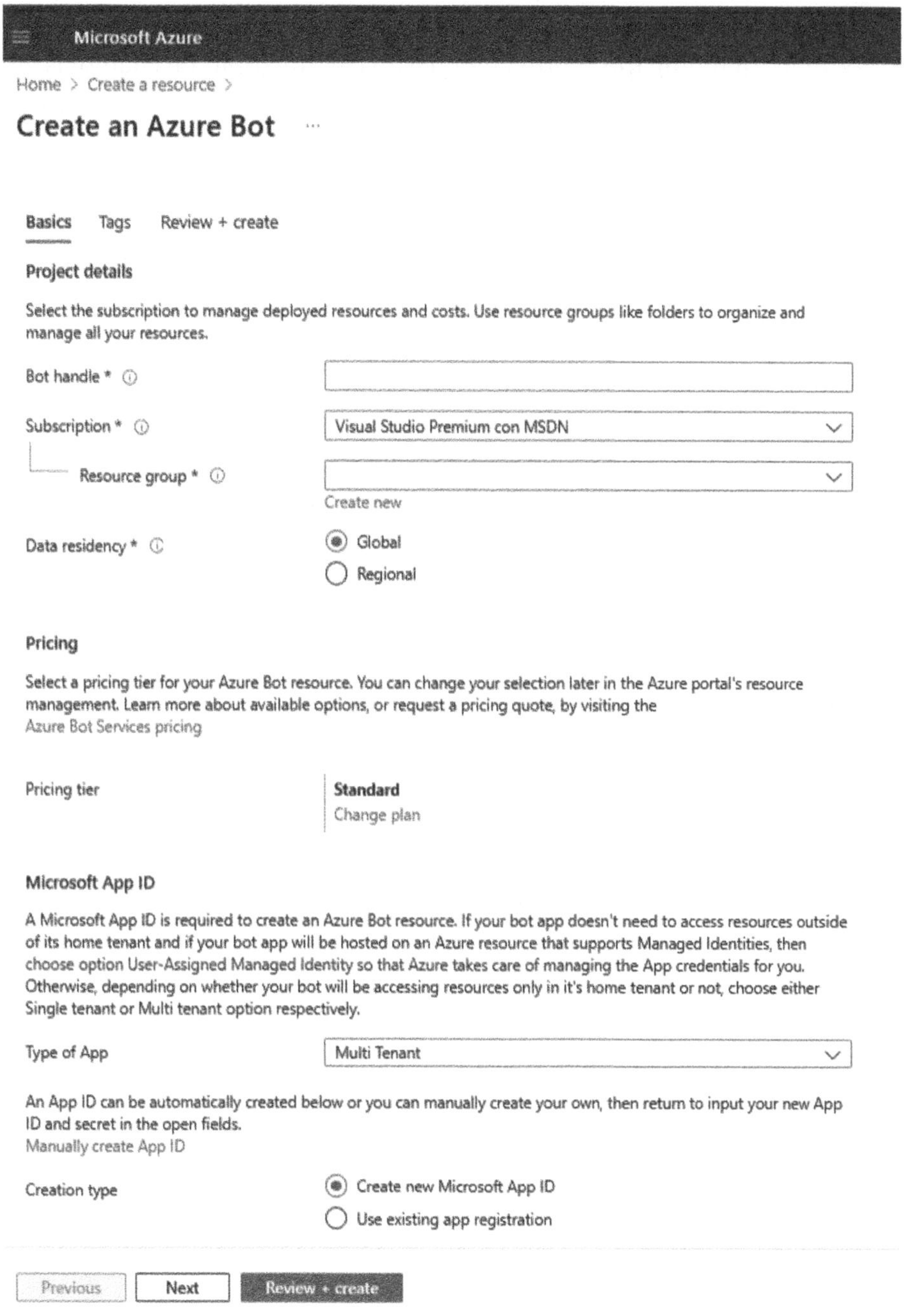

Figure 5-1. *Create an Azure bot screen on the Azure portal*

Once deployment is complete, go to your newly created resource as shown in Figure 5-2. When expanding the *Settings* menu, you can find that the chatbot is already connected through Direct Line, using REST API or inside a Web Chat. More available channels are listed in the Available Channels part.

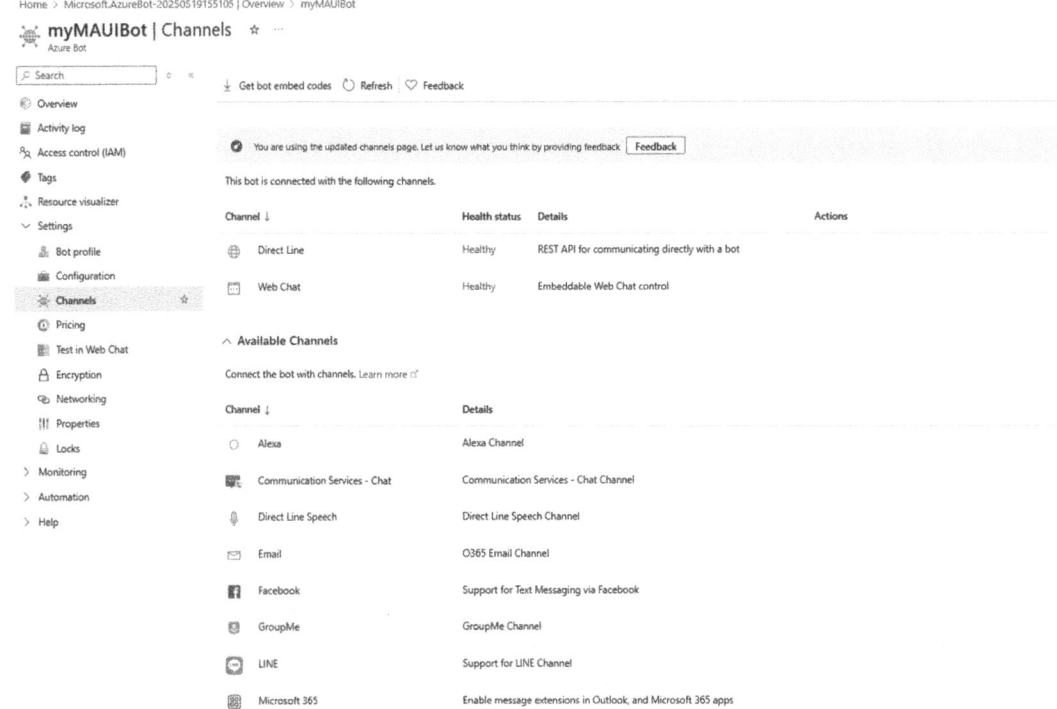

Figure 5-2. *Newly created bot Channels page*

If we focus at the Web Chat view, we can see that there is an `Embeddable Web Chat` control so that means we can embed it into our MAUI application.

By clicking the Web Chat option, we can see that the sample of an *iframe* is created in the Embedded code box, as shown in Figure 5-3. You can find the *iframe* content in Listing 5-1.

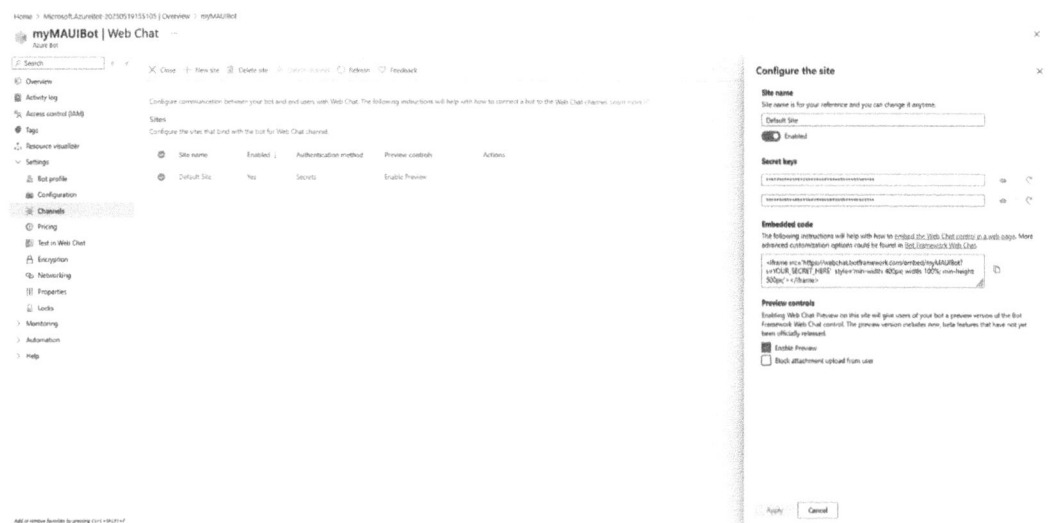

Figure 5-3. *Web Chat page and iframe*

Listing 5-1. Azure bot iframe

```
<iframe src='https://webchat.botframework.com/embed/myMAUIBot?s=YOUR_
SECRET_HERE' style='min-width: 400px; width: 100%; min-height: 500px;'>
</iframe>
```

If you are used to HTML, the <iframe> tag indicates an inline frame that is used to embed another document into the main html. In our MAUI app, we can create a new XAML page that will contain a WebView control. Inside the source property of the control, we can paste the *src* property content of the iframe, as shown in Listing 5-2, and substitute YOUR_RESOURCE_NAME with the name of your newly created resource and YOUR_SECRET_HERE with our secret key. We will also set a height and width for the WebView.

Listing 5-2. WebView for xaml page

```
<WebView x:Name="myWebView" Source="https://webchat.botframework.com/embed/
YOUR_RESOURCE_NAME?s=YOUR_SECRET_HERE "          HeightRequest="600"
WidthRequest="400" />
```

What we have created and embedded is just an empty bot. It already provides a basic UI so you can start interacting with it from your MAUI app. You can see it in Figure 5-4.

Figure 5-4. *Rendered bot inside a .NET MAUI app*

To enhance your new bot, you can develop your bot with Bot Framework SDK or use Microsoft Copilot Studio. We only focused on adding an existing bot, and I invite you to create your own and add it to your application. You can learn more about creating a bot at https://learn.microsoft.com/en-us/azure/bot-service/bot-service-quickstart-create-bot?view=azure-bot-service-4.0&tabs=csharp%2Cvs using the

Bot Framework SDK or at `https://learn.microsoft.com/training/modules/power-virtual-agents-bots/` to create your bot with Microsoft Copilot Studio. You can embed the bot in the app and develop it separately.

Integrate ChatGPT

ChatGPT can be defined as more than just a simple bot as it uses generative AI. With Azure, we can create our own version of ChatGPT, tailor it to our needs, and add it to a .NET MAUI application. We can use all the features that ChatGPT has like answering questions, generating creative content, and even writing stories and base its answers on our data.

As magic as it might seem, ChatGPT has its limitations. Sometimes it may generate plausible answers or nonsensical ones that just sound good. Make sure you check all the information provided. It is also sensitive to the input prompt, that is why it is important to be precise so the model can understand the input. Sometimes the model is excessively verbose and might overuse certain phrases due to its overoptimization. You can tweak that in the initial prompt. If the prompt is ambiguous, sometimes ChatGPT tries to guess what the user needs and might get it wrong; once again, the precision of the prompt is important.

ChatGPT is powered by OpenAI's GPT (generative pretrained transformer) models. As of today, the latest model is GPT-5 and can be used by default by the logged users into the platform. If you are curious about how people around the world use ChatGPT, you can read the following article at `https://www.nber.org/papers/w34255`.

As we have already used the Azure portal so far and thanks to OpenAI and Microsoft partnership, you can have ChatGPT hosted in Azure OpenAI service. Let's log in to Azure portal and create a new resource. From the left menu, if we select `AI Apps and Agents` category, we will find `Azure OpenAI` resource, as shown in Figure 5-5.

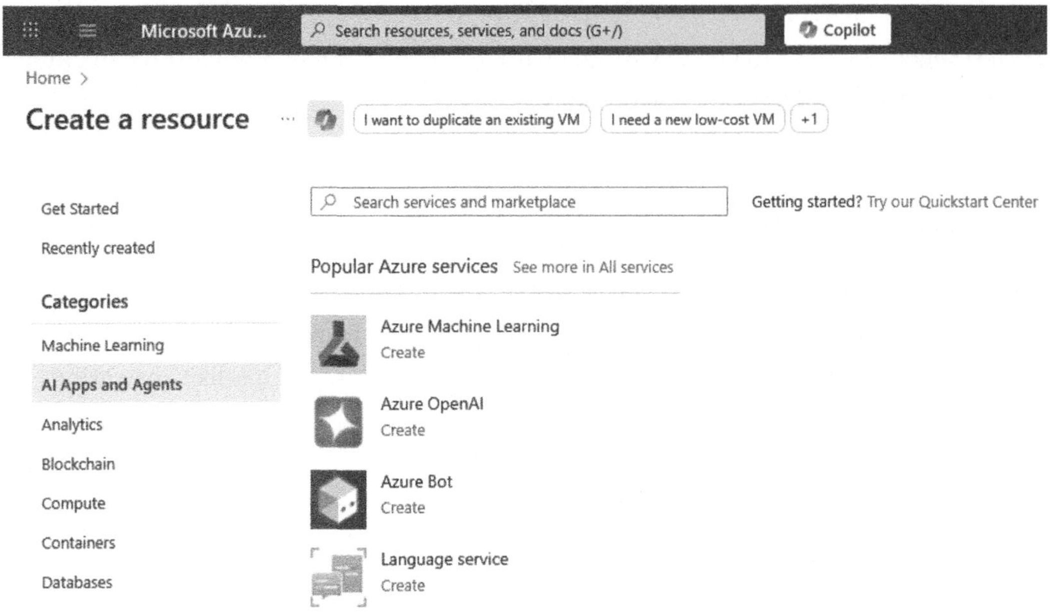

Figure 5-5. *Create new resource*

Click Create underneath AzureOpen AI and fill in the required information, as shown in Figure 5-6. You can use an existing resource; make sure you use the right subscription and give your resource a unique name. There is no free tier for this resource, so we will choose the Standard pricing tier that is a pay as you go for input and output tokens option.

Then click Next.

Home > Create a resource >

Create Azure OpenAI   ⋯   ✕

---

① Basics   ② Network   ③ Tags   ④ Review + submit

Azure OpenAI Service provides access to OpenAI's powerful language models, including all the latest OpenAI models.
These models can be easily adapted to your specific tasks, including but not limited to content generation,
summarization, image understanding, semantic search, and natural language to code translation. Top use cases include
Call Centers, Virtual Assistants, Accessibility, Content Generation, and Code Development. The service also features the
Assistants API, Fine Tuning capabilities and many ways to connect your data to the service for conversational
experiences. The service can be scaled through Standard (tokens) and Provisioned (PTUs) deployment types.

Learn more

Project Details

Subscription * ⓘ | Visual Studio Premium con MSDN   ∨ |

    Resource group * ⓘ | mauiResource   ∨ |
                               Create new

Instance Details

Region ⓘ | East US   ∨ |

Name * ⓘ | azureopenaich5   ✓ |

Pricing tier * ⓘ | Standard S0   ∨ |

View full pricing details

Content review policy

To detect and mitigate harmful use of the Azure OpenAI Service, Microsoft logs the content you send to the
Completions and image generations APIs as well as the content it sends back. If content is flagged by the service's filters,
it may be reviewed by a Microsoft full-time employee.

Learn more about how Microsoft processes, uses, and stores your data

Apply for modified content filters and abuse monitoring

| Previous | **Next** | ⓡ Give feedback

Figure 5-6. Create Azure OpenAI page

In the Network tab, we can leave the default "All networks" selected, as shown in
Figure 5-7, and click Next.

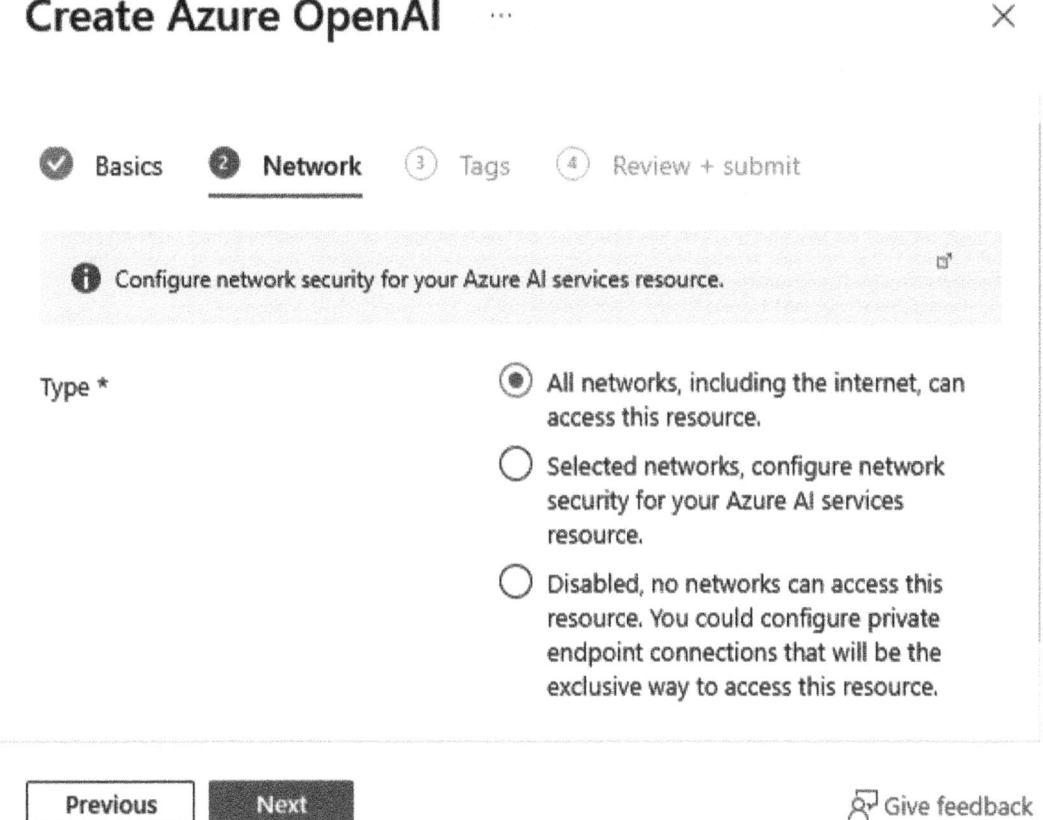

Figure 5-7. *Create Azure OpenAI–Network tab*

On the Tags tab, if you want you can create tags to categorize the resources that you have. After you have set your tags, as shown in Figure 5-8, click Next.

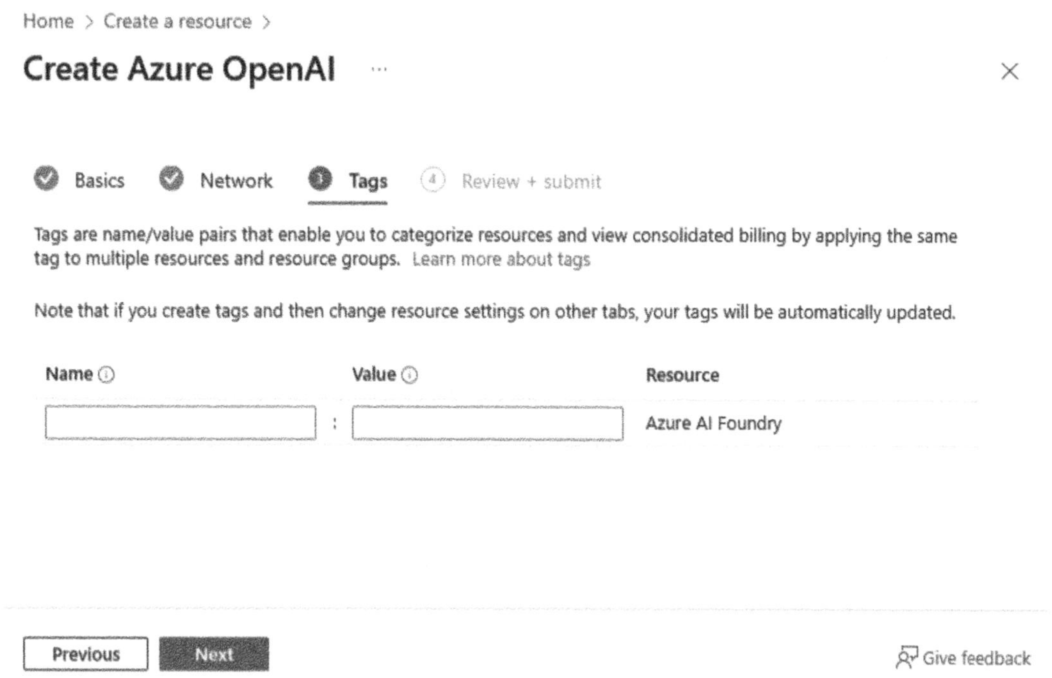

Home > Create a resource >

Create Azure OpenAI   ···   ×

✓ Basics   ✓ Network   ❸ Tags   ④ Review + submit

Tags are name/value pairs that enable you to categorize resources and view consolidated billing by applying the same tag to multiple resources and resource groups. Learn more about tags

Note that if you create tags and then change resource settings on other tabs, your tags will be automatically updated.

Name ⓘ		Value ⓘ	Resource
	:		Azure AI Foundry

Previous   Next   ℞ Give feedback

Figure 5-8. *Create Azure OpenAI–Tags tab*

On the Review + submit tab, review all your info, as shown in Figure 5-9, and click Create to create your OpenAI resource on Azure.

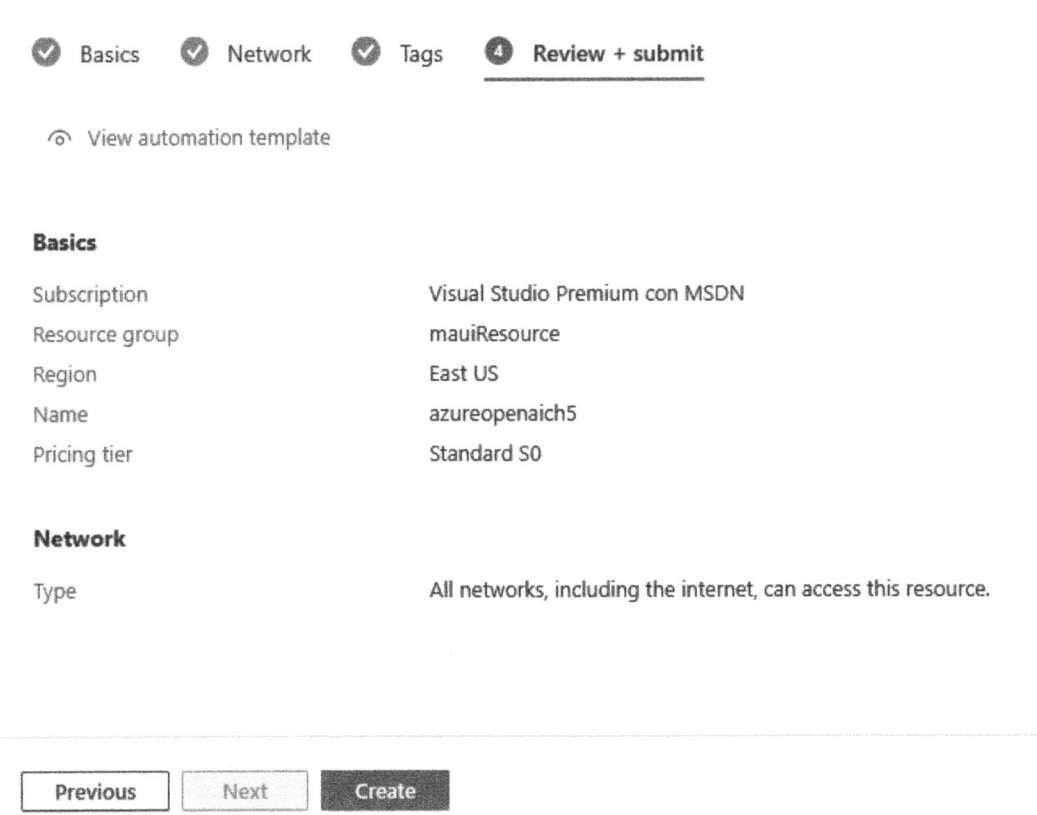

Figure 5-9. *Create Azure OpenAI–Review + submit tab*

Once we have our Azure OpenAI resource created, log in with your Azure account to https://ai.azure.com/. Previously known as Azure AI Studio, Azure AI Foundry is the new name for the AI Space on Azure, a unified platform for building, managing, and deploying AI solutions. It brings together tools and services that were previously spread across Azure AI Studio and other portals, providing a single environment for developers and data scientists to collaborate.

With Azure AI Foundry, you can explore a catalog of models (such as GPT-4, GPT-35-Turbo, Phi-3, and more), test prompts in a playground, deploy and manage models in your own Azure resources, and evaluate their performance and safety before releasing them to production. It also integrates with other Azure services, allowing you to connect storage, search, and cognitive resources into a single project. In short, Azure AI Foundry streamlines the entire AI life cycle—from experimenting with models to integrate them into applications like your .NET MAUI app.

Here you can find your newly created resource, as shown in Figure 5-10. After you click on it, select Deployments from the left menu.

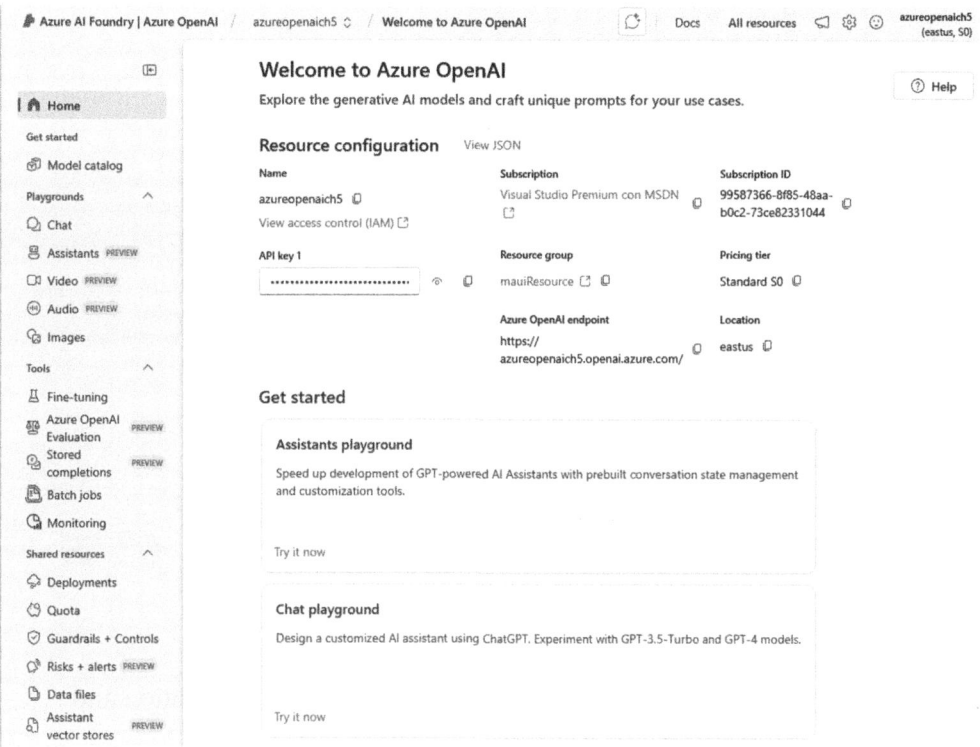

Figure 5-10. *Newly created resource*

Click + Deploy model and choose Deploy base model from the dropdown menu. In the pop-up, as shown in Figure 5-11, select gpt-g-mini or use the search box to search for gpt-5-mini. Based on your pricing tier, more or less models can be used.

Then click the Confirm button.

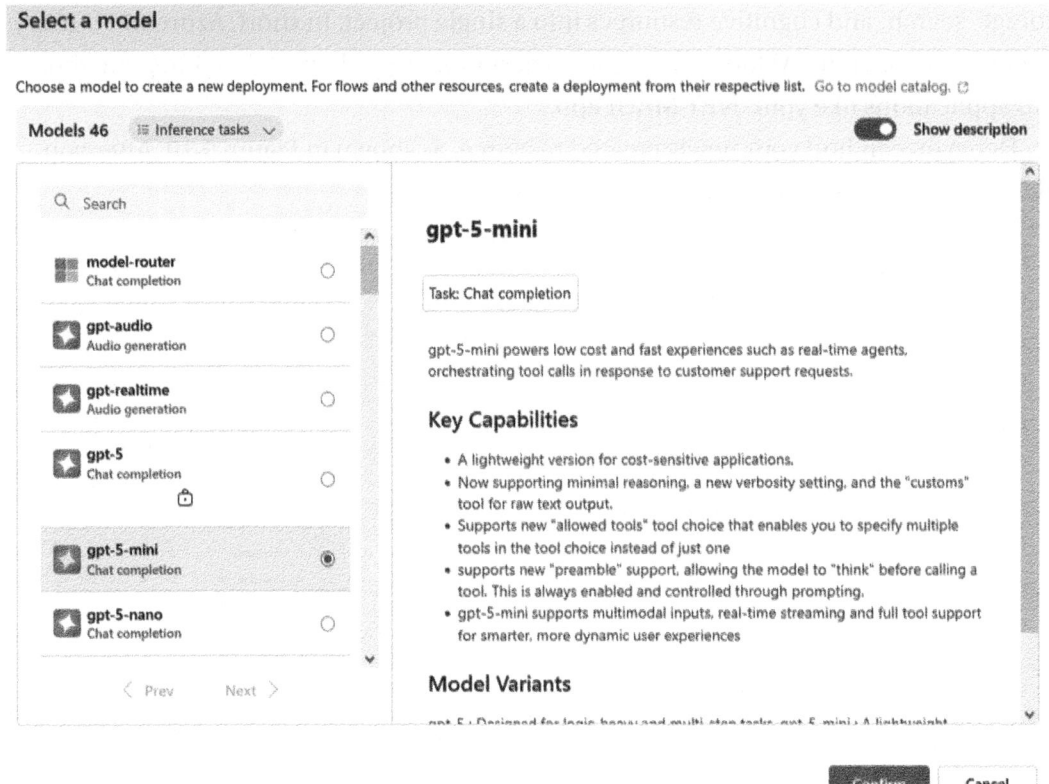

Figure 5-11. *Deploy–select model*

In the next screen, as shown in Figure 5-12, check all the information and click Deploy.

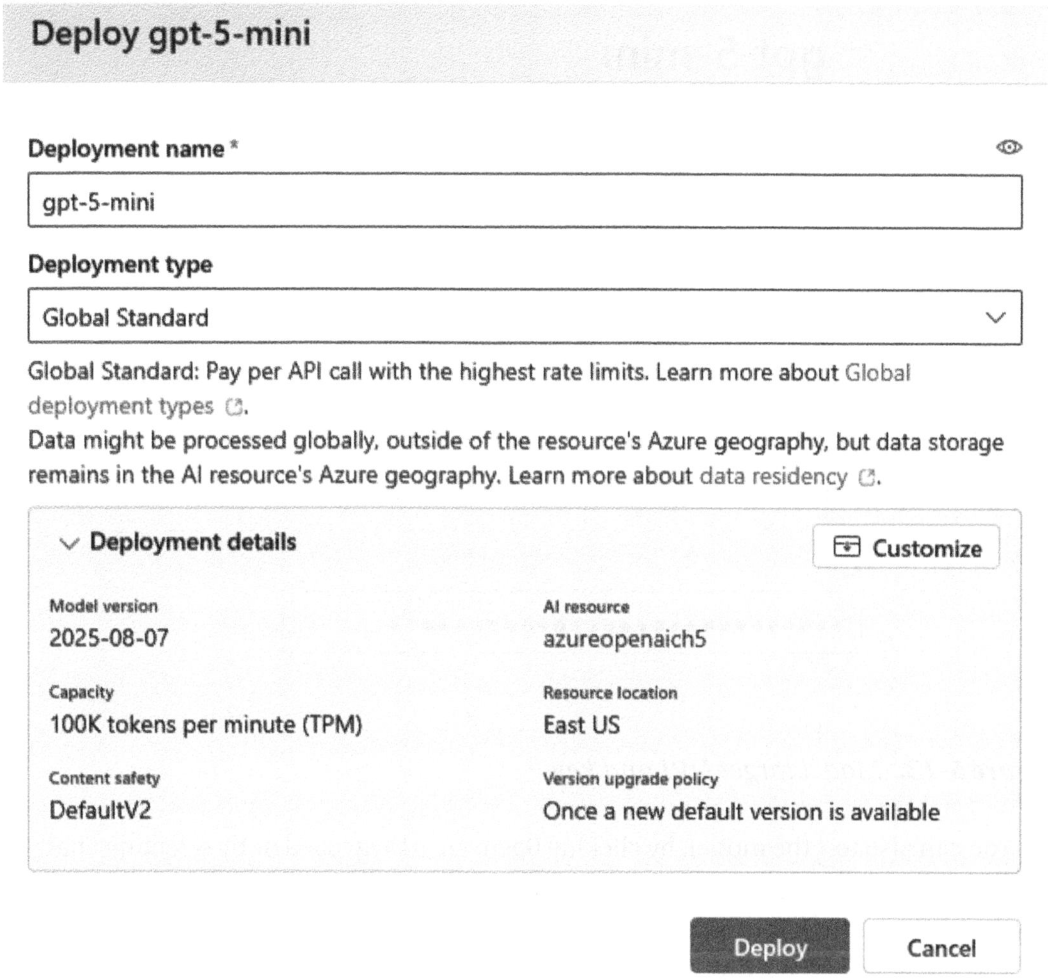

Deploy gpt-5-mini

Deployment name *   👁

> gpt-5-mini

Deployment type

> Global Standard   ⌄

Global Standard: Pay per API call with the highest rate limits. Learn more about Global deployment types ⧉.
Data might be processed globally, outside of the resource's Azure geography, but data storage remains in the AI resource's Azure geography. Learn more about data residency ⧉.

⌄ **Deployment details**   ⊞ Customize

Model version
2025-08-07

AI resource
azureopenaich5

Capacity
100K tokens per minute (TPM)

Resource location
East US

Content safety
DefaultV2

Version upgrade policy
Once a new default version is available

Deploy   Cancel

Figure 5-12. *Deploy model page*

We might already be redirected to the Deployments part or select Deployments from the left menu to check your Target URI (endpoint) and your key (API key) for the resource as shown in Figure 5-13.

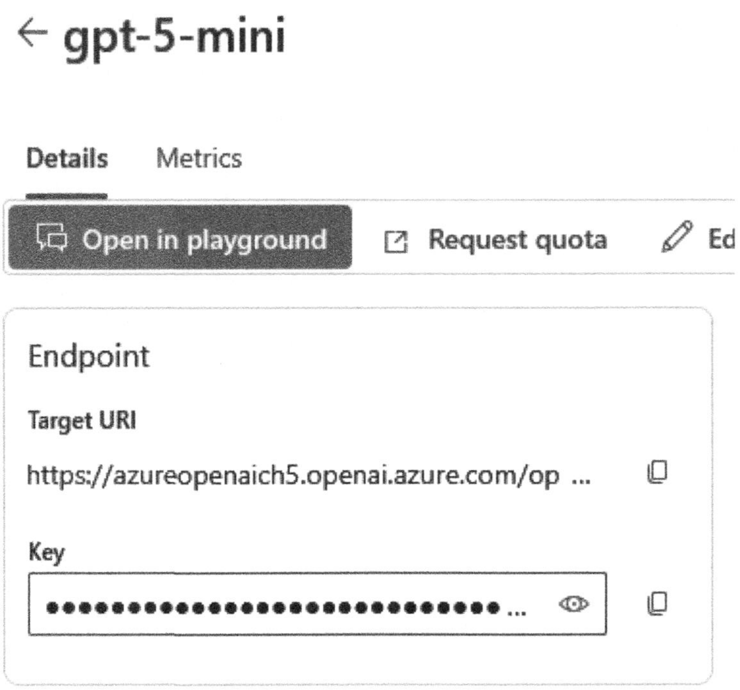

← gpt-5-mini

Details   Metrics

[💬 Open in playground]   [↗ **Request quota**]   ✎ Ed

> **Endpoint**
>
> **Target URI**
>
> https://azureopenaich5.openai.azure.com/op ...   📋
>
> **Key**
>
> •••••••••••••••••••••••••••••••• ...   👁   📋

Figure 5-13. *Model target URI and key*

You can also test the model, by clicking Open in playground or by selecting Chat from the left menu. You can select your deployment and explore gpt-5-mini model capabilities.

You can play with the sample prompt or use your own to see the model in action, as shown in Figure 5-14.

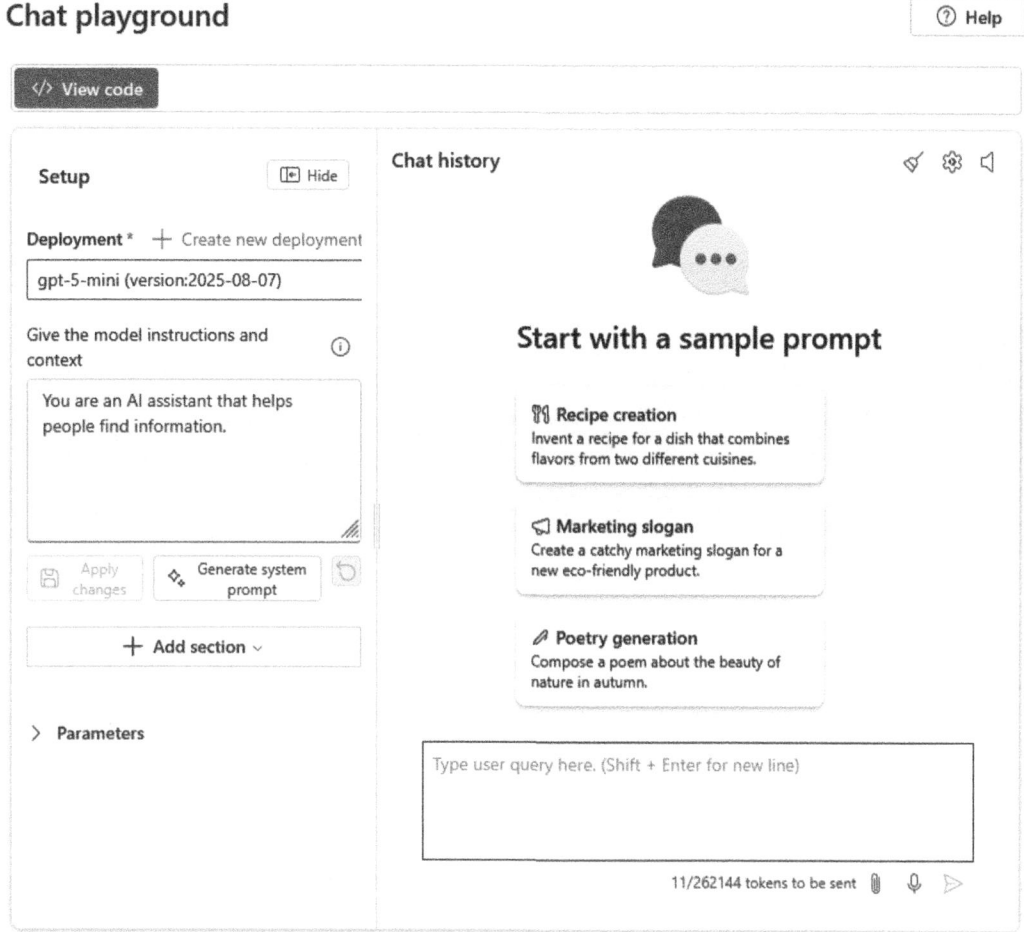

Figure 5-14. *Chat playground*

In the chat playground, when you click View code then select Key authentication, you will find the chat endpoint and key to use in our application. In the same page, you can see how the API works by clicking the </> View code button. You can also choose your preferred programming language and SDK to start integrating it into your application, as shown in Figure 5-15.

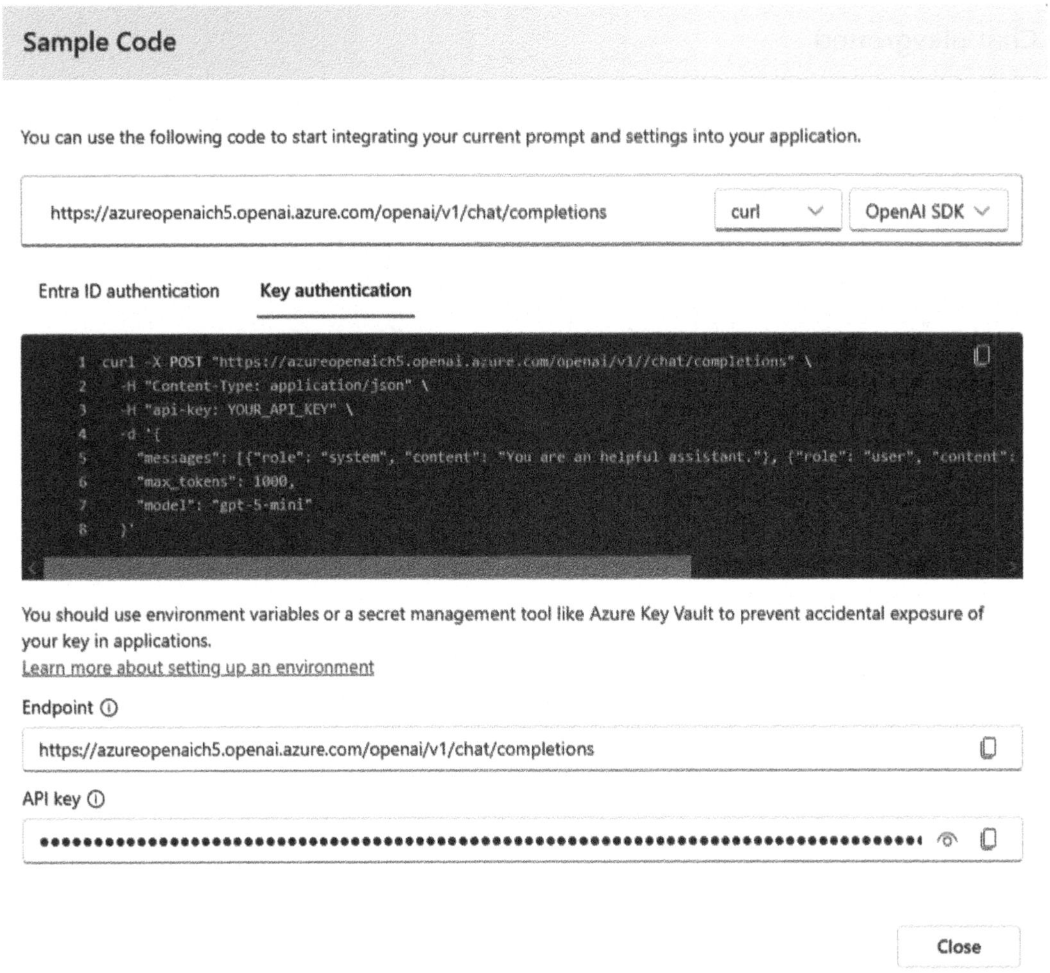

Figure 5-15. *Sample code for implementing the model*

Once we are ready with our model, we can integrate it into a .NET MAUI application. We will be creating a new .NET MAUI application that will gather the user prompt and send it to the model, then displaying the responses on the same page.

In our UI, we will do a similar UI as in the *Chat playground*, with an Entry on the bottom part of the page where the user will insert the prompt, and the rest part of the page will display the conversation between user and model.

So, let's start with creating a new .NET MAUI project and start with our UI. I usually use the Grid element to organize the page into rows and columns.

In our `MainPage.xaml`, we will create a Grid layout, with a `ScrollView` where we will display the chat messages in the top part of the page, and on the bottom part, we will have an `Editor` element and a `Button` element to send our request to the API.

We will modify `MainPage.xaml` with the code from Listing 5-3.

Listing 5-3. MainPage.xaml new Grid content

```
<ContentPage xmlns="http://schemas.microsoft.com/dotnet/2021/maui"
             xmlns:x="http://schemas.microsoft.com/winfx/2009/xaml"
             x:Class="Chapter5.MainPage">

  <Grid RowDefinitions="*,Auto" Padding="10">

    <ScrollView Grid.Row="0">
        <VerticalStackLayout x:Name="MessagesStack"
                                Spacing="10"
                                VerticalOptions="End"/>
    </ScrollView>

    <Grid Grid.Row="1" ColumnDefinitions="*,Auto" Padding="5">
        <Editor x:Name="InputEditor"
                Placeholder="Type a message..."
                AutoSize="TextChanges"
                HeightRequest="50"
                VerticalOptions="Center"/>
        <Button Grid.Column="1"
                Text="Send"
                Clicked="Button_Clicked"
                VerticalOptions="Center"/>
    </Grid>

  </Grid>

</ContentPage>
```

We will then need to get from Azure, in the sample code view of the chat, our key and endpoint. We will create an APIParameters class and store the info. We will also need the deployment name that we can find in the Deployment tab on the portal *e.g. gpt-5-mini.* You can find the calss implementation in Listing 5-4, just eplace YOUR_RESOURCE_NAME with your resurce name and YOUR_DEPLOYMENT_NAME with your deployment name.

Listing 5-4. APIParameters.cs class

```
public static class APIParameters
{
        public const string chatGPT_endpoint = "https://YOUR_RESOURCE_
        NAME.openai.azure.com"; // remember to delete /openai/v1/chat/
        completions from the endpoit
        public const string chatGPT_deploymentName = "YOUR_DEPLOYMENT_
        NAME"; // e.g. gpt-5-mini
        public const string chatGPT_apiVersion = "2024-02-15-preview";
        public const string chatGPT_apiKey = "YOUR_KEY_HERE";
    }
```

For the service class, we can use the official OpenAI SDK and the example provided in the portal. Just install the OpenAI NuGet package from the Package Manager. Next, create a new ChatGPTService.cs class inside your Services folder and use the code from Listing 5-5.

Listing 5-5. Call the OpenAI endpoint using OpenAI SDK

```
using OpenAI;
using OpenAI.Chat;
using System.ClientModel;
using System.Data;
using System.Net;
using System.Net.Http.Headers;
using System.Text;
using System.Text.Json;

namespace Chapter5.Services
{
    public class ChatGPTService
    {
```

```csharp
    private readonly ChatClient _client;

    public ChatGPTService()
    {

        _client = new(
        credential: new ApiKeyCredential(APIParameters.chatGPT_apiKey),
            model: APIParameters.chatGPT_deploymentName,
                options: new OpenAIClientOptions()
                {
                    Endpoint = new($"{APIParameters.chatGPT_endpoint}"),
                });

    }


    public async Task<string> AskAsync(string userMessage)
    {
        // Create a chat request
        var response = await _client.CompleteChatAsync(
            new[]
            {
                new UserChatMessage(userMessage)
            }
        );

        // Return the assistant reply
        return response.Value.Content[0].Text;

    }
  }
}
```

Once our service is ready, we can call it from MainPage.xaml.cs in the Button_ Clicked method and add the reply inside a new label in the UI. We will then also delete the content in the InputEditor to be ready to continue the conversation. You can find the MainPage.xaml.cs implementation in Listing 5-6.

Listing 5-6. Call OpenAI service from Button_Clicked method

```csharp
using Chapter5.Services;
using System.Net;
using System.Text.Json;

namespace Chapter5
{
    public partial class MainPage : ContentPage
    {
        private readonly ChatGPTService _chatGPTService;

        public MainPage()
        {
            InitializeComponent();
            _chatGPTService = new ChatGPTService();
        }

        private async void Button_Clicked(object sender, EventArgs e)
        {
            var userMessage = InputEditor.Text.ToString();
            if (string.IsNullOrWhiteSpace(userMessage))
                return;
            // Add user message to UI
            MessagesStack.Children.Add(new Label { Text = $"You:
            {userMessage}" });
            // Call Azure OpenAI via service
            string reply = await _chatGPTService.AskAsync(userMessage);
            // Add assistant response to UI
            MessagesStack.Children.Add(new Label { Text = $"chatGPT:
            {reply}" });
            InputEditor.Text = string.Empty;
        }
    }
}
```

Now, we are ready to build and run our application so we can start to chat with our ChatGPT bot. In *Figure 5-16,* you can see a sample conversation.

≡   Chapter4b   —   □   ×

Home

You: hi

chatGPT: Hi — how can I help you today?

You: tell me more about chatbots

chatGPT: Broadly, a chatbot is a software agent that interacts with people through text, voice, or other conversational modalities. They range from simple scripted helpers to advanced systems powered by large language models (LLMs). Here's a concise overview to give you a clear picture:

What chatbots do
- Answer questions (FAQ-style)
- Guide users through tasks (booking, form filling, onboarding)
- Automate routine support and transactions (order status, password resets)
- Provide recommendations and personalized experiences
- Serve as interfaces for services or devices (smart home, voice assistants)

Main types
- Rule-based (scripted): follow predefined flows and pattern-matching rules. Predictable and safe but limited and brittle.
- Retrieval-based: choose the best response from a fixed set using similarity or ranking (often combined with an FAQ or knowledge base).
- Generative (LLM-based): create responses on the fly using machine learning models. Flexible and natural but can hallucinate or be inconsistent.
- Hybrid: combine retrieval + generation (e.g., use the knowledge base to ground LLM responses).

How they work (typical components)
- Input processing: text normalization, speech-to-text for voice bots.
- NLP core: intent detection (what the user wants) and entity extraction (important details like dates, names).
- Dialogue manager: decides the next step (reply, ask for clarification, call an API).

Type a message...   Send

Figure 5-16. *.NET MAUI app output with ChatGPT*

Integrate Gemini Chatbot

Google has its own AI with its Google Gemini models that are designed to process and understand different types of data simultaneously including text, images, audio, video, and code. You can play around with their generative chatbot at `https://gemini.google.com/` or through the mobile app. It can help you the same way ChatGPT does with tasks like generating content or answering questions. We will take a deeper dive into the world of Google Gemini in Chapter 11.

For now, we will just integrate it in our app. You can call Gemini almost like you call OpenAI's ChatGPT API, by adjusting base URLs and using the correct model names. You can find the full API reference at `https://ai.google.dev/api`.

For example, you can use the latest gemini-2.5-flash model, and you can use the same key we used in Chapter 3 or create a new one. You can learn more about the models and their supported languages at `https://ai.google.dev/gemini-api/docs/models` and choose the one that works for you.

You can also explore example prompts at `https://ai.google.dev/gemini-api/prompts`.

We will use our API key to authenticate to `https://generativelanguage.googleapis.com/v1beta/models/gemini-2.5-flash:generateContent` to generate content in the chatbot. Like ChatGPT, the user will answer a question and the API will reply.

We will need to create a request body and send our request in the `parts` following the structure from Listing 5-7.

Listing 5-7. JSON structure of the request

```
"contents": [
{
     "role": "user",
     "parts": [
     { "text": "Hello." }
     ]
}
```

The response body has a similar structure as the one in Listing 5-8.

Listing 5-8. JSON structure of the response

```
{
  "candidates": [
    {
      "content": {
        "parts": [
          {
            "text": "At its core, Artificial Intelligence works by learning
            from vast amounts of data ..."
          }
        ],
        "role": "model"
      },
      "finishReason": "STOP",
      "index": 1
    }
  ],
}
```

For our app, we will be using text-only requests and responses to bind them in the UI. You can find the full API reference at https://ai.google.dev/api, including all primary endpoints and how to use multimodal prompt which includes text and images.

We will need to add the Google API key and the model's name, for example, gemini-2.5-flash-lite, into our APIParameters.cs. You can find the contants to modify in Listing 5-9, just replace YOUR_API_KEY_HERE with your key.

Listing 5-9. Google constants

```
public const string googleGemini_modelName = "gemini-2.5-flash-lite";
public const string googleGemini_apiKey = "YOUR_API_KEY_HERE";
```

Now, let's create another service class in our solution called GoogleGeminiService. cs. As there is no official SDK yet, we will be calling the REST API directly. You can find the implementation in Listing 5-10.

Listing 5-10. Call Google Gemini from REST API

```
using System.Net.Http;
using System.Net.Http.Headers;
using System.Text;
using System.Text.Json;

namespace Chapter5.Services
{
    public class GoogleGeminiService
    {
        private readonly HttpClient _httpClient;

        public GoogleGeminiService()
        {

            _httpClient = new HttpClient();
        }

        public async Task<string> AskAsync(string userMessage)
        {
            var url = $"https://generativelanguage.googleapis.com/v1beta/
            models/{APIParameters.googleGemini_modelName}:generateContent?
            key={APIParameters.googleGemini_apiKey}";

            var requestBody = new
            {
                contents = new[]
                {
                new {
                        role = "user",
                        parts = new[]
                        {
                            new { text = userMessage }
                        }
                    }
                }
            };
```

```
var json = JsonSerializer.Serialize(requestBody);
var content = new StringContent(json, Encoding.UTF8,
"application/json");

var response = await _httpClient.PostAsync(url, content);
response.EnsureSuccessStatusCode();

var responseText = await response.Content.ReadAsStringAsync();
using var doc = JsonDocument.Parse(responseText);

var candidate = doc.RootElement
                .GetProperty("candidates")[0]
                .GetProperty("content")
                .GetProperty("parts")[0]
                .GetProperty("text")
                .GetString();

        return candidate ?? string.Empty;
    }
  }
}
```

We can use the same MainPage.xaml page to display our chatbot, comment on the OpenAI call, and call the newly created service. I have also changed the label to see that now Google Gemini is replying. The updated code is shown in *Listing* 5-11.

Listing 5-11. Modified MainPage.xaml.cs to call the Google Gemini service

```
using Chapter5.Services;
using System.Net;
using System.Text.Json;

namespace Chapter5
{
    public partial class MainPage : ContentPage
    {
        private readonly ChatGPTService _chatGPTService;
        private readonly GoogleGeminiService _googleGeminiService;
```

```
public MainPage()
{
    InitializeComponent();
    _chatGPTService = new ChatGPTService();
    _googleGeminiService = new GoogleGeminiService();
}

private async void Button_Clicked(object sender, EventArgs e)
{
    var userMessage = InputEditor.Text.ToString();
    if (string.IsNullOrWhiteSpace(userMessage))
        return;

    // Add user message to UI
    MessagesStack.Children.Add(new Label { Text = $"You:
    {userMessage}" });

    // Call Azure OpenAI via service
    //string reply = await _chatGPTService.AskAsync(userMessage);

    // Or call Google Gemini via service
    string reply = await _googleGeminiService.
    AskAsync(userMessage);

    // Add assistant response to UI
    //MessagesStack.Children.Add(new Label { Text = $"chatGPT:
    {reply}" });
    MessagesStack.Children.Add(new Label { Text = $"Google Gemini:
    {reply}" });

    InputEditor.Text = string.Empty;
}
}
}
```

You: hi

Google Gemini: Hello there! How can I help you today?

You: tell me more about chatbots

Google Gemini: Chatbots are a fascinating and rapidly evolving technology that are becoming increasingly integrated into our daily lives. In essence, a **chatbot is a computer program designed to simulate conversation with human users, especially over the internet.**

Here's a deeper dive into what chatbots are, how they work, their different types, applications, and the future of this technology:

How Do Chatbots Work?

The underlying technology of chatbots can vary, but generally, they rely on a combination of these principles:

*   **Natural Language Processing (NLP):** This is the core of most chatbots. NLP allows computers to understand, interpret, and generate human language. It involves:
    *   **Natural Language Understanding (NLU):** Breaking down user input into its constituent parts, identifying keywords, intent (what the user wants to achieve), and entities (specific pieces of information like names, dates, locations).
    *   **Natural Language Generation (NLG):** Constructing human-like responses based on the processed input and retrieved information.

*   **Machine Learning (ML):** Many advanced chatbots utilize ML to learn from vast amounts of data. This allows them to:
    *   **Improve accuracy over time:** By analyzing past conversations, they can refine their understanding of language and provide more relevant responses.
    *   **Handle variations in language:** They can learn to recognize synonyms, slang, and

Type a message...

Send

Figure 5-17. *.NET MAUI app output with Google Gemini*

You can see in Figure 5-17 that I have used the same question and that Google Gemini response has some words or part of the sentences in **–we can parse that, so we make those words bold, translate simple * to bullet point, and style all the responses as we wish.

Custom UI AI Chatbot

In our app, we have created a simple user interface (UI) for the chatbot, but I am sure we can enhance it to make it more on brand for our application. Common chatbots have a unique name and might use as their avatar the company logo, but some companies have created their own identity for their bot, giving it a human-like name. You might remember that Eliza was the first one, already had a human-like name, and companies might want their users to have the feeling that they are speaking with a person.

Sometimes chatbots are called virtual assistant or AI assistant. What we want to achieve is that the user has a conversation with our bot/assistant through a conversational user interface (CUI). A CUI is a type of user interface that allows people to interact with computers using natural language, either through text or voice. Instead of using traditional buttons and menus, a CUI emulates a human-like conversation to achieve the final scope of the conversation. If you are using AI, this human-centric approach is made possible by using technologies like natural language processing (NLP), which allows the system to not only recognize words but to truly understand the intent and context behind them. It's a continuous, dynamic process where the CUI analyzes user input, manages the flow of dialogue to maintain coherence, and learns from each interaction to improve its ability to respond accurately and helpfully in the future.

One of the most compelling advantages of conversational UIs lies in their ability to democratize and streamline digital interactions. For the average user, this translates to unparalleled convenience, as they can bypass the complex process of navigating intricate menus, sifting through endless forms, or clicking through multiple screens. Instead, they can simply articulate their needs in natural language, and the system instantly understands and executes the request. This simplicity also makes CUIs a powerful tool for accessibility too, opening technology to individuals who might face physical or visual barriers. For the elderly or those with disabilities, voice-enabled interfaces eliminate the need for precise motor skills or keen eyesight, empowering them to interact with devices and services with remarkable ease. From a business perspective, this technology offers immense scalability, enabling companies to handle a vast and continuous volume of customer inquiries through automated chatbots and voice assistants. This not only provides 24/7 support but also frees up human employees to focus on more complex issues, leading to significant cost savings. Ultimately, by offering instant, personalized, and efficient support, CUIs fundamentally enhance customer experience, fostering greater satisfaction and loyalty.

Not only UI is important, but also the user experience (UX). The goal of a great chatbot UX is to make the user feel like they are having a productive and helpful conversation, even though they are interacting with an automated system. This involves a blend of smart technology and thoughtful design. A good chatbot UX is built on several key principles and components that work together to create a smooth and engaging experience. At the core is conversational design, where the chatbot's persona (fictional character that represents your chatbot's personality and communication style) and tone should align with the brand, whether that means being friendly and informal or formal and professional. It should use natural language to handle variations in phrasing, typos, or slang and be transparent about its capabilities by managing expectations and offering a clear path to a human agent when needed. Equally important is flow and efficiency, ensuring conversations are goal-oriented, minimizing unnecessary steps, and leveraging contextual awareness to remember past exchanges. Well-designed fallbacks also keep interactions productive when misunderstandings occur. On the visual and interaction design side, the chatbot's interface should be clean, consistent with the brand, and easy to read, while enhancing engagement with quick replies, buttons, and rich media. Message pacing adds a natural, human-like touch by avoiding instant, robotic responses. Finally, data-driven improvement ensures the chatbot evolve over time through continuous learning, analyzing real conversations, and integrating user feedback loops like quick surveys on helpfulness.

While we design our assistant, we can think of the UX elements and the UI ones. We have seen also in the examples chatbots use plain text messages to interact with the user. Chat cards are a type of chatbot message that goes beyond plain text. Instead of just sending a single or multiple line of text, a chat card is like a mini-interactive panel within the chat that can include multiple elements such as

- **Title and Subtitle:** To summarize the information or highlight a key point.

- **Images or Icons:** To make the message more visually appealing.

- **Buttons or Quick Actions**: So the user can tap to take an action (e.g., "View Menu," "Get Directions," "Order Now").

- **Optional Additional Info**: Like ratings, prices, or descriptions.

Think of chat cards as mini cards in the chat that combine visual content, text, and interactivity in one message. They're widely used in ecommerce bots, travel assistants, or any chatbot that needs to present multiple options or rich content in an easy-to-digest format.

If we think about a pizza restaurant bot chat card, we can easily draw that using xaml or c#. For the greeting message, we can create a Border with some CornerRadius, images, and colored labels and buttons to style a card. You can find a sample implementation in Listing 5-12.

Listing 5-12. Xaml for our card

```xaml
<Border
    Stroke="#E0E0E0"
    StrokeThickness="1"
    Background="White"
    StrokeShape="RoundRectangle 20"
    Padding="10"
    Margin="5">

    <VerticalStackLayout Spacing="8">

        <!-- Image -->
        <Image Source="pizza.jpg"
               Aspect="AspectFill"
               HeightRequest="120"
               WidthRequest="250" />

        <!-- Title & Subtitle -->
        <Label Text="Pizza Place"
               FontSize="18"
               FontAttributes="Bold" />

        <Label Text="Best pizza in town, open until 11pm"
               FontSize="14"
```

```
        TextColor="Gray" />

    <!-- Actions -->
    <HorizontalStackLayout Spacing="10">
        <Button Text="View Menu"
                BackgroundColor="#9B2D1F"
                TextColor="White"
                CornerRadius="20" />

        <Button Text="Get Directions"
                BackgroundColor="#EEE"
                TextColor="Black"
                CornerRadius="20" />
    </HorizontalStackLayout>

  </VerticalStackLayout>

</Border>
```

And you can see the rendered frame in Figure 5-18.

Figure 5-18. *Rendered frame*

Or we can use a `collectionView` to style multiple cards and give the user more choices and control over the menu, for example, with a button that will add the pizza to their order. You can see the implementation in Listing 5-13.

Listing 5-13. Use a CollectionView to display chatbot cards

```
<CollectionView ItemsLayout="HorizontalList" HeightRequest="220">
    <CollectionView.ItemTemplate>
        <DataTemplate>
            <Frame CornerRadius="20" Padding="10" WidthRequest="250"
            Margin="5"
                BackgroundColor="White" BorderColor="#E0E0E0">
                <VerticalStackLayout Spacing="8">
                    <Image Source="{Binding Image}" Aspect="AspectFill"
                    HeightRequest="120" CornerRadius="15"/>
                    <Label Text="{Binding Title}" FontSize="16"
                    FontAttributes="Bold"/>
                    <Label Text="{Binding Subtitle}" FontSize="14"
                    TextColor="Gray"/>
                    <Button Text="Order" BackgroundColor="#9B2D1F"
                    TextColor="White" CornerRadius="20"/>
                </VerticalStackLayout>
            </Frame>
        </DataTemplate>
    </CollectionView.ItemTemplate>
</CollectionView>
```

Improve UX and UI for Your Chatbot

I am sure you can be more creative than I did with creating engaging conversational cards. You can also use the CommunityToolkit.Maui.Markup that might not be chat-specific, it simplifies building custom UIs in C# instead of XAML. Learn more about the amazing .NET MAUI Community Toolkit at https://learn.microsoft.com/en-us/dotnet/communitytoolkit/maui/.

Other third-party companies like DevExpress offers .NET MAUI UIs that can be used in chatbots. You can find more at https://www.devexpress.com/maui/. You can also check out the Giral kit at https://grialkit.com/.

There are also third parties' libraries specifically for chatbots and conversational UI like Syncfusion for .Net MAUI. The .NET MAUI Chat control, also called a conversational UI, delivers a modern and interactive chat experience. It is a versatile component that can display conversations between multiple users in a fully customizable layout. The control supports various types of content, including text, images, hyperlinks, and cards, and can be seamlessly integrated with chatbot frameworks to create intelligent, interactive conversations. You can find it at `https://www.syncfusion.com/maui-controls/maui-chat`.

You can instead use Telerik, which supports integration with major conversational UI APIs and is part of the Telerik UI for .NET MAUI library, which includes over 60 professionally designed UI controls. The package also provides comprehensive documentation, demos, learning resources, and dedicated support to help you build modern, interactive applications. You can find it at `https://www.telerik.com/maui-ui/chat-(conversational-ui)`.

These libraries provide a NuGet package ready to be installed and used. In your Visual Studio project, open the NuGet Package Manager and search for the specific package. Install the package into your .NET MAUI project and you are ready to use it in your projects.

Summary

In this chapter, we have learned more about chatbots. We started with ChatGPT and integrated it into our app, then moved to Google Gemini and changed the initial app. At the end of the chapter, we have seen how to create custom UI for our chatbots or use third-party libraries to create beautiful chatbots and how to create the UX for conversational chatbots that also please the user, not only help him.

In the next chapter, we will focus on adding image capabilities to a .NET MAUI application using Azure Vision. We will generate alternate text for our pictures and use the image recognition features to detect and count objects inside a picture.

CHAPTER 6

AI-Based Image Capabilities

Introduction

In this chapter, you will get an overview of how to use Azure AI Vision to generate alternate text and to detect objects inside a picture using *image recognition*.

Azure AI Vision is a unified service that offers innovative computer vision capabilities. Enhance your apps with powerful vision capabilities that let them understand and interact with the world around them. With just a few lines of code, you can enable your applications to analyze and tag images automatically, read printed or handwritten text using advanced OCR (optical character recognition), and detect faces in a responsible and secure way. We will start in this chapter to understand how we can use these capabilities with our images.

Inside an Image

An image can say more than a thousand words, but sometimes images don't say anything. Alternate text or alt text is important for describing what is inside a picture when it can't be displayed or for users who are visually impaired. For accessibility, it is crucial to set this property as screen readers use it to give a meaning of the image for the users who cannot see it on the screen.

Images are displayed all over the Internet, but what happens when an image might fail to load or is for some reason broken? We rely on its description. I know it might be overwhelming to add descriptions to a multitude of images across websites and apps. In .NET MAUI, we use the semantic properties to define which information of each control

© Codrina Merigo 2026
C. Merigo, *AI-Enabled Apps with .NET MAUI*, https://doi.org/10.1007/979-8-8688-1817-2_6

can be used by screen readers and should be read aloud to the user. While a *Label* element or a *Button* already has the *Text* property that is easily accessed by screen reader, for *Images, ImageButton, Switch,* or other elements do not have this property.

There are three semantic properties:

- *Description*, of type string, which represents a description that will be read aloud by the screen reader

- *Hint*, of type string, which is like *Description*, but provides additional context such as the purpose of a control

- *HeadingLevel*, of type SemanticHeadingLevel, which enables an element to be marked as a heading to organize the UI and make it easier to navigate

You can combine both Description and Hint for your images as in the XAML sample below.

```
<Image Source="image.png"
    SemanticProperties.Description="my Image"
    SemanticProperties.Hint="This is my Image." />
```

Or you can use c#.

```
Image image = new Image { Source = "myImage.png" };
SemanticProperties.SetDescription(image, "my Image");
SemanticProperties.SetHint(image, "This is my Image.");
```

Generate Image Description

Artificial intelligence can help to save a significant amount of time by using Image description capabilities. With this service, we can generate comprehensive descriptions and just copy-paste them to your image *Description* of the *Semantic* property. It will increase the accessibility of our app as screen readers will use it to read aloud to the user what is displayed on the screen.

Azure AI Vision Studio offers a playground to test their Apps. We can start by heading to https://portal.vision.cognitive.azure.com/demo/image-captioning to see how captions or alternate texts are generated. You can use the sample images or upload your own as shown in Figure 6-1.

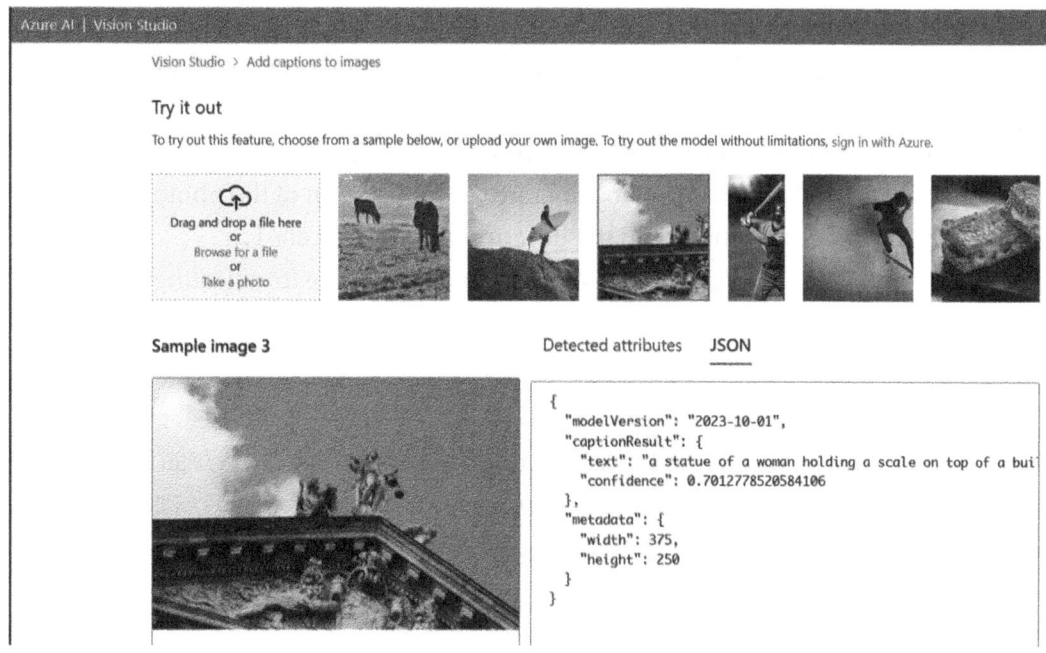

Figure 6-1. *Azure AI Vision Studio*

If we click on the JSON tab, we can see all the properties that the API will give us in return. We can check the *modelVersion* and *captionResult* together with some metadata. You can find the JSON in Listing 6-1.

Listing 6-1. JSON results

```
{
  "modelVersion": "2023-10-01",
  "captionResult": {
    "text": "a statue of a woman holding a scale on top of a building",
    "confidence": 0.7012778520584106
  },
  "metadata": {
    "width": 375,
    "height": 250
  }
}
```

We will use *captionResult.text* to get the description of our image and bind it in our app. We can also see, as in the previous examples, the *confidence* score and we might be doing some additional logic based on it.

Let's start by creating a new .NET MAUI project. In this project, we will be taking a picture and using the image caption to generate the description of the photo. We will then display the image and then bind the description inside a `Label`.

We can start by modifying the `MainPage.xaml` with the code from Listing 6-2.

Listing 6-2. XAML page

```
<?xml version="1.0" encoding="utf-8" ?>
<ContentPage xmlns="http://schemas.microsoft.com/dotnet/2021/maui"
             xmlns:x="http://schemas.microsoft.com/winfx/2009/xaml"
             x:Class="Chapter7.MainPage">

    <ScrollView>
        <VerticalStackLayout
            Padding="30,0"
            Spacing="25">
<Label x:Name="WelcomeLabel" FontSize="18" TextColor="Purple" Text="Let's
try the Image AI Model"></Label>
<Button Text="Take Photo" Clicked=" PhotoButton _Clicked"/>
<Image x:Name="CapturedImage" HeightRequest="300"/>
<Label x:Name="CaptionLabel" FontSize="18" Text="Your caption will
appear here"/>
    </ScrollView>
</ContentPage>
```

We will get the `PhotoButton_Clicked` method in a second; now it's time to create the API we will be using in a service class.

To get our API and secret key, log in to `https://portal.azure.com/` and make sure you have an active subscription.

Click on create a resource button and search for Computer Vision as shown in Figure 6-2.

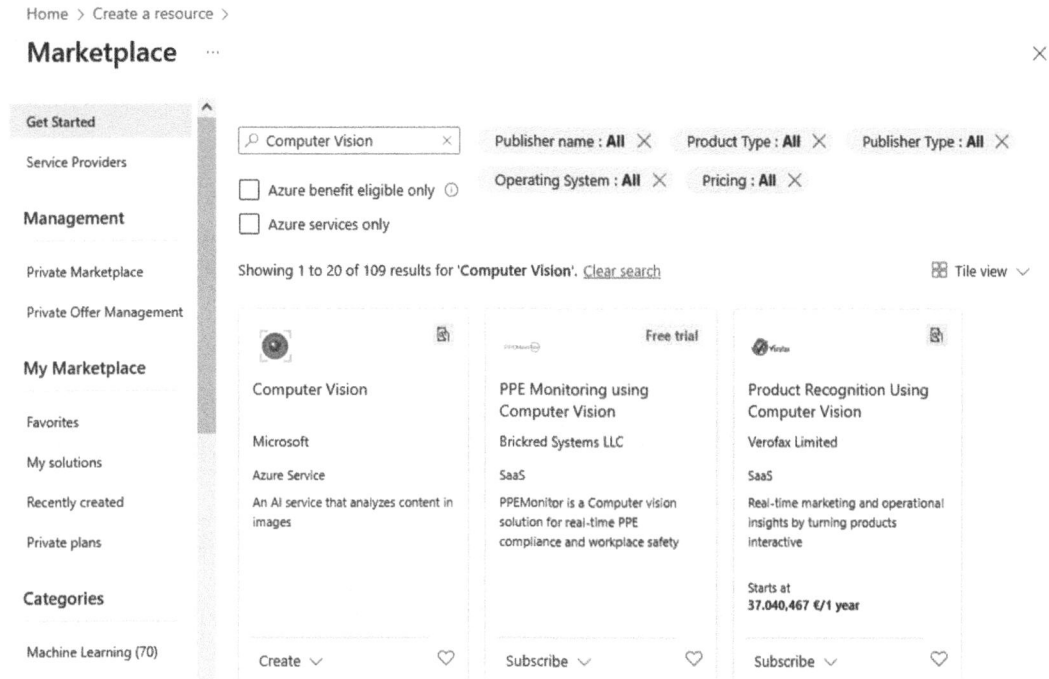

Figure 6-2. *Search on Azure portal*

Click Computer Vision box and check your subscription from the dropdown menu and then click Create as shown in Figure 6-3.

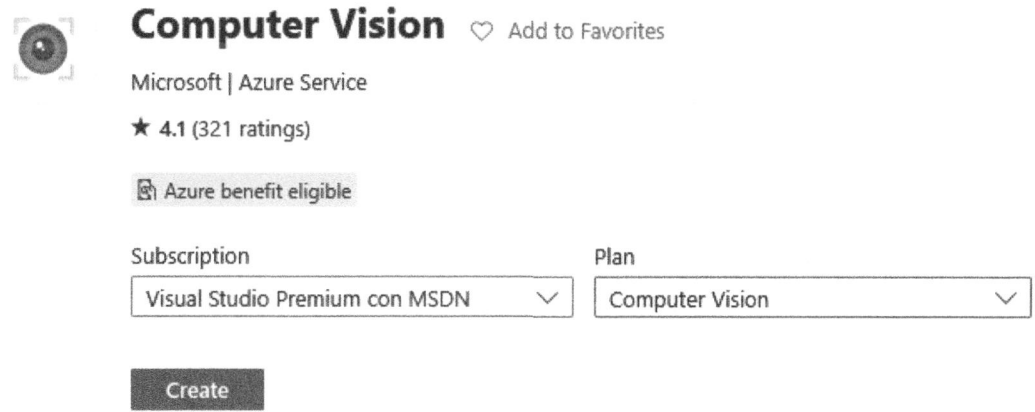

Figure 6-3. *Computer Vision create page*

On the creation page, fill in all the required information. You can use an existing resource group or create a new one, give this resource a name, select a pricing tier, check the acknowledgment, and click `Review + create` as shown in Figure 6-4.

Home > Create a resource > Marketplace > Computer Vision >

Create Computer Vision   ···

Boost content discoverability, accelerate text extraction, and create products that more people can use by embedding vision capabilities in your apps. Use visual data processing to label content (from objects to concepts), extract printed and handwritten text, recognize familiar subjects like brands and landmarks, and moderate content. No machine learning expertise is required.

Learn more

Project Details

Subscription * ⓘ

Visual Studio Premium con MSDN

Resource group * ⓘ

mauiResource

Create new

Instance Details

Region ⓘ

East US

Name * ⓒ

image6

Pricing tier * ⓘ

Free F0 (20 Calls per minute, 5K Calls per month)

View full pricing details

Responsible AI Notice

Microsoft provides technical documentation regarding the appropriate operation applicable to this Azure AI service that is made available by Microsoft. Customer acknowledges and agrees that they have reviewed this documentation and will use this service in accordance with it. This Azure AI services is intended to process Customer Data that includes Biometric Data (as may be further described in product documentation) that Customer may incorporate into its own systems used for personal identification or other purposes. Customer acknowledges and agrees that it is responsible for complying with the Biometric Data obligations contained in the Online Services DPA.

Online Services DPA

Responsible Use of AI documentation for Spatial Analysis

By checking this box I certify that I have reviewed and acknowledge the all the terms above. *

| Previous | Next | Review + create |

Figure 6-4. *Create your resource*

Check the information provided and click Create to create your resource as shown in Figure 6-5.

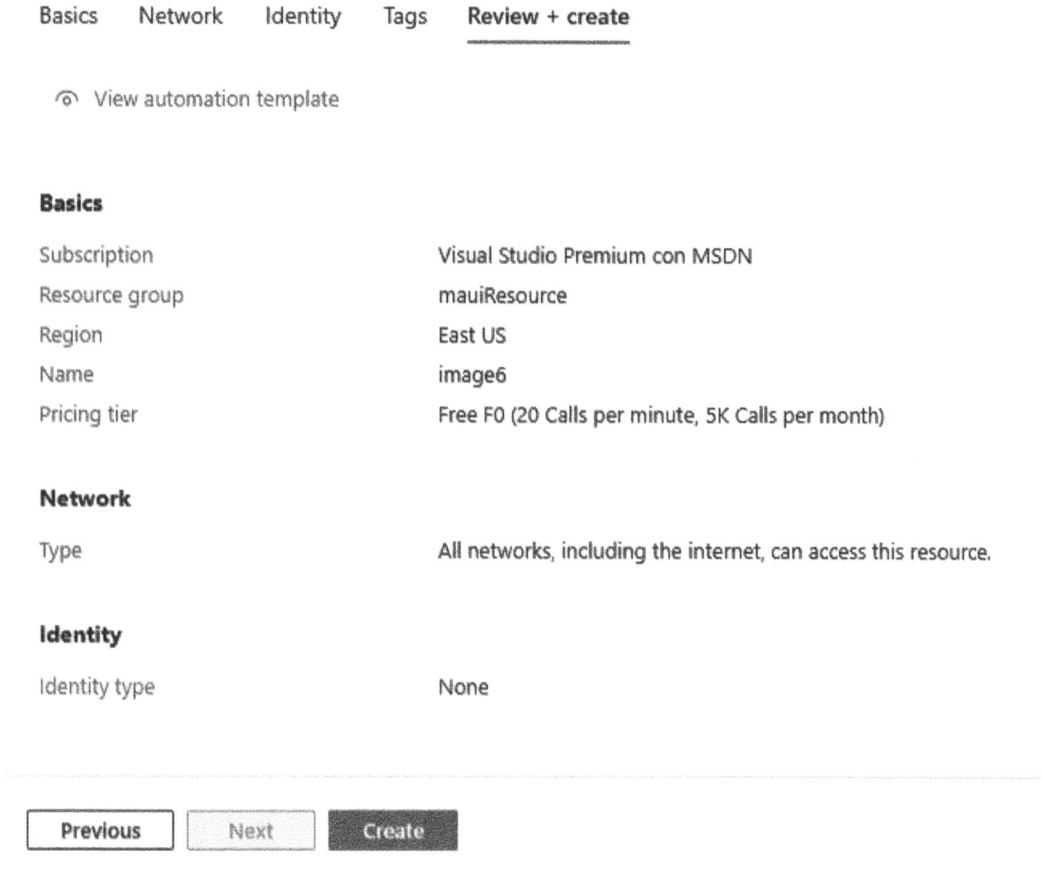

Figure 6-5. *Create your Custom Vision resource*

Once deployment is complete, as shown in Figure 6-6, you will be redirected to a new page. Click Go to resource to see your resource.

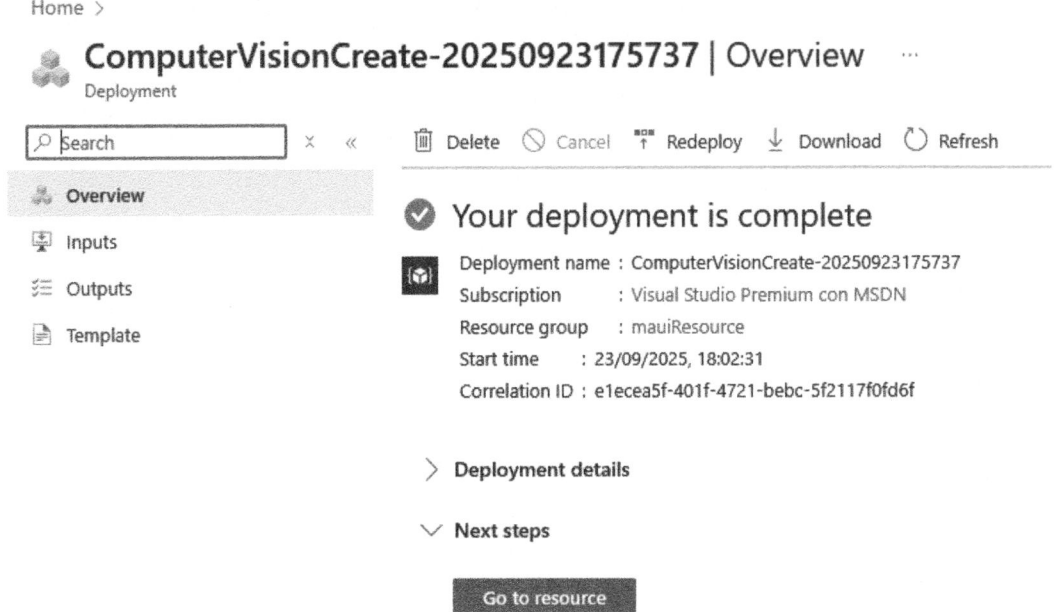

Figure 6-6. Custom Vision deployment result page

On the resource page, select the new created one in the group as shown in Figure 6-7. I called it image6.

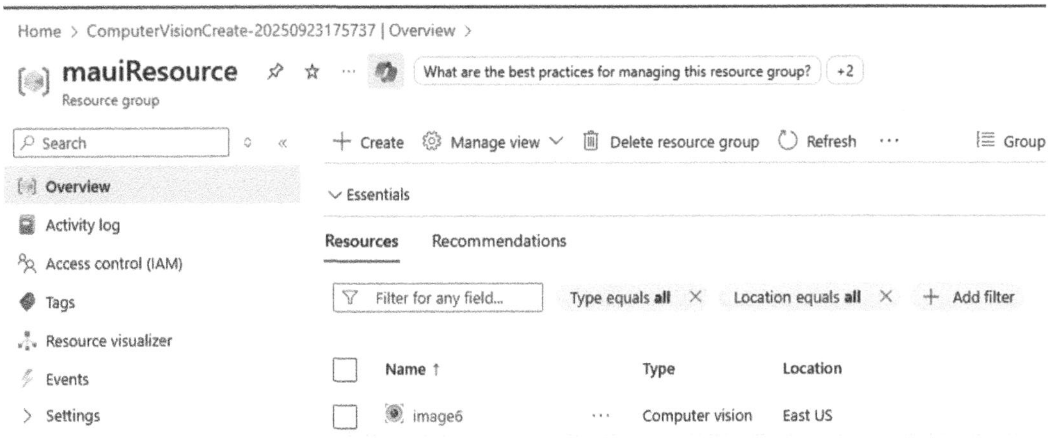

Figure 6-7. Resource group page

On the resource page, we will land on the Overview part as shown in Figure 6-8. Here, we can see our endpoint and manage our keys.

Save the endpoint for later and select Click here to manage keys.

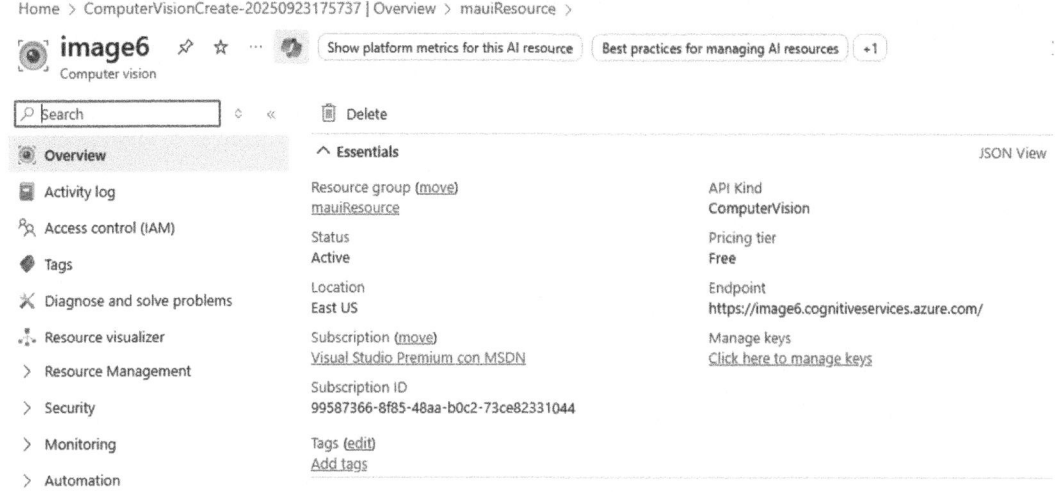

Figure 6-8. *Computer Vision overview*

You can also use the left menu. Navigate to Resource management and then Keys and Endpoint, as shown in Figure 6-9, to get your endpoint and keys. Copy a key that we will use in our application.

You will see two keys; usually one is for development and one is for production.

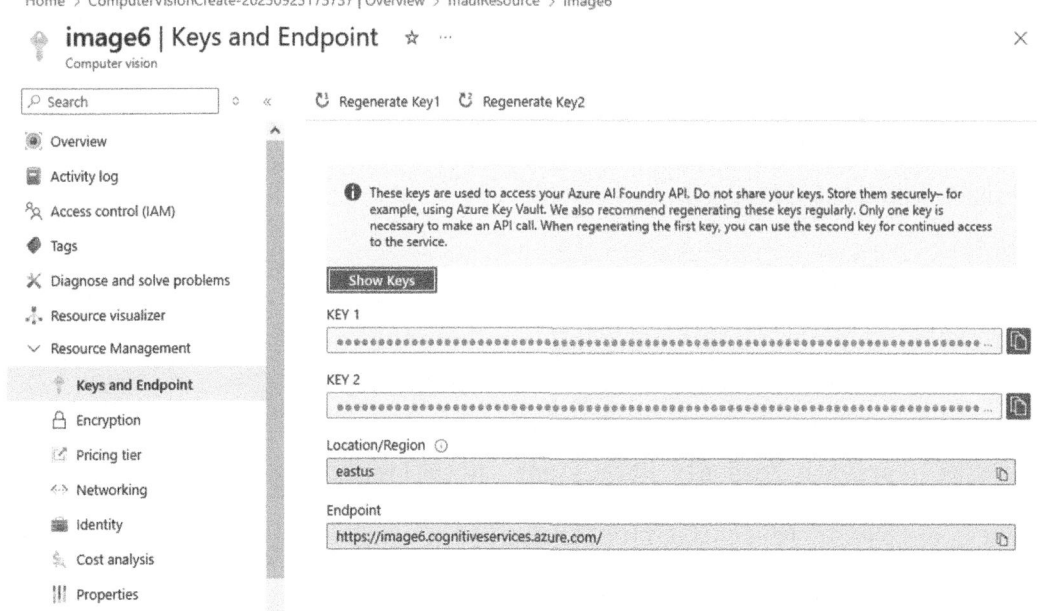

Figure 6-9. *Endpoint and keys page*

Next, we will create a new class called APIParameters.cs where we will save our endpoint and the API key. You can find the class implementation in Listing 6-3, just replace YOUR_API_Key with your key.

Listing 6-3. APIParameters class

```
public static class APIParameters
{
    public const string APIKey = "YOUR_API_KEY";
    public const string APIEndpoint = "https://<your-custom-endpoint>.
cognitiveservices.azure.com/";
}
```

Then, create a new folder inside the solution called Services and a new class AzureAICaptureServices.cs. You can find the full class implmentation in Listing 6-4.

Listing 6-4. Azure API service class

```
using System;
using System.Collections.Generic;
using System.Linq;
using System.Net.Http.Headers;
using System.Text;
using System.Text.Json;
using System.Threading.Tasks;

namespace Chapter6.Services
{

        public class AzureAICaptionService
        {
            private readonly string _endpoint;
            private readonly string _apiKey;
            private readonly HttpClient _httpClient;

            public AzureAICaptionService()
            {
                _endpoint = APIParameters.APIEndpoint;
                _apiKey = APIParameters.APIKey;
```

```csharp
    _httpClient = new HttpClient();
    _httpClient.DefaultRequestHeaders.Add("Ocp-Apim-
    Subscription-Key", _apiKey);
}

public async Task<string> GenerateCaptionAsync(MemoryStream
imageStream)
{
    try
    {
        var url = $"{_endpoint}/computervision/
        imageanalysis:analyze" +
        "?api-version=2024-02-01&features=caption&language=
        en&gender-neutral-caption=true";

        using var content = new StreamContent(imageStream);
        content.Headers.ContentType = new MediaTypeHeaderValue(
        "application/octet-stream");

        var response = await _httpClient.PostAsync(url,
        content);

        if (!response.IsSuccessStatusCode)
        {
            var errorMsg = await response.Content.
            ReadAsStringAsync();
            return $"API Error: {response.StatusCode} -
            {errorMsg}";
        }

        var json = await response.Content.ReadAsStringAsync();
        using var doc = JsonDocument.Parse(json);

        var caption = doc.RootElement
                        .GetProperty("captionResult")
                        .GetProperty("text")
                        .GetString();
```

```
                var confidence = doc.RootElement
                            .GetProperty("captionResult")
                            .GetProperty("confidence")
                            .GetDouble();

            return $"{caption} (confidence: {confidence:P0})";
        }
        catch (Exception ex)
        {
            return $"Exception: {ex.Message}";
        }
    }
  }
}
```

Once we have our service, we can go back to the `Button_Clicked` class inside `MainPage.xaml.cs` and replace it with the code in Listing 6-5. We also need to resize the captured image. I have used 300px width and 300px height to pass it to the Azure AI service.

When working with images, I prefer SkiaSharp. SkiaSharp is a cross-platform 2D graphics library for .NET that gives developers a powerful, flexible, and high-performance way to draw anything using C#. Developers can draw from simple shapes to fully custom UI components. It's essentially a .NET wrapper around Google's Skia engine, the same graphics engine used by major products like Google Chrome, Android, Flutter, and countless high-performance rendering systems. This means you get access to a production-grade, battle-tested graphics stack while staying fully inside the .NET ecosystem.

With SkiaSharp, you can render lines, curves, paths, images, text, gradients, shadows, and complex visual compositions with precise control over pixels, colors, blending modes, and transformations. It's extremely useful when you need to go beyond what standard UI frameworks can offer, whether that's drawing custom charts, rendering PDFs, building games, generating images dynamically, creating custom controls in .NET MAUI, or performing advanced image processing. Because SkiaSharp is designed to be fast and efficient, it supports hardware acceleration where available and behaves consistently across platforms, meaning your drawings look and perform the same on Windows, macOS, iOS, Android, Linux, and web (via WASM).

For .NET MAUI developers, SkiaSharp integrates smoothly through the SKCanvasView and SKGLView controls, allowing you to plug custom drawing logic right into the UI. You simply subscribe to a paint callback and draw with SkiaSharp's API, and the library takes care of rendering, scaling, and device-specific details. This makes it a great choice for scenarios where precision, performance, and cross-platform consistency matter. In short, SkiaSharp empowers developers to take full creative control of the rendering pipeline and build rich, visually unique experiences far beyond the limitations of standard UI components. We will use this library also later on to draw some rectangles inside our captured image, and you will see how simple it is to achieve this using this library.

You can learn more about SkiaSharp at `https://github.com/mono/SkiaSharp`.

You start by adding SkiaSharp through NuGet so you can start using it in your projects.

Listing 6-5. MainPage.xaml.cs page and logic

```
using Chapter6.Services;
using SkiaSharp;
using System.IO.Pipelines;

namespace Chapter6
{
    public partial class MainPage : ContentPage
    {
        private readonly AzureAICaptionService _azureAICaptionService;
        public MainPage()
        {
            InitializeComponent();
            _azureAICaptionService = new AzureAICaptionService();

        }

        private async void PhotoButton_Clicked(object sender, EventArgs e)
        {
            try
            {
                var photo = await MediaPicker.Default.CapturePhotoAsync();
                if (photo == null) return;
```

```
        // Copy the photo into a memory stream
        using var originalStream = await photo.OpenReadAsync();
        var memoryStream = new MemoryStream();
        await originalStream.CopyToAsync(memoryStream);

        // Display photo
        memoryStream.Position = 0; // reset for ImageSource
        CapturedImage.Source = ImageSource.FromStream(() =>
        {
            memoryStream.Position = 0;
            return memoryStream;
        });

        // Send a new copy of the stream to Azure
        var resizedStream = ResizeImage(originalStream, 300, 300);

        // Display image
        CapturedImage.Source = ImageSource.FromStream(() =>
        {
            resizedStream.Position = 0;
            return resizedStream;
        });

        // Send a copy to Azure
        var apiStream = new MemoryStream(resizedStream.ToArray());
        apiStream.Position = 0;
        var caption = await _azureAICaptionService.GenerateCaptionA
        sync(apiStream);
        CaptionLabel.Text = caption;
    }
    catch (Exception ex)
    {
        await DisplayAlert("Error", ex.Message, "OK");
    }
}
```

```
public static MemoryStream ResizeImage(Stream originalStream, int
width, int height)
{
    originalStream.Position = 0;

    using var input = SKBitmap.Decode(originalStream);
    using var resized = input.Resize(new SKImageInfo(width,
    height), SKSamplingOptions.Default);

    if (resized == null)
        throw new Exception("Failed to resize image.");

    using var image = SKImage.FromBitmap(resized);
    var ms = new MemoryStream();
    image.Encode(SKEncodedImageFormat.Png, 100).SaveTo(ms);
    ms.Position = 0;
    return ms;
}

}
}
```

As we are using the camera to take the photo, we will need to give the app the right permission in the AndroidManifest.xml, or equivalent in the iOS Info.plist file.

```
<uses-permission android:name="android.permission.CAMERA" />
```

```
<key>NSCameraUsageDescription</key>
<string>PROVIDE YOUR REASON HERE</string>
```

We will also need permission to WRITE_EXTERNAL_STORAGE in the manifest. You can learn more about permissions in .NET MAUI at https://learn.microsoft.com/dotnet/maui/platform-integration/appmodel/permissions.

After you fix the permissions, you can try the app on your device. I have deployed on an Android phone, took a picture of a pen, and waited for the caption. I have also displayed the confidence score in parenthesis.

You can see the result in Figure 6-10.

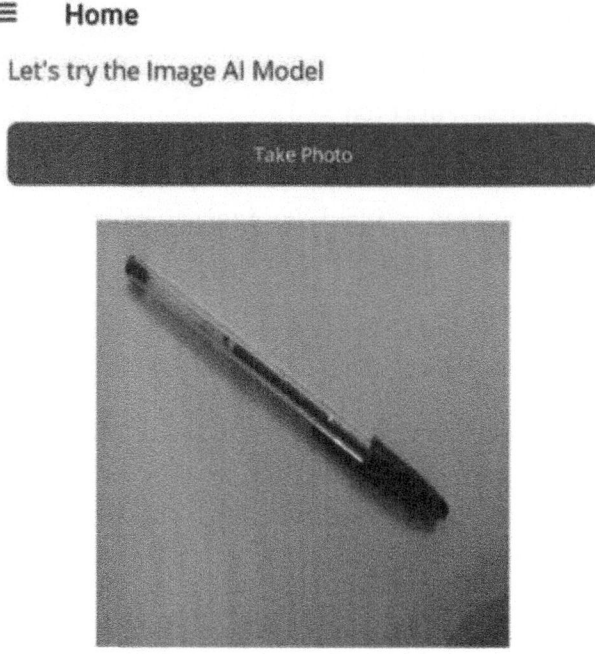

Figure 6-10. *Output of our app*

Detect Object Inside Images

Object detection is a smart feature in Azure AI Vision that allows your app or AI assistant to find and locate specific objects within an image. Instead of just knowing what is in a picture after creating the caption of the images, object detection tells you where those things are by drawing boxes around them. For example, if you upload a photo of your desk, object detection can identify and highlight items like a mouse, keyboard, a pen, or your favorite coffee mug—showing not only their names but also their exact positions in the image.

Azure AI Vision uses powerful machine learning models trained on millions of images to recognize a wide variety of everyday objects. When you send an image to the *Object Detection API*, it analyzes the picture pixel by pixel, searching for familiar patterns and shapes that match objects it knows. Once it detects an object, it returns the object's label (like "dog" or "car") along with coordinates that outline the area where the object appears.

This process happens very quickly and can handle multiple objects in the same image—so your AI assistant can understand complex scenes, not just single items. The API is designed to be easy to use, so developers can integrate it into apps without deep AI expertise.

You can go to `https://portal.vision.cognitive.azure.com/demo/generic-object-detection` to test this API, as shown in Figure 6-11. Here, you will find a slider that will allow you to set a threshold value; in this way, the service will return you the object identified only if the probability is above the set value. By default, the threashold value is set to 15.

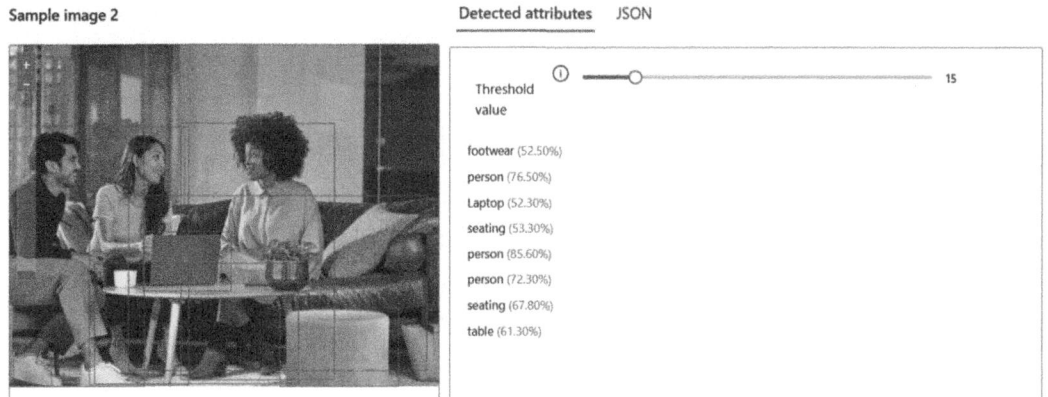

Figure 6-11. *Object detection page*

When you switch to the JSON view, you will find a little more complex JSON, but only because it contains lot of information for you. Apart from the tag and the confidence score, it also returns to you the exact box coordinates of where the object is detected. If we take, for example, the first person on the left side of the sample image, the API will return the following object inside the JSON, as shown in Listing 6-6.

Listing 6-6. JSON result

```
"boundingBox": {
        "x": 0,
        "y": 102,
        "w": 175,
        "h": 328
    },
```

```
    "tags": [
      {
        "name": "person",
        "confidence": 0.856
      }
    ]
```

Let's use this API with our app and enhance the image sample by also using this API. As in the previous sample, we will call our API and handle the information we get in response.

We will create a grid inside our MainPage.xaml.cs that will contain our image and an AbsoluteOverlay. You can find the Grid implementation in Listing 6-7.

Listing 6-7. New grid element

```
<Grid HorizontalOptions="Center" VerticalOptions="Center">
    <Image x:Name="CapturedImage" HeightRequest="300"/>
    <AbsoluteLayout x:Name="OverlayCanvas"
  IsVisible="True"        InputTransparent="True"/>
</Grid>
```

We will use the AbsoluteLayout to draw on the picture the blue box that we see on the Azure Vision Studio sample images. By placing both elements inside the Grid element, we can simply achieve that.

We can also add another label, to display the counted elements too, as in Listing 6-8.

Listing 6-8. New label element

```
<Label x:Name="ObjectCountLabel" FontSize="18" Text="Your detected objects
will appear here"/>
```

At the end, your new xaml will have the image capture and the new image detection information. You can find the full implmentation in Listing 6-9.

Listing 6-9. Complete MainPage.xaml

```
<ContentPage xmlns="http://schemas.microsoft.com/dotnet/2021/maui"
             xmlns:x="http://schemas.microsoft.com/winfx/2009/xaml"
             x:Class="Chapter6.MainPage">
    <ScrollView>
```

```
<VerticalStackLayout
    Padding="30,0"
    Spacing="25">
    <Label x:Name="WelcomeLabel" FontSize="18" TextColor="Purple"
    Text="Let's try the Image AI Model"></Label>
    <Button Text="Take Photo" Clicked="Button_Clicked"/>
    <Grid HorizontalOptions="Center" VerticalOptions="Center">
        <Image x:Name="CapturedImage" HeightRequest="300"/>
        <AbsoluteLayout x:Name="OverlayCanvas"
     IsVisible="True"
     InputTransparent="True"/>
    </Grid>
    <Label x:Name="CaptionLabel" FontSize="18" Text="Your caption
    will appear here"/>
    <Label x:Name="ObjectCountLabel" FontSize="18" Text="Your
    detected objects will appear here"/>
</VerticalStackLayout>
    </ScrollView>
</ContentPage>
```

We will create a new class for the detection API, like the AzureAICapture.cs class.

In this class, we will pass the results JSON, draw a red border on the OverlayCanvas element, and add also a yellow label. I have used the latest API version as of today, which replaced the boundingBox property from the example page with a rectangle property.

I suggest you always check the API and model versions at https://learn. microsoft.com/rest/api/computer-vision/?view=rest-computervision-v4.

To keep the services separated, create a new folder inside the solution called Services. Go to your newly created Services folder and add a new class called AzureAIDetectionService.

We will then parse our results JSON to get the coordinates x,y and width and height of the boxes that identify the detected object. You can see the JSON in Listing 6-10.

Listing 6-10. Results JSON used to draw the border and label

```
"rectangles": {
        "x": 50,
        "y": 84,
        "w": 175,
        "h": 126
    },
    "tags": [
      {
        "name": "pen",
        "confidence": 0.842
      }
```

We will use these information to draw a red `Border` element inside the OverlayCanvas. We will also create a yellow label element with a black background and place it on the top of our border, and we will display the content of the `name` property. I have added an alpha property to make the background more transparent WithAlpha(0.5f).

Once we have drawn the red border and placed the label, we can also update the object count label with the `name` property from the results JSON and confidence score. We will do this for each element in the image.

Inside the class `AzureAIDetectionService.cs`, it is important to add to our content header the "application/octet-stream" property. Application/octet-stream indicates that the payload is raw bytes, and we will be receiving a streaming binary content from the service. The complete code can be found in Listing 6-11.

Listing 6-11. `AzureAIDetectionService.cs`

```
using Microsoft.Maui.Graphics.Platform;
using Microsoft.Maui.Layouts;
using System;
using System.Collections.Generic;
using System.Linq;
using System.Net.Http.Headers;
using System.Text;
using System.Text.Json;
```

```csharp
using System.Threading.Tasks;

namespace Chapter6.Services
{
    public class AzureAIDetectionService
    {
        private readonly string _endpoint;
        private readonly string _apiKey;
        private readonly HttpClient _httpClient;

        public AzureAIDetectionService()
        {
            _endpoint = APIParameters.APIEndpoint;
            _apiKey = APIParameters.APIKey;
            _httpClient = new HttpClient();
            _httpClient.DefaultRequestHeaders.Add("Ocp-Apim-Subscription-
            Key", _apiKey);
        }

        public async Task<string> DetectObjectsAsync(Stream imageStream,
        AbsoluteLayout overlayCanvas)
        {
            var url = $"{_endpoint}/vision/v3.2/detect?overload=stream";

            using var content = new StreamContent(imageStream);
            content.Headers.ContentType = new MediaTypeHeaderValue
            ("application/octet-stream");

            var response = await _httpClient.PostAsync(url, content);
            response.EnsureSuccessStatusCode();

            var json = await response.Content.ReadAsStringAsync();
            using var doc = JsonDocument.Parse(json);

            if (!doc.RootElement.TryGetProperty("objects", out var
            objects))
            {
                // The 'objects' property was not found directly in the
                    root element.
```

```
        return "No objects detected.";
    }

    //our image has been resized to 300x300
    imageStream.Position = 0;
    using var img = PlatformImage.FromStream(imageStream);

    overlayCanvas.Children.Clear();

    var detected = new List<string>();

    // start drawing borders and the labels
    foreach (var obj in objects.EnumerateArray())
    {
        var name = obj.GetProperty("object").GetString();
        var confidence = obj.GetProperty("confidence").GetDouble();
        detected.Add($"{name} ({confidence:P0})");

        //Draw border from the rectangle property
        if (obj.TryGetProperty("rectangle", out var box))
        {
            float x = box.GetProperty("x").GetSingle();
            float y = box.GetProperty("y").GetSingle();
            float w = box.GetProperty("w").GetSingle();
            float h = box.GetProperty("h").GetSingle();

            // Border
            var border = new Border
            {
                BackgroundColor = Colors.Transparent,
                Stroke = Colors.Red,
                StrokeThickness = 2,
                WidthRequest = w,
                HeightRequest = h
            };
```

```
AbsoluteLayout.SetLayoutBounds(border, new Rect
(x, y, w, h));
overlayCanvas.Children.Add(border);

// Label
var label = new Label
{
    Text = name,
    TextColor = Colors.Yellow,
    FontSize = 14,
    BackgroundColor = Colors.Black.WithAlpha(0.5f)
};

AbsoluteLayout.SetLayoutBounds(label,
new Rect(x, y - 20, w, 20));
overlayCanvas.Children.Add(label);
        }
    }

//Now you can use the 'detected' list, which will contain the
detected objects
return detected.Count > 0 ? string.Join(", ", detected) : "No
objects detected.";
    }
  }

}
```

Now, build and run your application and test it. Take a picture of some elements and see the power of these services. You can see the app in action in Figure 6-12.

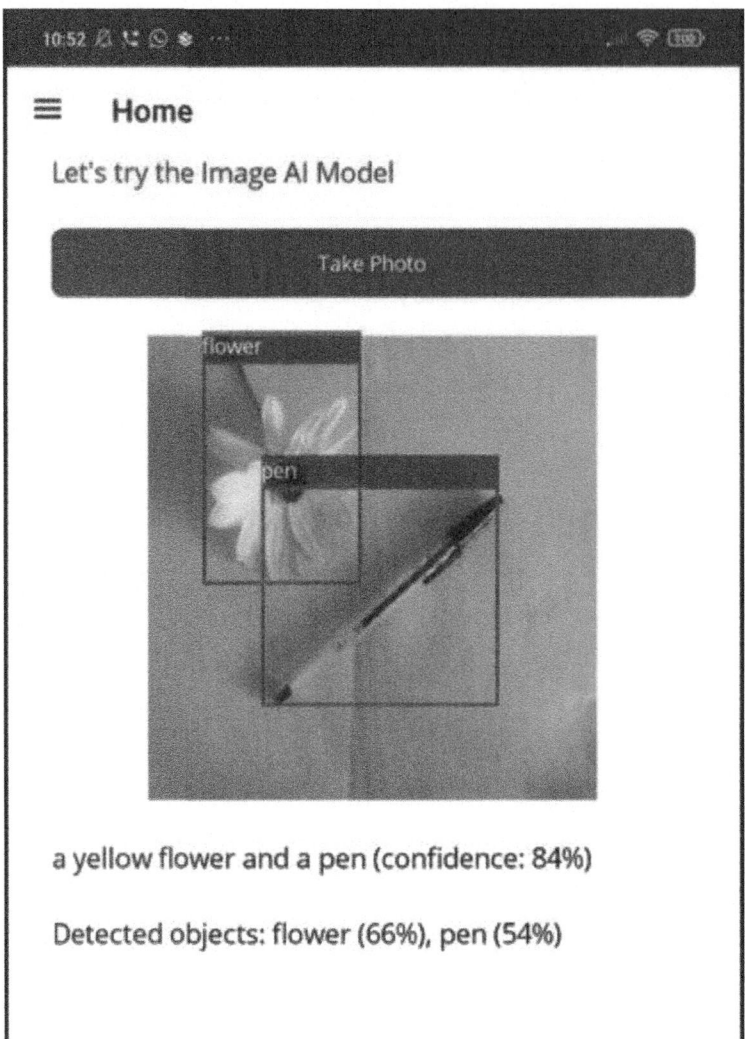

Figure 6-12. *Output of the updated app*

Object detection opens lots of possibilities for your AI assistant or app. It can help with tasks like

- Counting items in an image (e.g., how many products are on my desk)

- Detecting specific objects for automated inventory or quality control

- Enabling interactive experiences where users point their camera at objects and get instant information

- Enhancing accessibility by identifying objects in a scene and describing them to users with vision impairments as we know that accessibility is very important in our .NET MAUI apps

Because Azure AI Vision handles, as always, the heavy AI lifting, you get accurate, reliable results without needing to build and train your own complex models.

Your Photos, Your Power

Imagine your AI assistant being able to truly see and understand the content of an image. With Azure AI Vision's Image Analysis, it can identify objects and people within photos—whether it's a pen, a flower, or a famous landmark. We have seen how we can generate automatic descriptions in natural language, offering concise and accurate captions that make content more accessible.

You can use Image Analysis to create image description and bind the description inside the `SemanticProperties.Description` property. Semantic properties specify which controls should receive accessibility focus and determine the text that will be read aloud to the user. Accessibility for your application focuses on creating experiences that make your apps inclusive for users with diverse needs and ways of interacting with technology. While legal requirements may sometimes motivate developers to address accessibility, it's always the best practice to build inclusive apps to reach the widest possible audience. With Azure AI Vision, we can describe images and provide accessibility info dynamically, improving inclusivity for visually impaired users. Your app can also detect various characteristics of an image, such as where the objects are inside the picture, whether it's a photo or an illustration, its dominant colors, or if it contains potentially sensitive content—ideal for moderation scenarios. On top of that, *Image Analysis* can recognize thousands of celebrities and landmarks, enabling the assistant to instantly respond to an image with context like *"That's the Colosseum in Rome"* or *"This looks like the Beatles performing live."* All of this happens seamlessly, allowing your AI assistant to interact with the visual world in intelligent and meaningful ways. Below you can find an overview of the Image Analysis feature you can try right away. You can see the Capabilities of Vision Studio in Figure 6-13.

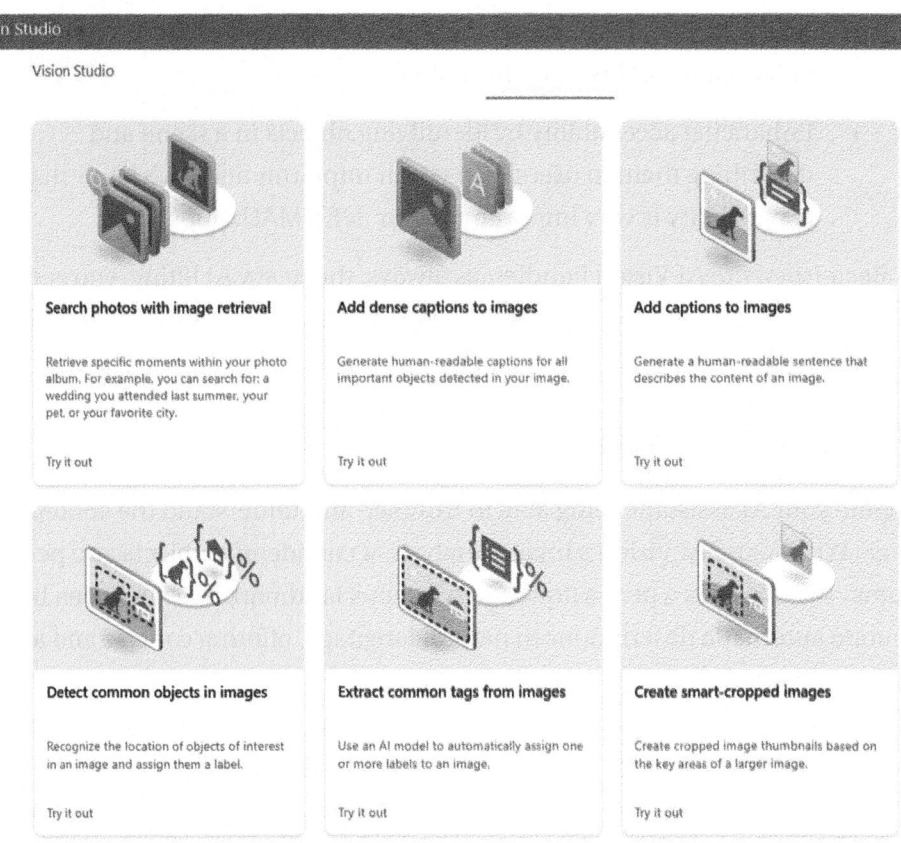

Figure 6-13. *Overview of capabilities of Vision Studio*

By integrating Azure Image Analysis, your AI assistant can offer a wide range of enhanced capabilities that make it more interactive and intelligent. It can power visual search experiences—like identifying similar products from a user-submitted photo—automatically tag uploaded images for better organization and discoverability and provide real-time content moderation to ensure a safe and appropriate user environment. Additionally, it enables more dynamic and context-aware conversations by responding to both images and text, while also supporting accessibility by generating helpful image descriptions for users with visual impairments. These are just some simple ideas on how you enhance your image capabilities inside your assistant. I would love to hear your ideas!

Summary

In this chapter, we have looked into Azure AI Vision services and learnt how to generate image description using AI. We have also used the service to detect objects inside images and draw a rectangle inside the image to see where the object has been detected. By the end of the chapter, we have seen all the vision capabilities we can try in the playground and start using them in our application.

In the next chapter, we will focus on more services related to AI Vision and more specific to optical character recognition (OCR). We will learn how we can detect handwritten text or use OCR to detect what is written inside an image.

CHAPTER 7

OCR—Optical Character Recognition

Introduction

In this chapter, you will get an overview of how to use Azure AI Vision optical character recognition capability to extract printed or handwritten text from images. It can also be used for documents and already supports mixed languages.

Azure AI Vision offers an advanced OCR (optical character recognition) API for us to use. The roots of optical character recognition (OCR) go back over a century, starting with inventions aimed at helping with telegraph communication and assisting people who are blind. In 1914, a scientist named Emanuel Goldberg created a device that could read printed characters and turn them into telegraph code. Around the same time, another inventor, Edmund Fournier d'Albe, built the *optophone*—a handheld scanner that played different tones as it moved over printed text, allowing users to "hear" the letters. Later, in the 1920s and 1930s, Goldberg continued innovating with a device he called the statistical machine. This early technology could search through microfilm archives by recognizing coded symbols—an early glimpse at the power of machine-based text recognition. Optical character recognition (OCR) targets typewritten text, one glyph or character at a time. Some advanced models can also target words and even handwritten or cursive text.

Detect Handwritten Notes

We all live in a digital world, but maybe you, like me, still prefer to write your notes on an actual piece of paper, perhaps a sticky note, and place them around your home. Sometimes we just need to digitalize this, maybe it is an item that will go directly into our grocery or shopping list. Our AI assistant can help here by using Azure AI Vision OCR capabilities.

We will just take a picture of our memo and call the API, and we will have the memo in a digital way, ready to be pasted in the right place.

Once again, artificial intelligence can help to save a significant amount of time by using the *Extract text from images capability*. Azure AI Vision Studio offers a playground to test their apps. We can start by heading to `https://portal.vision.cognitive.azure.com/demo/extract-text-from-images` to see how text extraction works. You can find an example in Figure 7-1.

Figure 7-1. *Sample form of Handwritten Notes detection*

When you switch to the JSON view, you will find a similar JSON as we have seen in the previous chapter, as it contains lot of information for you. Apart from the tag and the confidence score, it also returns to you the exact box coordinates of where the text is detected in the *boundingPolygon* object. You can find the JSON IN Listing 7-1.

Listing 7-1. Results JSON

```
{
        "text": "You",
        "boundingPolygon": [
          {
            "x": 252,
            "y": 267
          },
          {
            "x": 307,
            "y": 265
          },
          {
            "x": 307,
            "y": 318
          },
          {
            "x": 253,
            "y": 318
          }
        ],
        "confidence": 0.996
      }
```

Let's start by creating a new .NET MAUI project, very similar to the one in Chapter 6. In this project, we will be taking a picture of some handwritten text, use the *Extract text from images* capability to extract the text, and bind it inside a label underneath the image. So we will need a Button to be able to take a picture, an Image where to store the captured image, and a Label where we will bind the extracted info after calling the API.

We can start by modifying the MainPage.xaml with the code from Listing 7-2.

Listing 7-2. XAML page

```xml
<?xml version="1.0" encoding="utf-8" ?>
<ContentPage xmlns="http://schemas.microsoft.com/dotnet/2021/maui"
             xmlns:x="http://schemas.microsoft.com/winfx/2009/xaml"
             x:Class="Chapter7.MainPage">

    <ScrollView>
        <VerticalStackLayout
            Padding="30,0"
            Spacing="25">
            <Label x:Name="WelcomeLabel" FontSize="18" TextColor="Purple"
            Text="Let's Extract text from images capability "></Label>
            <Button Text="Take Photo" Clicked="PhotoButton_Clicked"/>
            <Image x:Name="CapturedImage" HeightRequest="300"/>
            <Label x:Name="ExtractedTextLabel" FontSize="18"
            TextColor="darkred" Text="Your extracted text will appear here"/>

        </VerticalStackLayout>
    </ScrollView>

</ContentPage>
```

We will get the PhotoButton_Clicked method in a second; now it's time to create the API we will be using in a service class. We can use the same Computer Vision resource from Chapter 6. You can log in to https://portal.azure.com/, look for your existing Custom Vision resource, select it, then expand Resource Management.

Click Keys and Endpoint to get your endpoint and key as shown in Figure 7-2.

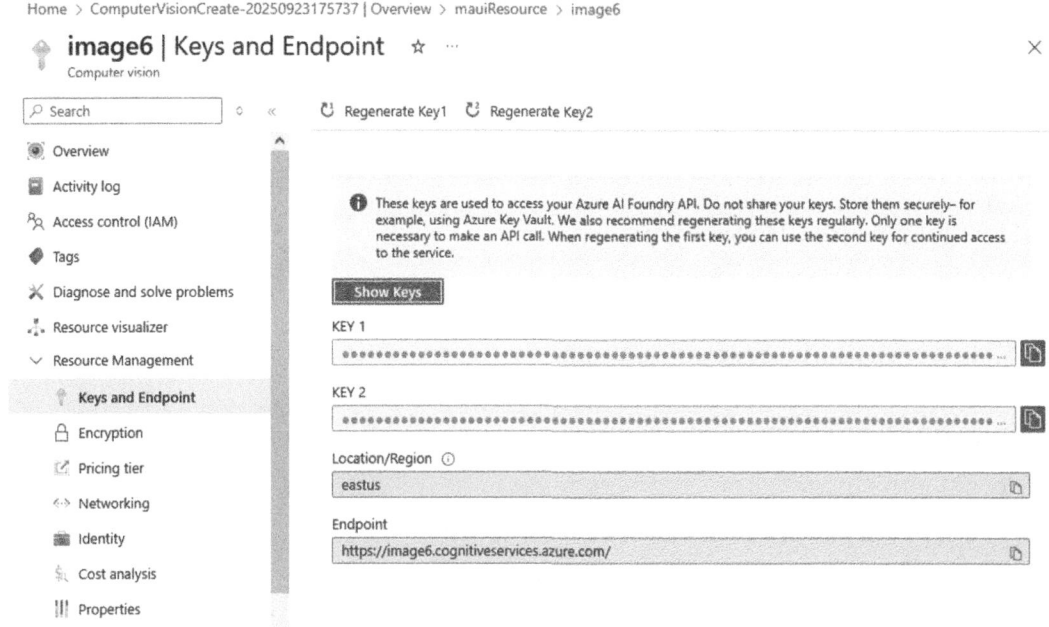

Figure 7-2. *Azure Custom Vision resource Keys and Endpoint*

Once we have the endpoint and the key, we can create a new class called APIParameters.cs where we will save our endpoint and the API key. You can find the APIParameters class in Listing 7-3, just replace YOUR_API_KEY with your key.

Listing 7-3. APIParameters class

```
public static class APIParameters
{
    public const string APIKey = "YOUR_API_KEY";
    public const string APIEndpoint = "https://<your-custom-endpoint>.
    cognitiveservices.azure.com/";
}
```

Now, we can call our endpoint and send the captured image. We will be using Analyze Image API /vision/v3.2/read/analyze.

You can learn more about this powerful API at https://learn.microsoft. com/erest/api/computervision/analyze-image/analyze-image?view=rest-computervision-v3.2&tabs=HTTP. We will extract all the text lines using the API and then save them in List<string>().

Next, we can create a new Services folder and add a new AzureAIOCRService.cs class. Inside the class, we need to add the following code from Listing 7-4 to be able to call the service.

Listing 7-4. Call the Analyze Image API from the services class

```
public class AzureAIOCRService
{
    private readonly string _endpoint;
    private readonly string _apiKey;
    private readonly HttpClient _httpClient;
    public AzureAIOCRService()
    {
        _endpoint = APIParameters.APIEndpoint;
        _apiKey = APIParameters.APIKey;
        _httpClient = new HttpClient();
        _httpClient.DefaultRequestHeaders.Add("Ocp-Apim-Subscription-Key",
        _apiKey);
    }
    public async Task<string> GenerateTextWithOCRAsync(Stream imageStream)
    {
        var url = $"{_endpoint}/vision/v3.2/read/analyze";

        using var content = new StreamContent(imageStream);
        content.Headers.ContentType = new MediaTypeHeaderValue("application/
        octet-stream");

        var response = await _httpClient.PostAsync(url, content);
        response.EnsureSuccessStatusCode();

        // The 'Operation-Location' header contains the URL to poll
        for result
        var operationLocation = response.Headers.GetValues("Operation-
        Location").FirstOrDefault();
        if (operationLocation == null)
            return "Failed to get operation location.";
```

```csharp
    // Poll for result
    while (true)
    {
        await Task.Delay(1000);
        var resultResponse = await _httpClient.
        GetAsync(operationLocation);
        resultResponse.EnsureSuccessStatusCode();
        var resultJson = await resultResponse.Content.
        ReadAsStringAsync();
        using var resultDoc = JsonDocument.Parse(resultJson);

        var status = resultDoc.RootElement.GetProperty("status").
        GetString();
        if (status == "succeeded")
        {
            // Extract text lines
            var lines = new List<string>();
            var analyzeResult = resultDoc.RootElement.
            GetProperty("analyzeResult");
            foreach (var readResult in analyzeResult.
            GetProperty("readResults").EnumerateArray())
            {
                foreach (var line in readResult.GetProperty("lines").
                EnumerateArray())
                {
                    lines.Add(line.GetProperty("text").GetString());
                }
            }
            return string.Join("\n", lines);
        }
        else if (status == "failed")
        {
            return "Text extraction failed.";
        }
    }
}
}
```

We can now modify the MainPage.xaml, as shown in Listing 7-5 or use the same we had in Chapter 6.

Listing 7-5. MainPage.xaml code

```
?xml version="1.0" encoding="utf-8" ?>
<ContentPage xmlns="http://schemas.microsoft.com/dotnet/2021/maui"
             xmlns:x="http://schemas.microsoft.com/winfx/2009/xaml"
             x:Class="Chapter7.MainPage">

    <ScrollView>
        <VerticalStackLayout
            Padding="30,0"
            Spacing="25">
            <Label x:Name="WelcomeLabel" FontSize="18" TextColor="Purple"
            Text="Let's Extract text from images capability "></Label>
            <Button Text="Take Photo" Clicked="PhotoButton_Clicked"/>
            <Image x:Name="CapturedImage" HeightRequest="300"/>
            <Label x:Name="ExtractedTextLabel" FontSize="18"
            TextColor="darkred" Text="Your extracted text will appear here"/>

        </VerticalStackLayout>
    </ScrollView>
</ContentPage>
```

Once we have the API, we can call it from our `MainPage.xaml.cs` by adding the call that you can find in Listing 7-6 inside PhotoButton_Clicked.

Listing 7-6. Call the new API

```
//call our API to detect text
var objects = await _azureAIOCRService.GenerateTextWithOCRAsync(apiStream);
ExtractedTextLabel.Text = $"Extracted text: {objects}";
```

The final MainPage.xaml.cs can be find in Listing 7-7 below.

Listing 7-7. MainPage.xaml.cs complete code

```
public partial class MainPage : ContentPage
{
    private readonly AzureAIOCRService _azureAIOCRService;
    public MainPage()
    {
        InitializeComponent();
        _azureAIOCRService = new AzureAIOCRService();
    }

    private async void PhotoButton_Clicked(object sender, EventArgs e)
    {
        try {
        var photo = await MediaPicker.Default.CapturePhotoAsync();
        if (photo == null) return;

        // Copy the photo into a memory stream
        using var originalStream = await photo.OpenReadAsync();
        var memoryStream = new MemoryStream();
        await originalStream.CopyToAsync(memoryStream);

        // Display photo
        memoryStream.Position = 0; // reset for ImageSource
        CapturedImage.Source = ImageSource.FromStream(() =>
        {
            memoryStream.Position = 0;
            return memoryStream;
        });

        // Send a new copy of the stream to Azure
        var resizedStream = ResizeImage(originalStream, 300, 300);

        // Display image
        CapturedImage.Source = ImageSource.FromStream(() =>
        {
            resizedStream.Position = 0;
            return resizedStream;
        });
```

```
        // Send a copy to Azure
        var apiStream = new MemoryStream(resizedStream.ToArray());
        apiStream.Position = 0;

        //call our API to detect text
        var objects = await _azureAIOCRService.GenerateTextWithOCRAsync(
        apiStream);
        ExtractedTextLabel.Text = $"Extracted text: {objects}";
    }

    catch (Exception ex)
    {
        await DisplayAlert("Error", ex.Message, "OK");
    }
}
    public static MemoryStream ResizeImage(Stream originalStream, int
    width, int height)
{
    originalStream.Position = 0;

    using var input = SKBitmap.Decode(originalStream);
    using var resized = input.Resize(new SKImageInfo(width, height),
    SKSamplingOptions.Default);

    if (resized == null)
        throw new Exception("Failed to resize image.");

    using var image = SKImage.FromBitmap(resized);
    var ms = new MemoryStream();
    image.Encode(SKEncodedImageFormat.Png, 100).SaveTo(ms);
    ms.Position = 0;
    return ms;
    }
}
```

We will still use SkiaSharp to resize the image as in Chapter 6. As we are using the camera to take photos, we will need to give the app the right permission in the AndroidManifest.xml file or equivalent in the iOS Info.plist file. We will also need permission to WRITE_EXTERNAL_STORAGE in the manifest.

After you fix the permissions, you can try the app on your device. I deployed on an Android phone and took a picture of my not so beautiful handwritten text on my notebook, which by chance also has lines.

You can see the result in Figure 7-3.

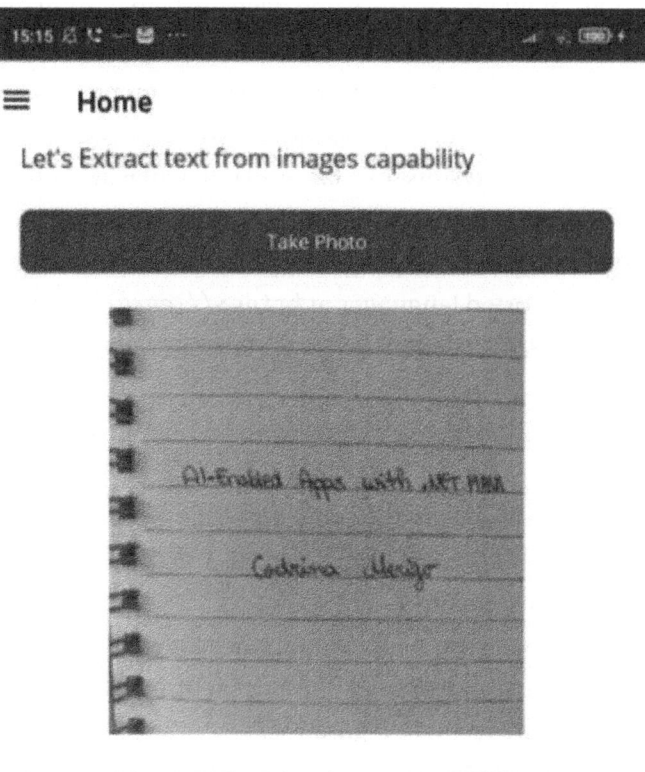

Extracted text: AI-Enabled Apps with .NET MAUI
Codrina Merigo

Figure 7-3. *Extracted handwritten text*

Detect Text Inside a Picture

As we have extracted handwritten text, you can imagine that we can also extract text from images, like product labels, documents, or advertising posters. The Read OCR model is available in both Azure AI Vision and Document Intelligence, providing a common set of core capabilities tailored to their specific scenarios.

With this model, you can easily extract printed and handwritten text across supported languages, while also capturing the structure of documents–including pages, lines, and words–along with their location and confidence scores. It also supports mixed content, meaning it can process documents that contain both printed and handwritten text, as well as multiple languages on the same page. As I am writing this chapter, it is important to mention the new Azure AI Vision Image Analysis 4.0 REST API makes it easier than ever to extract printed or handwritten text from images, thanks to its enhanced and unified API. With just one operation, you can access a complete set of image insights, including OCR results, in a fast and efficient way. Behind the scenes, the Read OCR engine is powered by advanced deep learning models and universal script-based technology, ensuring broad language support for users around the world. You can find the full list of supported languages at *https://learn.microsoft.com/en-us/ azure/ai-services/computer-vision/language-support#optical-character-recognition-ocr.*

There is more information you can extract from an image using the Image Analysis API.

For our scenario, similarly, like in the previous section, we will take a picture and call the REST API to extract all the text in the picture. The code is the same; we will take a picture and extract all the text inside it.

To test this, I will use the awesome book that my reviewer wrote on .NET MAUI. I bet you have already read it, but as a reminder, I took a picture of it and extracted all the text on the cover. You can find the result in Figure 7-4.

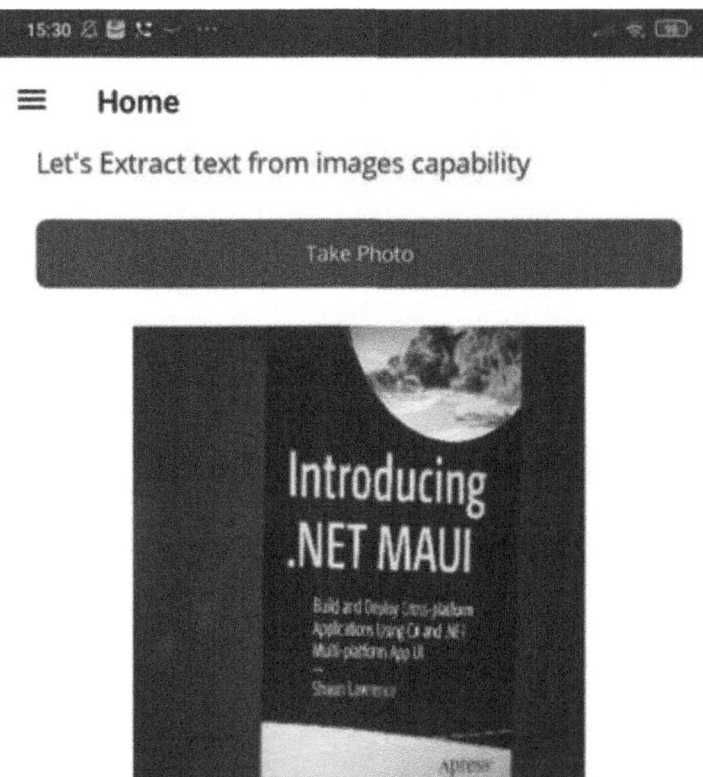

Figure 7-4. Extract text from printed text

Summary

In this chapter, we have looked deeper at the image analysis offered by Azure AI. We also learned more about OCR and created an app that can extract handwritten text. The same app can also extract printed text giving lot of opportunities.

In the next chapter, we will learn more about speech recognition and what Azure AI Voice services offer. We will be creating an app that registers voice and will transcribe the registration for us.

CHAPTER 8

Voice App with Speech Recognition

Introduction

In this chapter, you will get an overview of how to use speech recognition offered by Azure AI Speech Service. We will also see some real-life scenarios that can be easily implemented thanks to simple tools, flexible APIs, and support for dozens of languages.

Voice or Text?

Are you the type of person who loves sending voice messages, or do you prefer sticking to good old written texts? Honestly, if you saw my desk right now covered in sticky notes–or you might have imagined from the previous chapter on OCR scanning of handwritten notes—you'd probably guess that I'm firmly in the "text messages" camp. And you'd be right. I like things written down, easy to scan, easy to search, and no surprises.

But hey, we're not all done the same way. I'm sure you also have one friend who just loves sending voice messages. And not the quick "*Hey, I'm on my way!*" kind. No, I'm talking about those epic, multiminute audio messages that start with "*So, funny story, listen …*" and end with you wondering whether you should take notes just to keep up.

That's exactly why I'm such a fan of the speech-to-text feature in Azure AI's Speech Service. It feels like having a superpower: you can just hand over those marathon voice messages to the AI, and you have it—neatly transcribed text in just a few seconds. No more rewinding, pausing, or pretending you caught every word.

© Codrina Merigo 2026
C. Merigo, *AI-Enabled Apps with .NET MAUI*, https://doi.org/10.1007/979-8-8688-1817-2_8

In this chapter, we'll be integrating this speech-to-text capability into a .NET MAUI app. By the end, your app will be able to listen to audio clips or voice messages and effortlessly transform them into text—saving you time, patience, and the occasional *"Wait, what did they just say?"* moment.

Speech Recognition

Azure AI Speech Service won't just convert spoken words into text with impressive accuracy but will also generate natural and lifelike voices from text, translate spoken audio on the fly, and even recognize who's speaking in a conversation. It's an all-in-one toolkit to help your apps understand, speak, and interact just like a human would.

Azure AI Speech Studio can be found `https://speech.microsoft.com/`. You can also see the different models available as shown in Figure 8-1. We will start with the speech-to-text models.

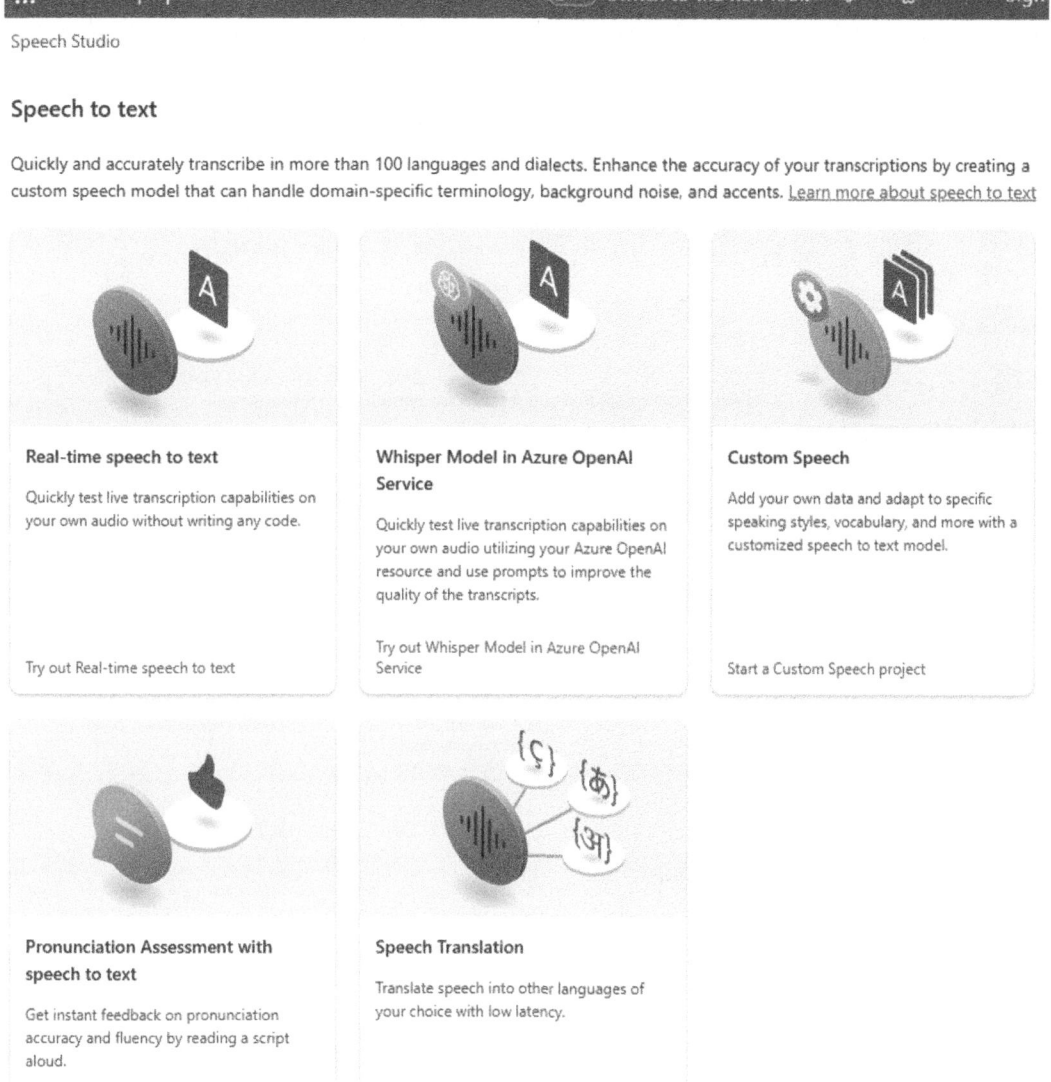

Figure 8-1. *Azure AI Speech Studio–speech-to-text models*

For our sample scenario, we will try the speech-to-text feature at `https://speech.microsoft.com/portal/speechtotexttool`. In the portal, you can upload an audio file or register up to a minute of audio and see the API in action.

We will start from the Azure portal, so log in to `https://portal.azure.com/` and click `create a new resource`. Search for `speech`, look for the Speech Service from `Microsoft` as shown in Figure 8-2, and click `Create`.

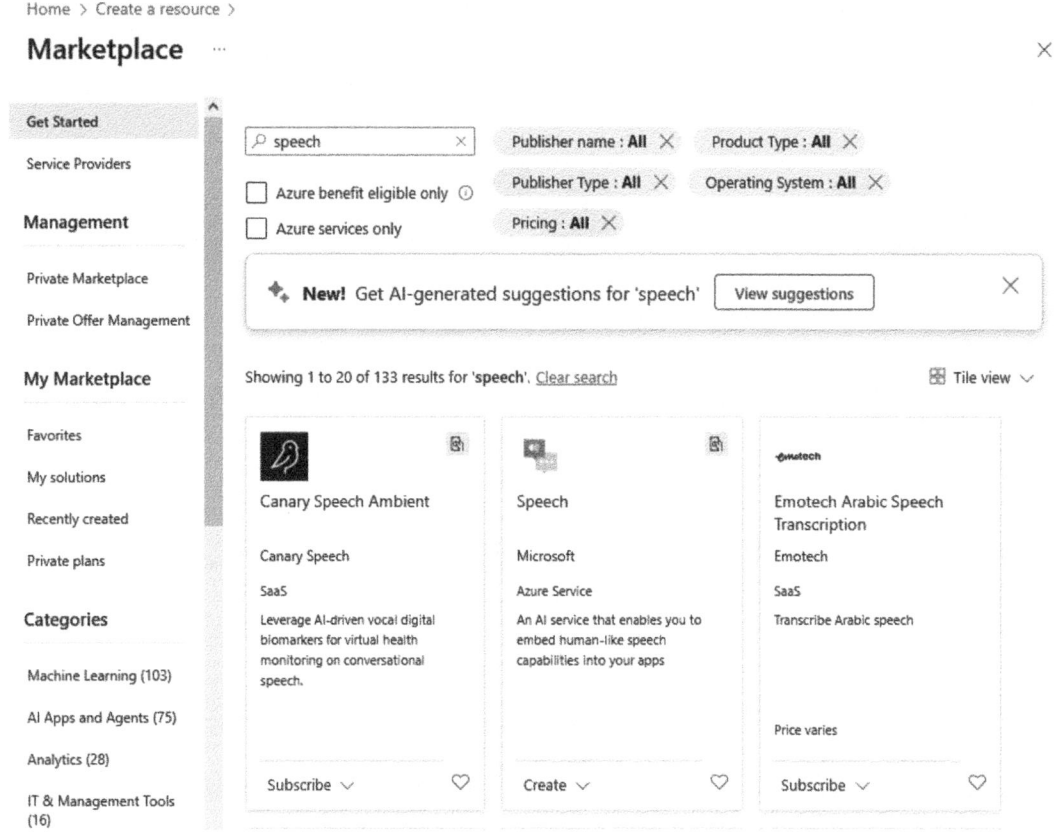

Figure 8-2. *Create new speech resource on Azure*

Select your Subscription as shown in Figure 8-3 and click Create.

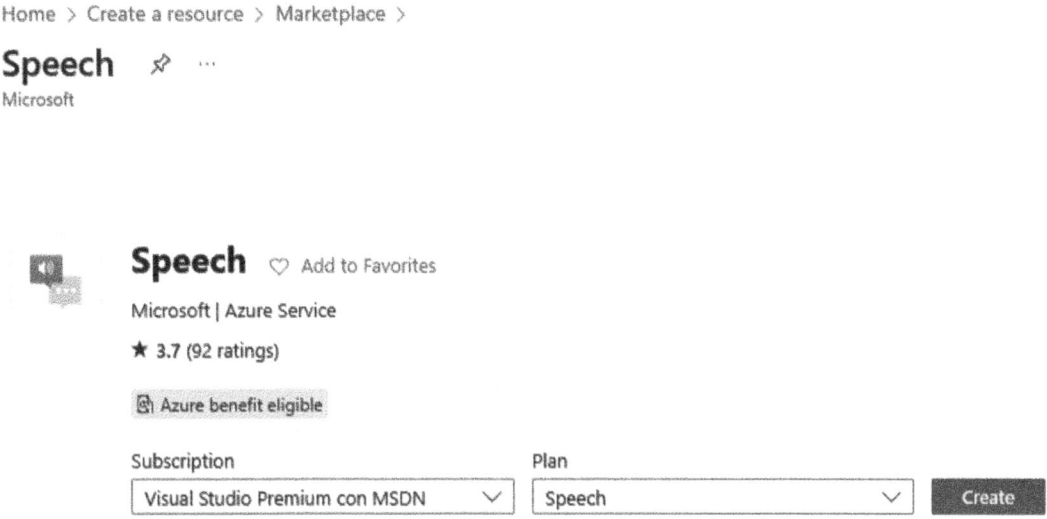

Figure 8-3. Speech resource

On the following screen, as shown in Figure 8-4, select an existing resource group or create a new one, select your region, give your resource a name, and select a Pricing Tier. Then click Review + create.

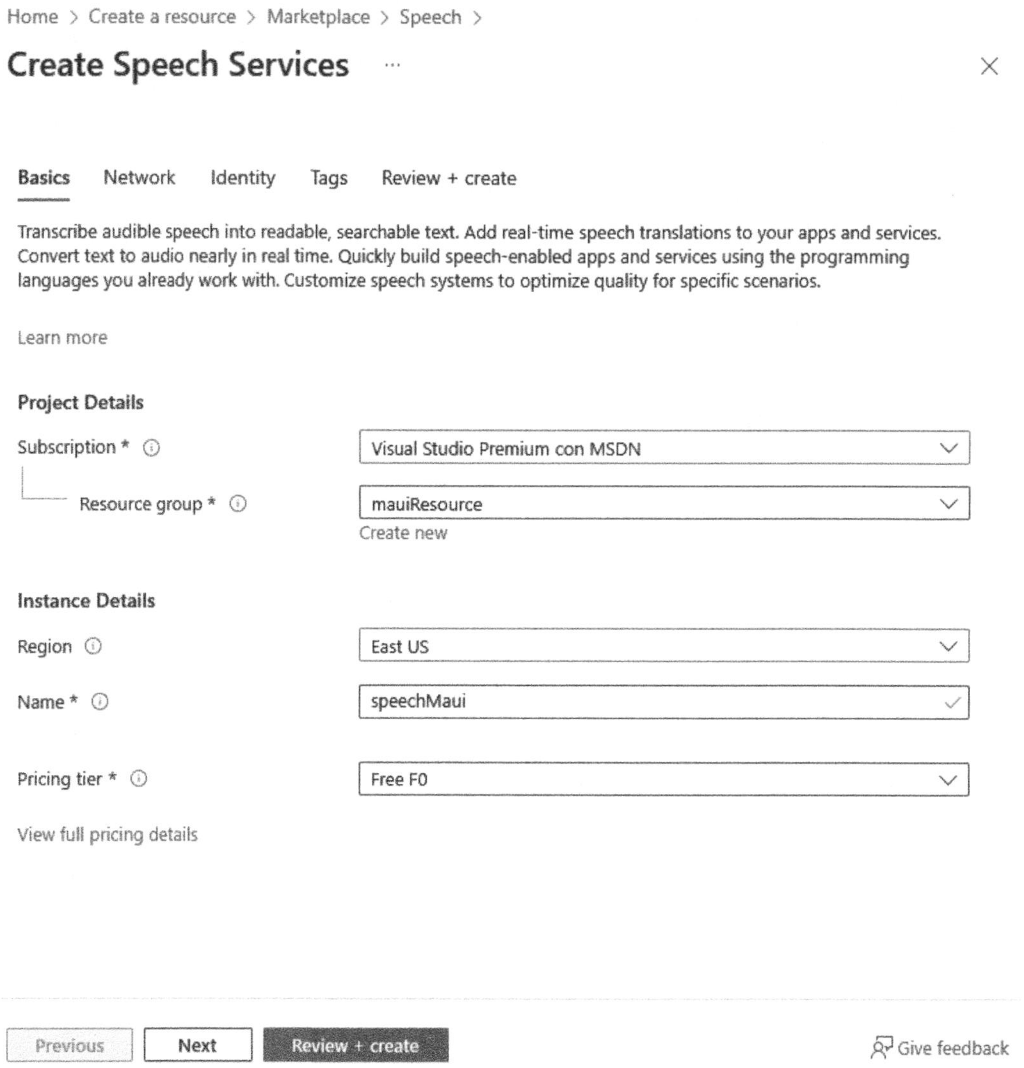

Home > Create a resource > Marketplace > Speech >

Create Speech Services ···   ✕

Basics   Network   Identity   Tags   Review + create

Transcribe audible speech into readable, searchable text. Add real-time speech translations to your apps and services. Convert text to audio nearly in real time. Quickly build speech-enabled apps and services using the programming languages you already work with. Customize speech systems to optimize quality for specific scenarios.

Learn more

Project Details

Subscription * ⓘ | Visual Studio Premium con MSDN   ⌄ |

    Resource group * ⓘ | mauiResource   ⌄ |
                         Create new

Instance Details

Region ⓘ | East US   ⌄ |

Name * ⓘ | speechMaui   ✓ |

Pricing tier * ⓘ | Free F0   ⌄ |

View full pricing details

| Previous | | **Next** | | Review + create | ⅗ Give feedback

Figure 8-4. *Create a new resource information page*

In the next page, as shown in Figure 8-5, review all the information and click Create.

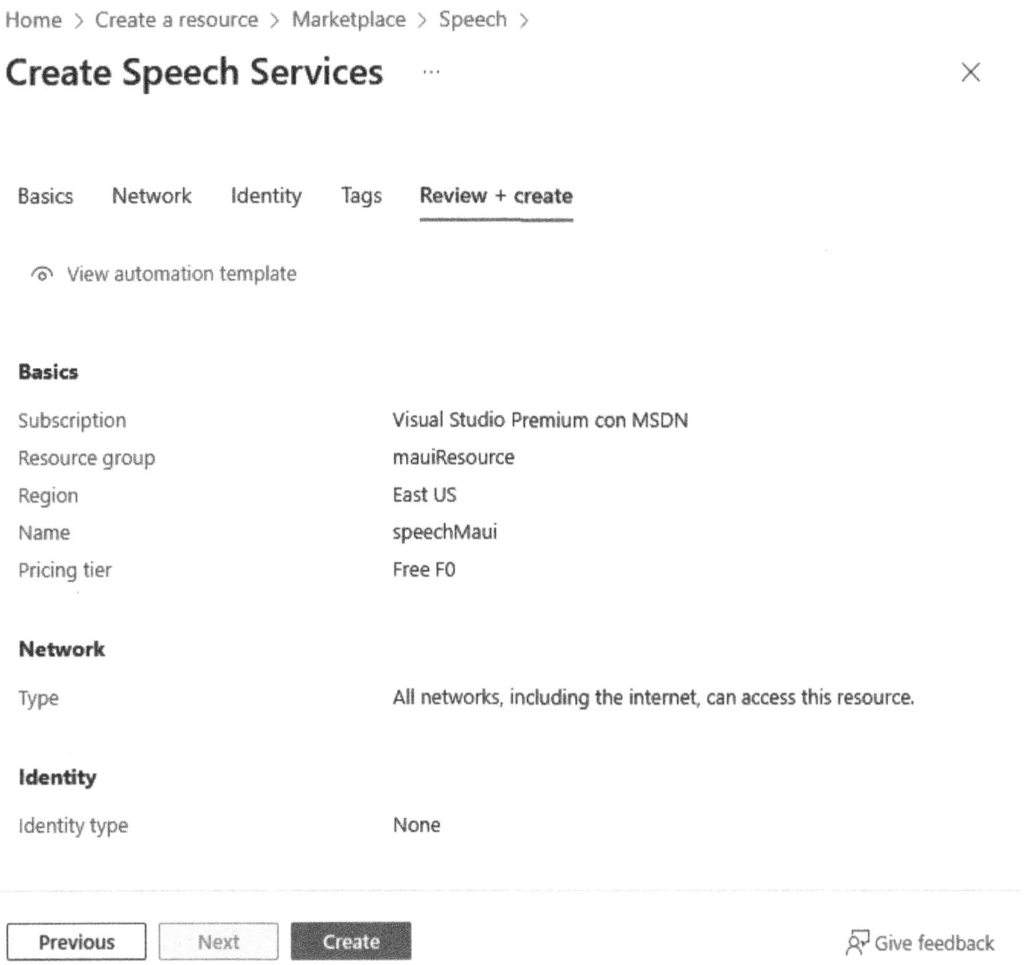

Home > Create a resource > Marketplace > Speech >

Create Speech Services   ···   ×

Basics   Network   Identity   Tags   **Review + create**

⌒ View automation template

Basics

Subscription	Visual Studio Premium con MSDN
Resource group	mauiResource
Region	East US
Name	speechMaui
Pricing tier	Free F0

Network

Type	All networks, including the internet, can access this resource.

Identity

Identity type	None

[Previous]   [Next]   [**Create**]   ⌂ Give feedback

Figure 8-5. *Create new resource information review page*

Wait for your resource to be deployed, and once deployment is complete as in Figure 8-6, go to your resource page as shown in Figure 8-7.

Home >

SpeechServicesCreate-20250926141753 | Ov...
Deployment

≫ Service menu

🗑 Delete   ⊘ Cancel   ⬆ Redeploy   ⬇ Download   ↻ Refresh

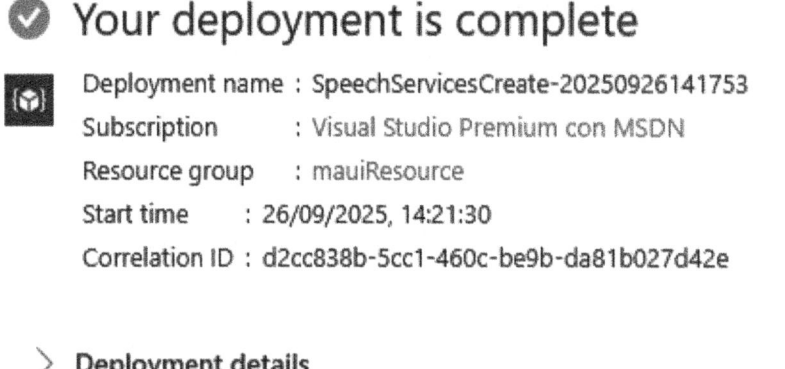

✓ **Your deployment is complete**

Deployment name : SpeechServicesCreate-20250926141753
Subscription   : Visual Studio Premium con MSDN
Resource group   : mauiResource
Start time   : 26/09/2025, 14:21:30
Correlation ID : d2cc838b-5cc1-460c-be9b-da81b027d42e

> **Deployment details**

∨ **Next steps**

Go to resource

Figure 8-6. *Resource deployment page*

In the resource page, you can check all the details and save the endpoint URL and keys for later.

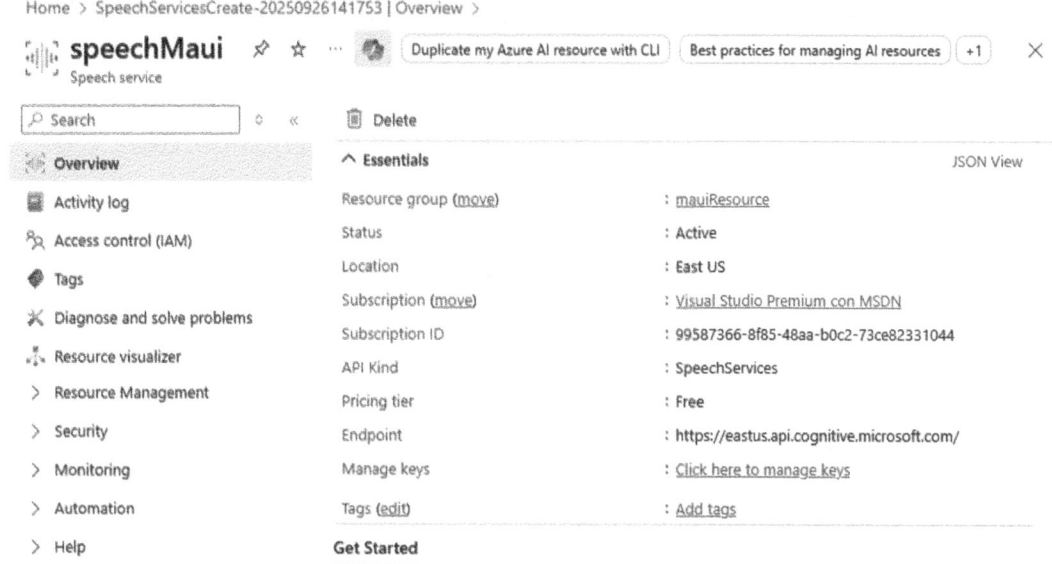

Figure 8-7. *Speech resource overview page*

Once we have our Azure resource created, we can create a new .NET MAUI application. In this application, the user will use the device microphone to record audio. We will then pass the recorded audio to the AI service to transform it into text and then we will display the text inside the page.

As we will be recording audio in our app, for Android, we will need to modify the AndroidManifest.xml file by enabling the RECORD_AUDIO flag. In your solution, click the Platforms folder and then Android. In the Required Permission list, scroll down and look for RECORD_AUDIO and select the checkbox.

For iOS, expand the iOS folder, inside the Platforms folder, and edit the Info.plist file by adding the following key named NSMicrophoneUsageDescription with a string value that explains why your app needs the microphone, for example: *This app needs access to the microphone to convert your speech to text.* If you are targeting a Mac, expand the MacCatalyst folder, Platforms folder, and add the same key to Info.plist file.

To target Windows, you will need to expand the Windows folder, Platforms folder, and open the Package.appxmanifest file. Inside the capabilities tag, add the following tag <DeviceCapability Name="microphone"/>.

You can target every platform that can have or connect to a microphone to test this AI service.

To record audio in our app, we will use the Plugin.Maui.Audio sponsored by two persons really dear to me and great members of the community: Gerald Versluis (https://github.com/jfversluis), the one that allowed me to do my first international session on Xamarin back in 2019, and Shaun Lawrence (https://github.com/bijington), technical editor for this book who helped me a lot with reviewing everything that I wrote. You can find more about the plugin at https://github.com/jfversluis/Plugin.Maui.Audio. Install the Plugin.Maui.Audio from the NuGet Manager into your project, along with the System.Net.Http.Json, as we will need to handle JSON structures.

To use the plugin, you will need to register it inside the builder in MauiProgram.cs. as shown in Listing 8-1.

Listing 8-1. Add the plugin to the builder

```
var builder = MauiApp.CreateBuilder();
builder
    .UseMauiApp<App>()
    .ConfigureFonts(fonts =>
    {
        fonts.AddFont("OpenSans-Regular.ttf", "OpenSansRegular");
        fonts.AddFont("OpenSans-Semibold.ttf", "OpenSansSemibold");
    })
    .AddAudio();
```

Next, let's create the UI for our application. In MainPage.xaml, we will create, apart from a title Label, a couple of Button elements, one to start the recording and one to stop the recording, disabled by default. Then we will bind the result of our API inside another Label element, the ResultLabel. The final MainPage.xaml implementation can be found in Listing 8-2.

Listing 8-2. MainPage.xaml source code

```
<?xml version="1.0" encoding="utf-8" ?>
<ContentPage xmlns="http://schemas.microsoft.com/dotnet/2021/maui"
             xmlns:x="http://schemas.microsoft.com/winfx/2009/xaml"
             x:Class="Chapter8.MainPage">
    <ScrollView>
```

```
<VerticalStackLayout
    Padding="30,0"
    Spacing="25">
    <Label  Text="Speech to Text AI service"/>
    <Button x:Name="StartButton" Text="Start Recording"
    Clicked="StartButton_Clicked"/>
    <Button x:Name="StopButton" Text="Stop Recording"
    Clicked="StopButton_Clicked" IsEnabled="False"/>
    <Label x:Name="ResultLabel" Text="Transcription will appear
    here..."
    TextColor="DarkRed" />
</VerticalStackLayout>
</ScrollView>

</ContentPage>
```

We will then create a new APIParameters.cs class where to store our API key and region from Azure as shown in Listing 8-3.

Listing 8-3. APIParameters.cs content

```
namespace Chapter8
{
    public static class APIParameters
    {
        public const string APIkey = t
        public const string APIRegion = "eastus";
    }
}
```

After that, we can create a new folder called Services and inside it a new class, AzureSpeechService.cs. In this service class, we will call the Azure Speech Service API and pass the audio stream added by the user. We will need to add a new audio/wav header to our call, together with the key. We will then call the API at https://{YOUR_REGION}.stt.speech.microsoft.com/speech/recognition/conversation/cognitiveservices/v1?language=en-US passing an English audio input. The result of the call will be a JSON file that will have our transcription in the DisplayText property. You can find the full implementation in Listing 8-4.

Listing 8-4. ApiSpeechService.cs implementation

```
using System;
using System.Collections.Generic;
using System.Linq;
using System.Net.Http.Headers;
using System.Text;
using System.Text.Json;
using System.Threading.Tasks;

namespace Chapter8.Services
{
    public class AzureSpeechService
    {
        private readonly HttpClient _httpClient;
        private readonly string _key;
        private readonly string _region;

        public AzureSpeechService()
        {
            _httpClient = new HttpClient();
            _key = APIParameters.APIkey;
            _region = APIParameters.APIRegion;
        }
        public async Task<string> TranscribeAudioAsync(Stream audioStream)
        {
            using var client = new HttpClient();
            client.DefaultRequestHeaders.Add("Ocp-Apim-Subscription-
            Key", _key);

            audioStream.Position = 0;
            using var content = new StreamContent(audioStream);
            content.Headers.ContentType = new
            MediaTypeHeaderValue("audio/wav");

            var url = $"https://{_region}.stt.speech.microsoft.com/speech/
            recognition/conversation/cognitiveservices/v1?language=en-US";
```

```
    var response = await client.PostAsync(url, content);

    var transcription = await response.Content.ReadAsStringAsync();

    if (!response.IsSuccessStatusCode)
        throw new Exception($"Azure returned {(int)response.
        StatusCode}: {transcription}");

    using var doc = JsonDocument.Parse(transcription);

    // Azure's REST response commonly contains "DisplayText"
    if (doc.RootElement.TryGetProperty("DisplayText", out var dt))
        return dt.GetString() ?? string.Empty;

    return transcription;
    }
}
```

On MainPage.xaml.cs, we will implement some logic that will create the audio stream and enable and disable the StartButton and StopButton based on whether we are already recording or not. We will also need to ask for the user's permission to use the microphone to record audio.

Once we stop the recording, we will call the Speech-to-Text API from Azure after the Speak Result button is clicked and bind the API result into ResultLabel. You can find the implementation in Listing 8-5.

Listing 8-5. MainPage.xaml.cs logic

```
using Chapter8.Services;
using Plugin.Maui.Audio;
using System.Net.Http.Headers;
using System.Text.Json;

namespace Chapter8;

public partial class MainPage : ContentPage
{
    private IAudioRecorder _recorder;

    private readonly Services.AzureSpeechService _azureSpeechService = new
    Services.AzureSpeechService();
```

```csharp
    public MainPage()
    {
        InitializeComponent();
        _recorder = AudioManager.Current.CreateRecorder();
        _azureSpeechService = new AzureSpeechService();
    }

    private async void StartButton_Clicked(object sender, EventArgs e)
    {
        StartButton.IsEnabled = false;
        StopButton.IsEnabled = true;

        // 1) Check/request microphone permission
        var status = await Permissions.CheckStatusAsync<Permissions.
        Microphone>();
        if (status != PermissionStatus.Granted)
            status = await Permissions.RequestAsync<Permissions.
            Microphone>();

        if (status != PermissionStatus.Granted)
        {
            await DisplayAlert("Permission required", "Microphone
            permission is required to record audio.", "OK");
            StartButton.IsEnabled = true;
            StopButton.IsEnabled = false;
            return;
        }

        _recorder = AudioManager.Current.CreateRecorder();

        await _recorder.StartAsync();

        ResultLabel.Text = "Recording...";
    }

    private async void StopButton_Clicked(object sender, EventArgs e)
    {
        StopButton.IsEnabled = false;
        StartButton.IsEnabled = true;
```

```csharp
    await _recorder.StopAsync();

    ResultLabel.Text = "Sending audio to Azure Speech Service...";

    var audioSource = await _recorder.StopAsync();

    // Get the stream of the recorded audio
    using var recordedStream = audioSource.GetAudioStream();

    // Copy to memory (easier to re-use)
    using var ms = new MemoryStream();
    await recordedStream.CopyToAsync(ms);
    ms.Position = 0;

    ResultLabel.Text = "Sending audio to Azure...";
    try
    {
        var transcription = await _azureSpeechService.
        TranscribeAudioAsync(ms);
        ResultLabel.Text = string.IsNullOrWhiteSpace(transcription) ?
        "No transcription returned" : transcription;
    }
    catch (Exception ex)
    {
        ResultLabel.Text = $"Error: {ex.Message}";
    }
    }
}
```

Now, we can build and deploy our application. I have used an Android device and recorded some text. You can see the result screen in Figure 8-8.

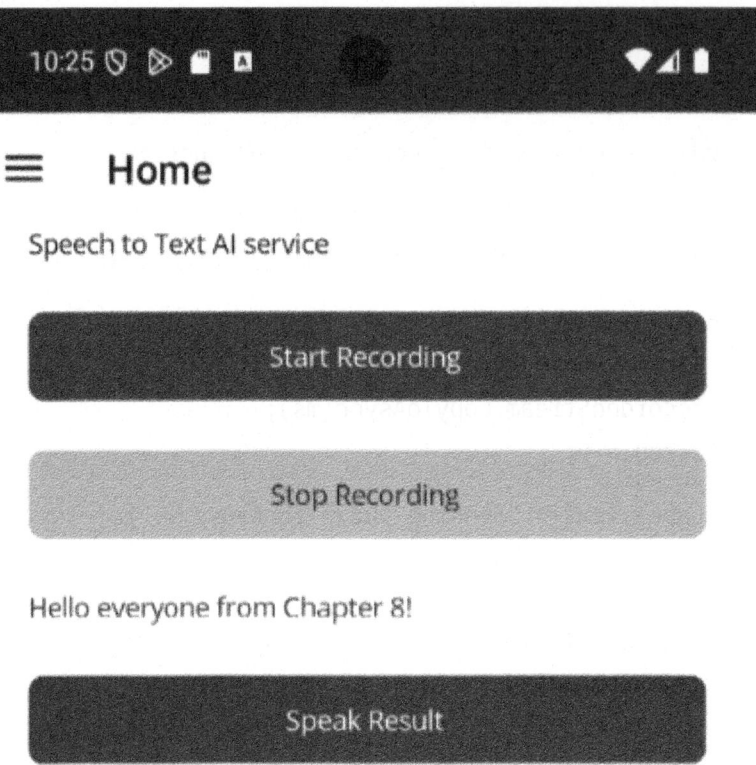

Figure 8-8. *Result screen*

From Text to Speech

The Speech Service provides both speech-to-text and text-to-speech (TTS) capabilities. We have used speech to text in our app. But this service will also allow your apps to transform text into human-like synthesized speech. The text-to-speech capability is also known as speech synthesis.

Text to speech leverages deep neural networks to produce computer-generated voices that sound almost identical to human recordings. By clearly articulating words, neural text to speech greatly minimizes listening fatigue during interactions with AI systems.

Prosody, the rhythm, stress, and intonation of speech, plays a key role in natural-sounding language. Conventional text-to-speech systems handle prosody through separate steps of linguistic analysis and acoustic prediction, each managed by independent models. This separation can lead to voices that sound muffled or buzzy. In contrast, neural TTS models learn these patterns end to end, allowing for expressive, natural-sounding speech that can convey emphasis, emotion, and subtle variations in tone. This makes neural TTS ideal for applications like voice assistants, audiobooks, accessibility tools, and branded voice experiences.

The text-to-speech feature in the Speech Service supports more than 400 voices and more than 140 languages and variants. You can find all the languages and voices available at `https://learn.microsoft.com/azure/ai-services/speech-service/ language-support?tabs=tts`.

There are many ways audio and speech capabilities can make your applications smarter, more engaging, and more accessible. With captioning, you can effortlessly synchronize captions with your audio content, helping viewers follow along in real time. You can apply profanity filters, see partial results as the audio is being processed, customize the captions to fit your brand, and even detect multiple spoken languages— perfect for multilingual webinars or international video content.

We can also add this feature to our app by creating a new button in the page, called `TextToSpeech`, to call the Text-to-Speech API, use one of the available voices, and play back the audio using the same plugin. You can find all the available voices and the languages supported at `https://learn.microsoft.com/azure/ai-services/speech- service/language-support#neural-voices`. You can also test the voices at `https:// speech.microsoft.com/portal/voicegallery`. I will use `en-US-LunaNeural`.

In our `MainPage.xaml`, we will add a new button `SpeakButton`. You can use the code from Listing 8-6.

Listing 8-6. New button added to MainPage.xaml

```
<Button x:Name="SpeakButton" Text="Speak Result" Clicked="SpeakButton_
Clicked" IsEnabled="True"/>
```

In our `Services` folder, we will add a new class called `AzureTextService.cs,` very similar to the `AzureSpeechService class,` to call the Text-to-Speech API. We can check the API documentation at `https://learn.microsoft.com/en-us/azure/ai-services/ speech-service/rest-text-to-speech?tabs=streaming#request-headers-1`. We will need an `application/ssml+xml` Content-Type for the header and to set the `X-Microsoft-OutputFormat` to one of the supported formats. For `.wav` format, we can use `riff-8khz-16bit-mono-pcm` already supported by the `Plugin`. We will then call the API at `https://{_region}.tts.speech.microsoft.com/cognitiveservices/v1` and pass the generated text. You can find the new method SpeackAudioAsync(string text) in Listing 8-7.

Listing 8-7. Speak audio method in the new service

```
...
public async Task<Stream> SpeakAudioAsync(string text)
{
    using var client = new HttpClient();
    client.DefaultRequestHeaders.Add("Ocp-Apim-Subscription-Key", _key);

    var ssml = $@"
                        <speak version='1.0' xml:lang='en-US'>
  <voice name='en-US-LunaNeural'>{System.Security.SecurityElement.
  Escape(text)}</voice>
                        </speak>";

    using var content = new StringContent(ssml, Encoding.UTF8,
    "application/ssml+xml");
    content.Headers.ContentType = new MediaTypeHeaderValue("application/
    ssml+xml");
    client.DefaultRequestHeaders.Add("X-Microsoft-OutputFormat",
    "riff-16khz-16bit-mono-pcm");

    var url = $"https://{_region}.tts.speech.microsoft.com/
    cognitiveservices/v1";

    var response = await client.PostAsync(url, content);
    if (!response.IsSuccessStatusCode)
    {
        var error = await response.Content.ReadAsStringAsync();
        throw new Exception(error);
    }

    var audioBytes = await response.Content.ReadAsByteArrayAsync();
    return new MemoryStream(audioBytes);
}
...
```

Once we have the service class, we can call it from MainPage.xaml.cs. Make sure you have initialized your service _azureTextService and created a new private readonly IAudioManager _audioManager;, initialized too as _audioManager = AudioManager. Current. You can find the new method SpeakButton_Clicked(object sender, EventArgs e) implementation in Listing 8-8.

Listing 8-8. New SpeakButton_Clicked method

```
private async void SpeakButton_Clicked(object sender, EventArgs e)
{
    var text = ResultLabel.Text;
    if (string.IsNullOrWhiteSpace(text) || text.StartsWith("Transcription"))
    {
        await DisplayAlert("Nothing to speak", "Record something
        first!", "OK");
        return;
    }

    ResultLabel.Text = "Calling Azure Text Service...";

    try
    {
        using var audioStream = await _azureTextService.
        SpeakAudioAsync(text);

        var player = _audioManager.CreatePlayer(audioStream);
        player.Play();
    }
    catch (Exception ex)
    {
        ResultLabel.Text = $"TTS error: {ex.Message}";
    }
}
```

Now is the time to build and deploy your application. For this one, you will have to believe me that it works as we cannot screenshot audio yet! Just give it a try, choose your preferred voice, and get creative on how you can implement these features.

The audio content creation features let you bring text to life using natural, expressive neural voices. Imagine turning an ebook into an audiobook that feels truly human, giving your chatbot or voice assistant a personality that users enjoy interacting with, or making in-car navigation instructions sound clear and friendly.

For call centers, you can transcribe conversations either in real time or in batches, automatically redact sensitive information, and extract useful insights such as customer sentiment. This helps teams understand trends, improve service quality, and make data-driven decisions.

For language learning, these tools provide real value by giving learners pronunciation feedback, offering real-time transcription for remote lessons, and reading teaching materials aloud with natural voices—making learning more interactive and effective.

Finally, Voice Live enables the creation of smooth, human-like conversational interfaces. Whether you're building a virtual agent, an interactive kiosk, or a voice-controlled application, this feature allows fast, reliable, and natural interaction between humans and machines. With Voice Live, conversations feel intuitive, responsive, and engaging, just like talking to a real person.

You can learn more about all the available capabilities at `https://learn.microsoft.com/en-us/azure/ai-services/speech-service/overview`.

Summary

In this chapter, we have learned more about Azure AI Speech Service capabilities. We also integrated this service into a .NET MAUI application. We used the service to transcribe audio into text. Afterwards, we used the transcribed text and a predefined voice to see the text-to-speech feature too.

In the next chapter, we will see how Azure AI translation services work and how to integrate it in a .NET MAUI application.

CHAPTER 9

AI-Powered Translations

Introduction

In this chapter, we will learn more about how AI translation works and how AI translation models are trained. We will see all the supported languages and their limitations. We will then integrate the Azure AI translation service with a .NET MAUI application.

Lost in Translation

Perhaps you have seen the *Lost in Translation* movie from the early 2000s–it is a movie about two strangers in Tokyo who form a quiet, meaningful connection while feeling a little lost in life and in a foreign city. Unless you have studied Japanese, it might sometimes feel as a very difficult language. There's also a famous scene with Bill Murray, the male character in the movie, filming a whiskey commercial in Tokyo. The director gives him long, passionate instructions in Japanese. The interpreter translates it into a few short words: "*He wants you to turn and look into the camera.*" A lot of nuances are lost in translation, which is both funny and frustrating.

As I moved to Italy when I was 15 years old, I felt also overwhelmed by the so-called "false friends" that are words that look similar in two languages but have very different meanings. Italian and Romanian, my native languages, they are both Latin languages and have plenty of those words. Also, Italian and English can get messed up, for example, in English, *library* is the place where you borrow a book, while in Italian, *libreria* is the bookstore. But a language is not only words that you can check in a dictionary to make sure you have the right translation; it is also sentences or idioms that can get a totally different sense in a context. If you say to someone *Break a leg* means you are wishing

© Codrina Merigo 2026
C. Merigo, *AI-Enabled Apps with .NET MAUI*, https://doi.org/10.1007/979-8-8688-1817-2_9

someone luck, not breaking their leg. Also, sometimes in the corporate world, there are lots of idioms used, and for nonnative speakers, sometimes they can feel funny or ambiguous.

AI can face the same struggle; it can get words right, but not the intended meaning. Despite AI's rapid advancement, it still can have difficulties with the fundamental linguistic challenge of semantic ambiguity, which is the same struggle human translators face. While AI models can accurately translate individual words or even short phrases, they often fail to grasp the intended meaning or deeper context of a sentence. This limitation is particularly evident when dealing with polysemous words (words with multiple meanings, like "bank") or idiomatic expressions that cannot be translated literally. To overcome these challenges, modern AI translation requires sophisticated models that are not just trained on word-to-word correspondences but are also designed to analyze the broader context of a sentence, paragraph, or even an entire document to properly disambiguate meaning. Furthermore, integrating a specialized domain vocabulary is crucial for technical, legal, or medical translation, as it prevents "false-friend mistakes" (words that look similar but have different meanings in different languages) and avoids the confusion resulting from overly literal translations, by ensuring the output is accurate, natural, and appropriate for its specific field.

How AI Translation Works

AI translation, also known as machine translation (MT), uses artificial intelligence to automatically translate text or speech from one language (the source language) to another (the target language). The most common and advanced method used today is neural machine translation (NMT), which relies on artificial neural networks (ANNs) to process and translate language. These models are modeled after the human brain structure and function and use artificial neurons to process the data, identify patterns, and make predictions.

NMT works through a three-step process that mimics human comprehension and learning. First, during input processing (encoding), the source sentence enters the neural network's encoder, which doesn't just look at single words but reads the entire sentence to grasp its complete meaning and context. This meaning is then condensed into a special mathematical code, or **context vector**, which holds the sentence's core idea independently of the original language. Next, in **translation generation (decoding),** this vector passes to the decoder, which uses the captured meaning and its training to generate the translation word by word in the target language. Crucially, a feature called the "attention mechanism" helps the decoder focus on the most relevant parts of the original sentence as it builds the new one, much like a careful human translator. Finally, the entire system excels due to learning and improvement (training): the models are continuously trained on enormous datasets of human-translated texts, comparing their own output to the perfect translations and constantly fine-tuning their internal parameters to ensure their translations become ever more accurate, fluent, and natural over time.

Though neural machine translation (NMT) is the current gold standard, it stands on the shoulders of earlier AI translation techniques. The first method, rule-based machine translation (RBMT), simply relied on extensive, preprogrammed linguistic rules and bilingual dictionaries. While fast, RBMT often produced stiff, inaccurate translations because it couldn't handle the nuances and exceptions inherent in human language. This was followed by statistical machine translation (SMT), which marked an advance by using machine learning to analyze massive amounts of human-translated texts, creating statistical models to predict the most likely translation for a word or phrase. SMT offered better results but still struggled with maintaining context over longer sentences, often leading to less coherent output.

Azure AI Translation

Azure AI Translator, which is a part of Microsoft's Azure AI services, is a sophisticated, cloud-based platform built on NMT technology. It is a robust service that developers can call primarily through REST APIs for various tasks.

Azure AI translation is part of the cognitive language services for languages, and you can find them at `https://language.cognitive.azure.com/` as shown in Figure 9-1 and learn more. You can translate short text or entire documents, and it currently supports 90 languages.

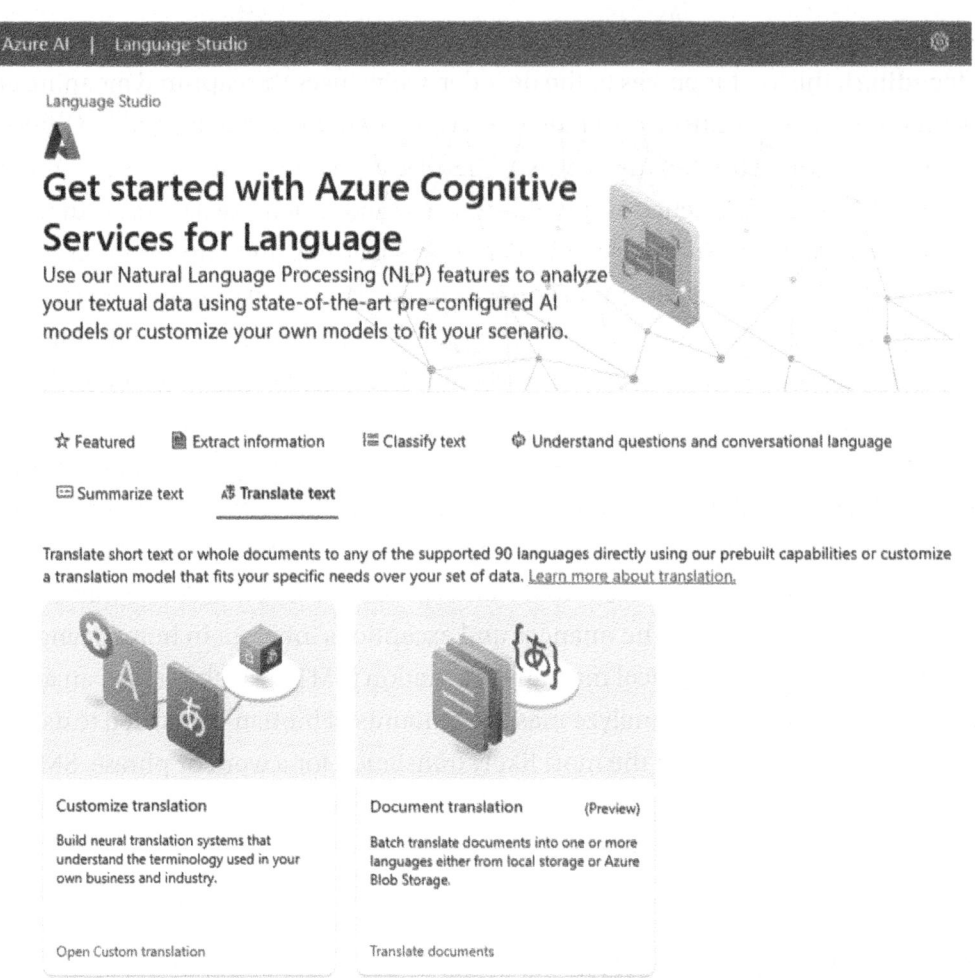

Figure 9-1. *Azure AI Language Studio*

To integrate this service with a .NET MAUI app, we will need to create a new resource on azure. Log in to `https://portal.azure.com` and click `Create new resource`.

In the search bar, look for `Azure Translation` as shown in Figure 9-2 and select the translator service from Microsoft.

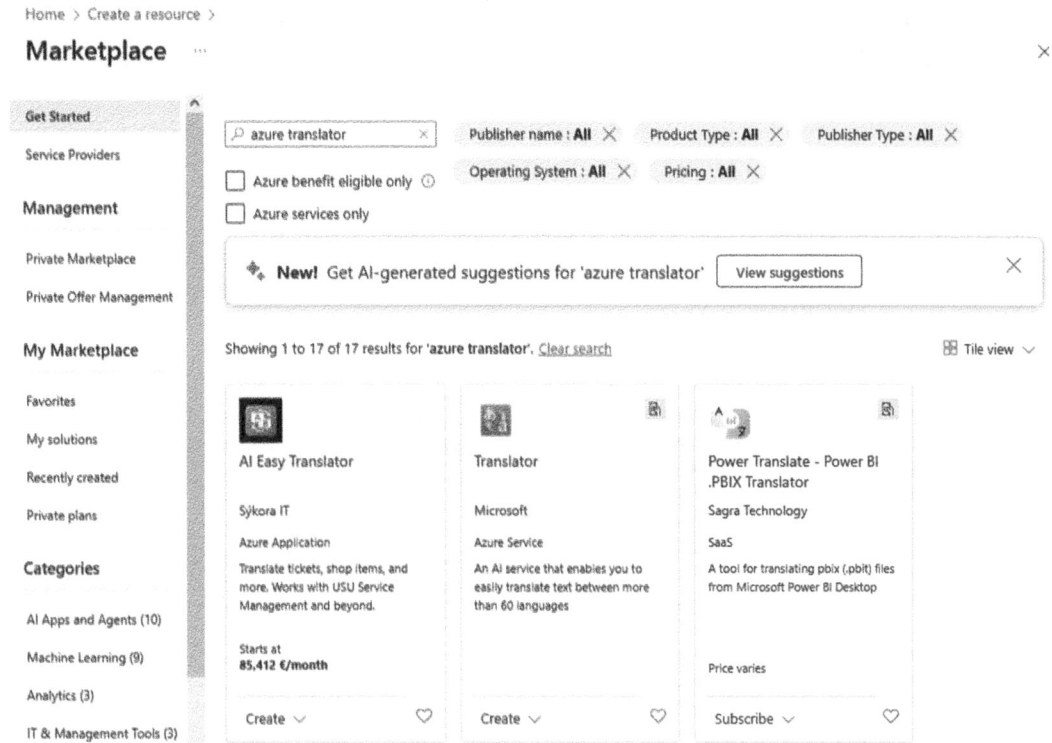

Figure 9-2. *Translator service*

Click Create, then in the new page, as shown in Figure 9-3, select your Subscription, and click Create.

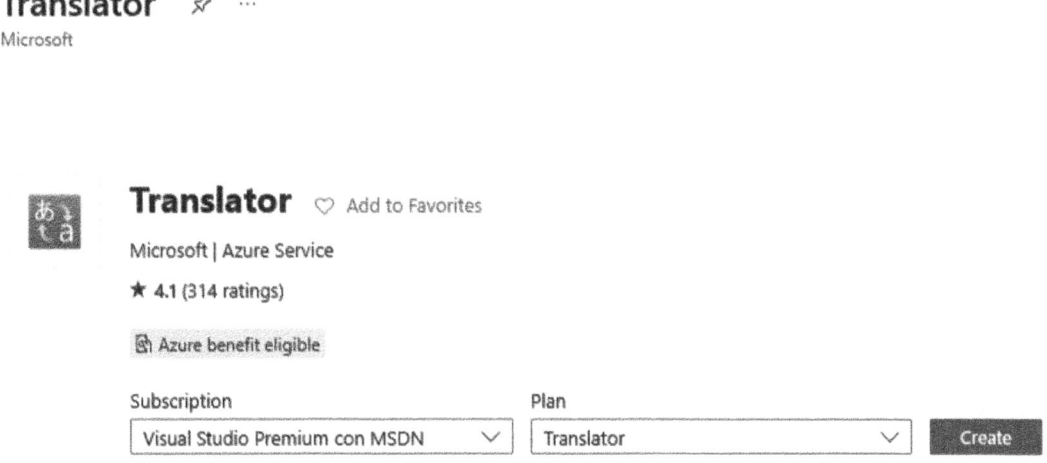

Figure 9-3. *Translator creation page*

In the next page, as shown in Figure 9-4, select an existing `resource` or create a new one, select a `Region`, give your resource a `name`, and select a `Pricing tier`. Check all the details and click `Review + create`.

Home > Create a resource > Marketplace > Translator >

Create Translator   ···   ✕

Basics   Network   Identity   Tags   Review + create

Easily integrate real-time text translation capabilities into your application's websites, tools, or any solution requiring multi-language support such as website localization, e-commerce, customer support, messaging applications, internal communication, and more.

Project Details

Subscription * ⓘ

| Visual Studio Premium con MSDN | ⌄ |

Resource group * ⓘ

| mauiResource | ⌄ |

Create new

Instance Details

ⓘ Please choose the Global region unless your business or application requires a specific region. Applications that do not offer a region selection use the Global region.

Region * ⓘ

| West Europe | ⌄ |

Name * ⓘ

| mauiTranslator | ✓ |

Pricing tier * ⓘ

| Free F0 (Up to 2M characters translated per month) | ⌄ |

View full pricing details

| Previous | **Next** | Review + create | ⤷ Give feedback

Figure 9-4. *New translation resource detail page*

In the following page, as shown in Figure 9-5, check the info and click Create.

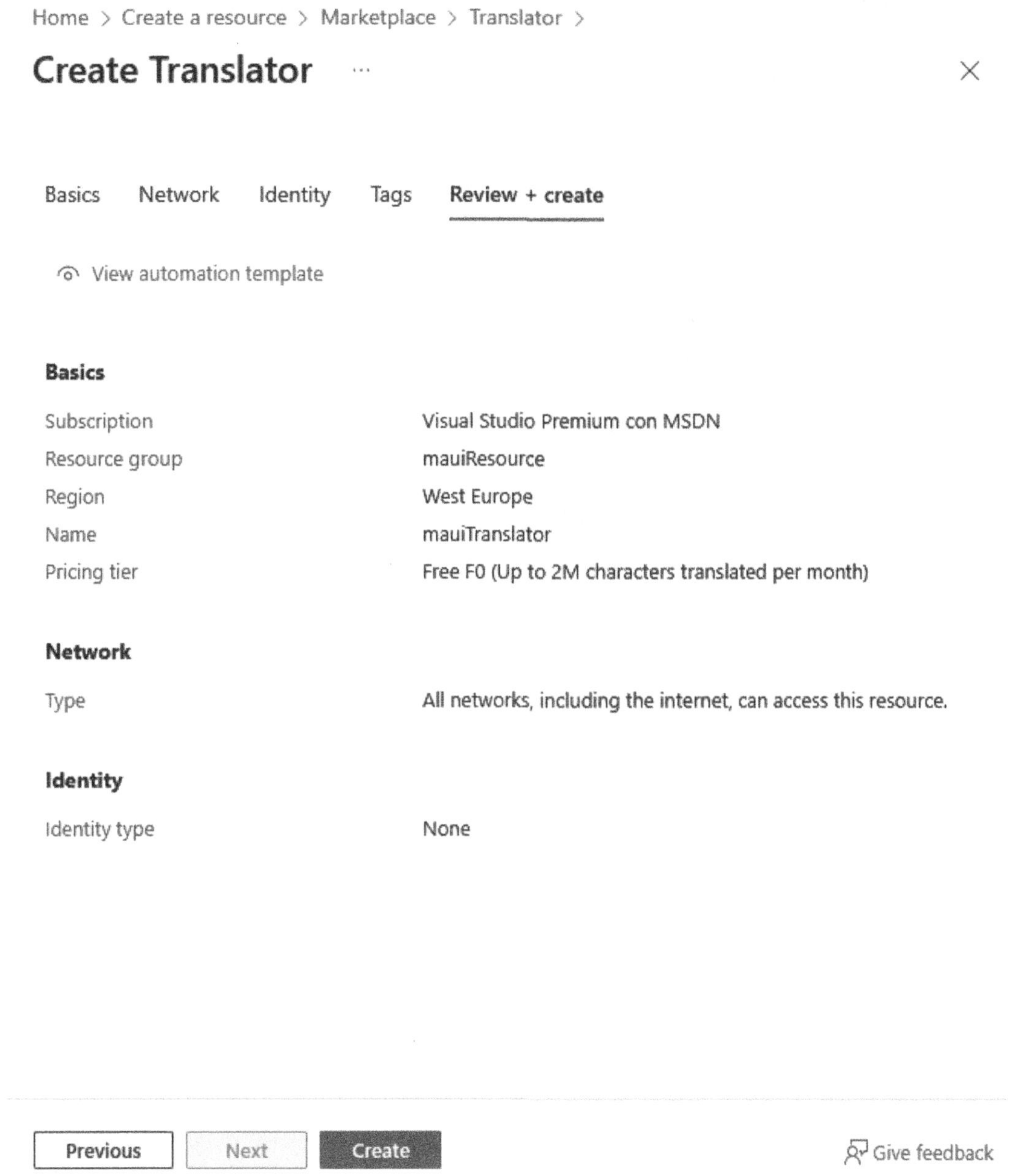

Home > Create a resource > Marketplace > Translator >

Create Translator   ⋯   ✕

Basics   Network   Identity   Tags   **Review + create**

⊙ View automation template

Basics

Subscription	Visual Studio Premium con MSDN
Resource group	mauiResource
Region	West Europe
Name	mauiTranslator
Pricing tier	Free F0 (Up to 2M characters translated per month)

Network

Type	All networks, including the internet, can access this resource.

Identity

Identity type	None

[Previous]   [Next]   **[Create]**   ⟲ Give feedback

Figure 9-5. *Review + create page for translator resource*

Once your resource has been deployed, as shown in Figure 9-6, go to your resource.

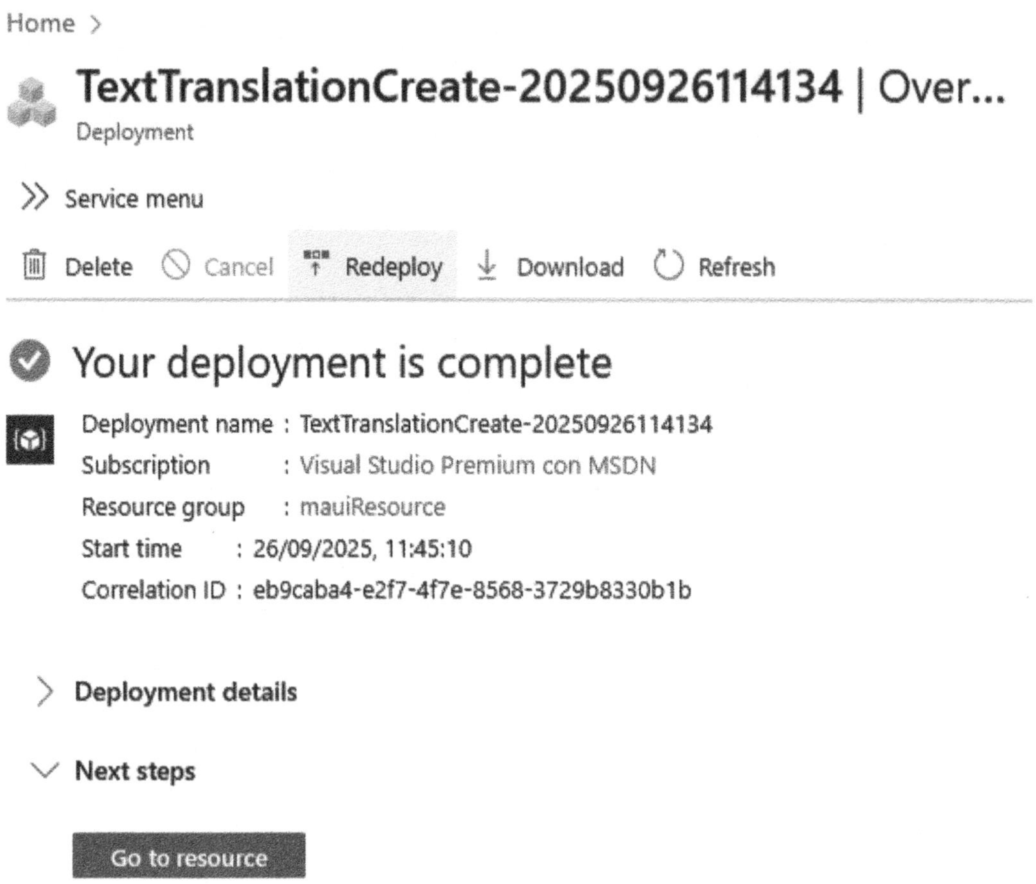

Home >

TextTranslationCreate-20250926114134 | Over...
Deployment

>> Service menu

🗑 Delete   ⃠ Cancel   ⬆ Redeploy   ⬇ Download   ⟳ Refresh

✅ Your deployment is complete

Deployment name : TextTranslationCreate-20250926114134
Subscription   : Visual Studio Premium con MSDN
Resource group   : mauiResource
Start time   : 26/09/2025, 11:45:10
Correlation ID : eb9caba4-e2f7-4f7e-8568-3729b8330b1b

> **Deployment details**

∨ **Next steps**

    Go to resource

Figure 9-6. *Deployment resource page*

In the resource page, as shown in Figure 9-7, select your newly created `Translator` resource. In the overview part, we can see in the `Essentials` group the endpoint and keys for our resource. Save them for later.

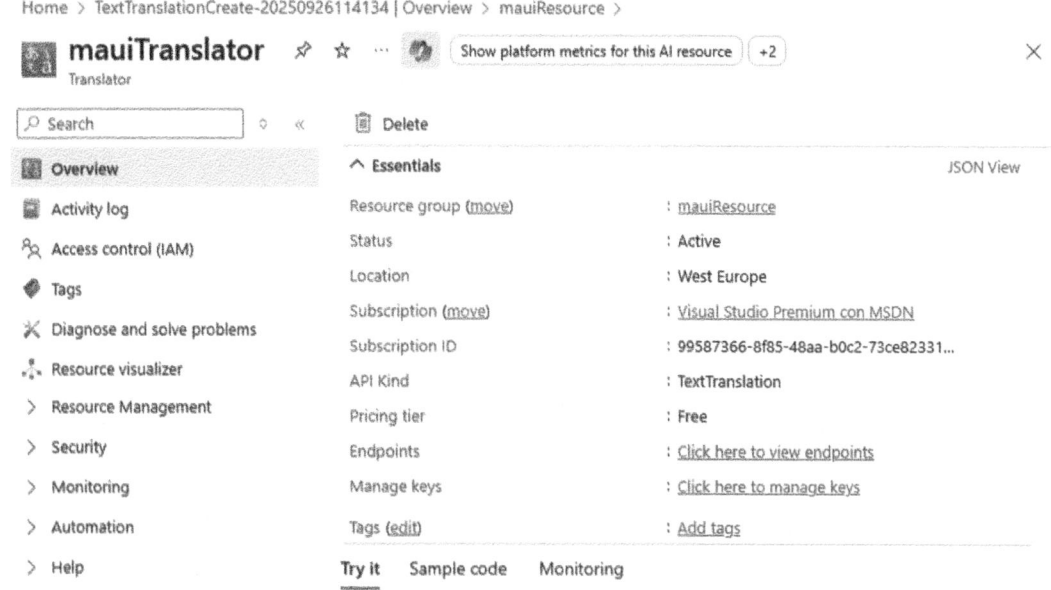

Figure 9-7. *Overview page–Essentials*

You can close the Essentials part and focus on the Try it menu. Here, as you can see in Figure 9-8, you can try your resource and check the request and response JSONs.

You can use the dropdown to select between the available languages, or use the Auto detect feature.

From the same part of the page, we can check the Sample code tab or the Monitoring tab. In the monitoring tab, you can check the request numbers or cost.

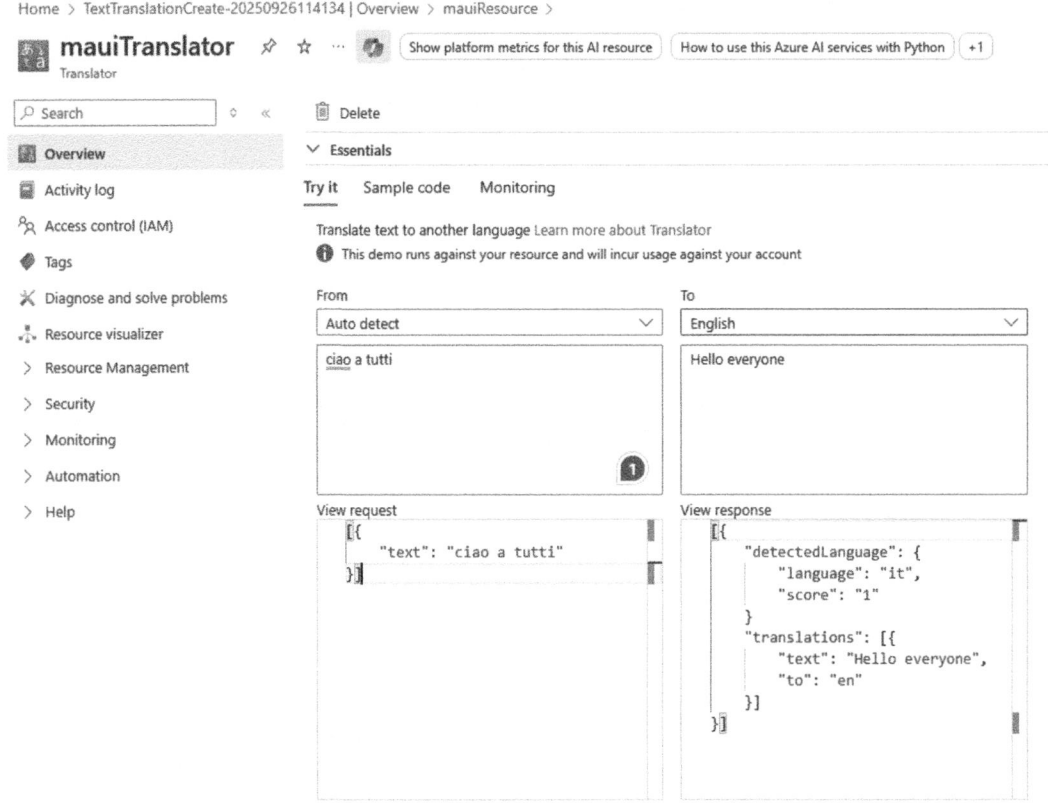

Figure 9-8. *Translator resource–Try it option*

Now that we have our resource, we tested it and checked the JSON formats, we can create a new .NET MAUI application.

In this application, our user will insert some English text into an Editor element and select the language into which we will translate the text from a Picker element. We will have some example languages such as Italian, Romanian, Spanish, French, and German. You can choose your preferred languages from the available languages.

The user will then click a Button to translate the text. We will display the translated text into a label underneath the Editor element.

We can start with the MainPage.xaml to modify the ContentPage and create our UI as shown in Listing 9-1.

Listing 9-1. MainPage.xaml content

```xml
<?xml version="1.0" encoding="utf-8" ?>
<ContentPage xmlns="http://schemas.microsoft.com/dotnet/2021/maui"
             xmlns:x="http://schemas.microsoft.com/winfx/2009/xaml"
             x:Class="Chapter9.MainPage">

    <ScrollView>
        <VerticalStackLayout
            Padding="30,0"
            Padding="30,0"
            Spacing="25">
            <Label Text="Enter text to translate:" FontSize="18" />

            <Editor x:Name="InputEditor"
                HeightRequest="100"
                laceholder="Type text here..." />
            <Picker x:Name="LanguagePicker" Title="Select target language">
                <Picker.Items>
                    <x:String>it</x:String>
                    <x:String>ro</x:String>
                    <x:String>es</x:String>
                    <x:String>fr</x:String>
                    <x:String>de</x:String>
                </Picker.Items>
            </Picker>

            <Button Text="Translate" Clicked="OnTranslateClicked" />
            <Label Text="Translation:" FontSize="18" />
            <Label x:Name="OutputLabel" FontSize="16"
                TextColor="DarkRed"
                LineBreakMode="WordWrap" />
        </VerticalStackLayout>
    </ScrollView>
</ContentPage>
```

After that, we can create an `APIParameters.cs` class where to store our API information. We will need the endpoint, key, and region. Retrieve your information from the Azure portal and save it into strings.

You can go to your resource in the Azure portal and expand `Resource Management` on the menu as shown in Figure 9-9. Then click Keys and Endpoints. As we will be translating simple text, we will be using the text translation endpoint. You can see also a document translation endpoint created, on the same resource and ready to be used.

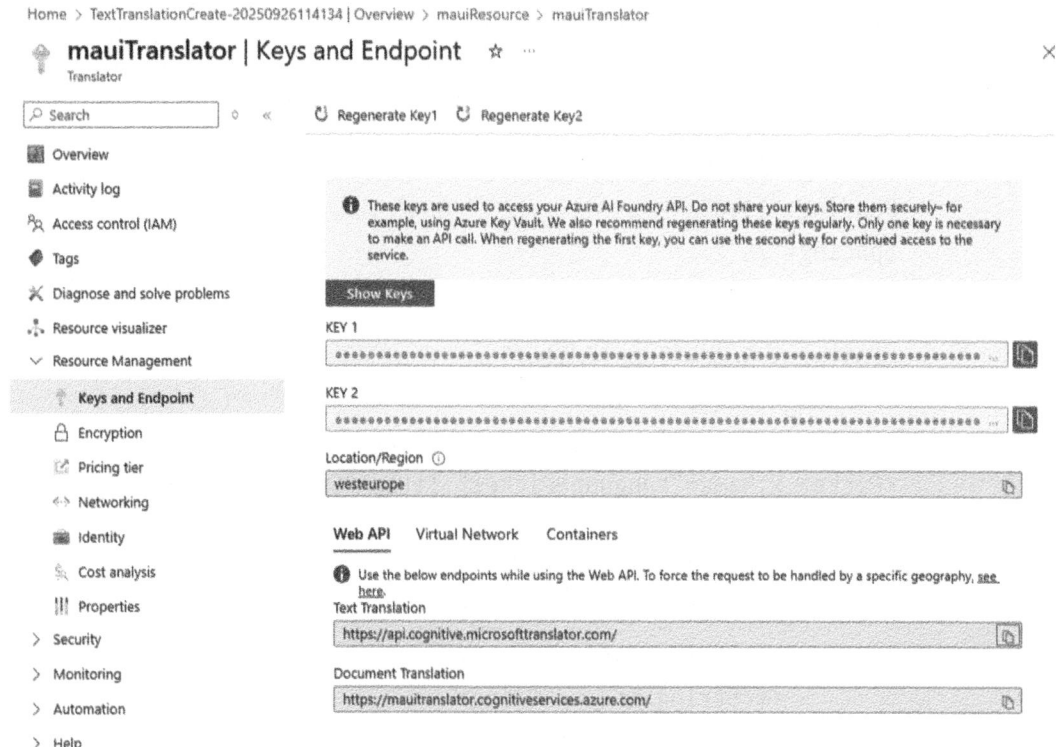

Figure 9-9. *Resource Management–Keys and Endpoint information*

With the retrieved info, our class will have the following constants, as shown in Listing 9-2. Replace YOUR_API_KEY, YOUR_ENDPOINT and YOUR_REGION with your values from the portal.

Listing 9-2. APIParameters.cs class

```
using System;
using System.Collections.Generic;
using System.Linq;
using System.Text;
using System.Threading.Tasks;
```

```
namespace Chapter9
{
    public static class APIParameters
    {
        public const string APIKey = "YOUR_API_KEY";
        public const string APIEndpoint = "YOUR_ENDPOINT";
        public const string APIRegion = "YOUR_REGION";
    }
}
```

Next, create a new folder called Services. Inside this folder, create a new class called *AzureTranslationService.cs*, where we will implement the call to the Azure Translator API. After checking the JSONs in the portal, we can parse the response and get the translated text. You can find the implementation in Listing 9-3.

Listing 9-3. AzureTranslationService.cs

```
using System;
using System.Collections.Generic;
using System.Linq;
using System.Text;
using System.Text.Json;
using System.Threading.Tasks;

namespace Chapter9.Services
{
    public  class AzureTranslationService
    {
        private readonly HttpClient _httpClient;
        private readonly string _endpoint;
        private readonly string _key;
        private readonly string _region;

        public AzureTranslationService()
        {
            _httpClient = new HttpClient();
            _endpoint = APIParameters.APIEndpoint;
            _key = APIParameters.APIKey;
```

```
        _region = APIParameters.APIRegion;

    }
    public async Task<string> TranslateTextAsync(string inputText,
    string targetLanguage)
    {
        if (string.IsNullOrWhiteSpace(inputText))
            throw new ArgumentException("Text cannot be empty",
            nameof(inputText));

        string url = $"{_endpoint}/translate?api-version=3.0&from=en&to
        ={targetLanguage}";

        _httpClient.DefaultRequestHeaders.Clear();
        _httpClient.DefaultRequestHeaders.Add("Ocp-Apim-Subscription-
        Key", _key);
        _httpClient.DefaultRequestHeaders.Add("Ocp-Apim-Subscription-
        Region", _region);

        var requestBody = new object[] { new { Text = inputText } };
        var requestJson = JsonSerializer.Serialize(requestBody);

        using var content = new StringContent(requestJson, Encoding.
        UTF8, "application/json");
        var response = await _httpClient.PostAsync(url, content);
        response.EnsureSuccessStatusCode();

        var result = await response.Content.ReadAsStringAsync();
        using var doc = JsonDocument.Parse(result);

        string translation = doc.RootElement[0]
            .GetProperty("translations")[0]
            .GetProperty("text").GetString();

        return translation;
    }
}
}
```

Once we have the service, we can create the `onTranslateClicked` method inside the `MainPage.xaml.cs` page and display the result back to the user. You can find the MainPage.xaml.cs implementation in Listing 9-4.

Listing 9-4. MainPage.xaml.cs updated code

```
namespace Chapter9
{
    public partial class MainPage : ContentPage
    {
        private readonly Services.AzureTranslationService _
        azureTranslationService = new Services.AzureTranslationService();
        public MainPage()
        {
            InitializeComponent();
        }
        private async void OnTranslateClicked(object sender, EventArgs e)
        {
            if (string.IsNullOrWhiteSpace(InputEditor.Text) ||
            LanguagePicker.SelectedItem == null)
            {
                await DisplayAlert("Error", "Please enter text and select a
                target language.", "OK");
                return;
            }

            string targetLang = LanguagePicker.SelectedItem.ToString();

            try
            {
                // Call the Translator service
                string translation = await _azureTranslationService.
                TranslateTextAsync(InputEditor.Text, targetLang);
                OutputLabel.Text = translation;
            }
```

```
            catch (Exception ex)
            {
                OutputLabel.Text = $"Error: {ex.Message}";
            }

        }

    }
}
```

We can now build our application and, why not, run it directly on Windows this time. Thanks to the power of .NET MAUI, you can just test on your Windows machine right away.

Just enter some English text, select your preferred language, and click the Translate button. You can see the reasult I got after translating "hello everyone" to romanian, by selecting "ro", in Figure 9-10.

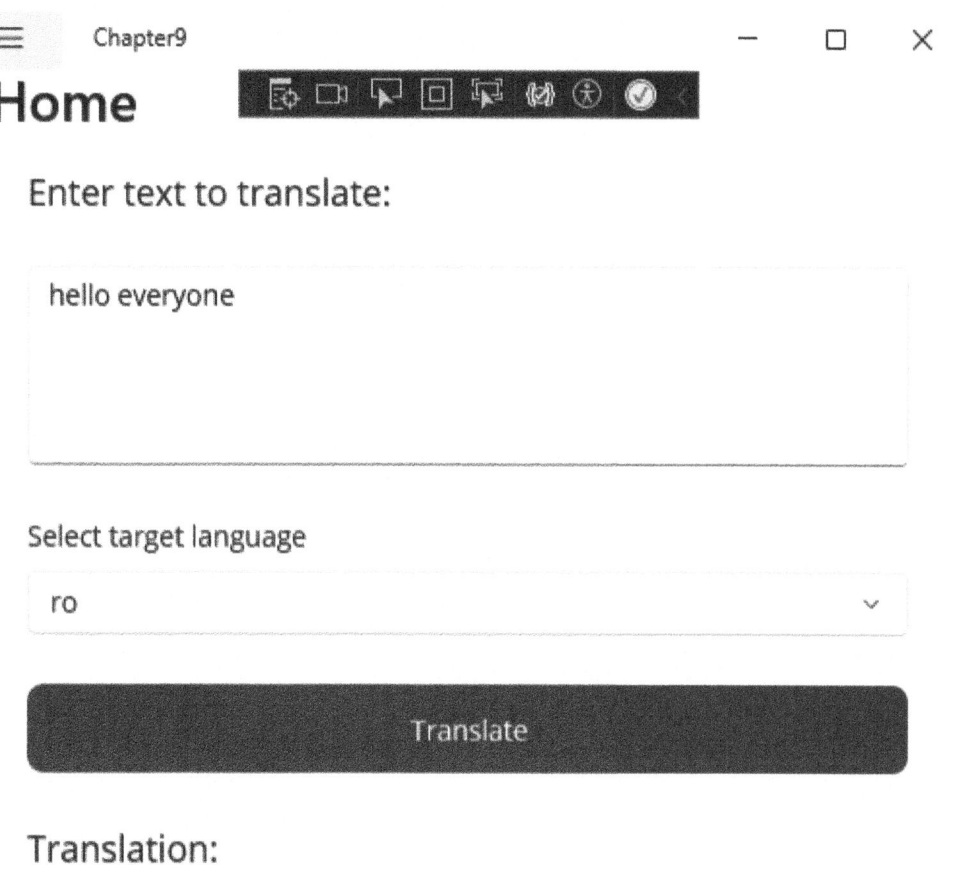

Figure 9-10. *Translation app result screen*

Summary

In this chapter, we have learned more about AI translation and how the Azure AI Translator service works. We used this service to integrate it into a .NET MAUI application that translated English text into a selected language and displayed it back to the user.

In the next chapter, we will focus on the OpenAI services, precisely the content summarizer model. We will learn more about it and how to integrate it in a .NET MAUI application.

CHAPTER 10

AI-Powered Content Summarizer

Introduction

In this chapter, we will see how we can use the content summarizer in a .NET MAUI app. We will also learn more about OpenAI models and how we can use them in our applications.

Beyond ChatGPT

We have seen in Chapter 5 how to integrate ChatGPT into your .NET MAUI application by using OpenAI's APIs. ChatGPT is maybe just the most famous application of the APIs provided by OpenAI, and when you call the OpenAI API with a request, you're interacting with the same powerful large language models (LLMs) that power the consumer-facing ChatGPT application. We have also seen in the second chapter that GPT is an acronym for *generative pretrained transformer*.

We can also use GPT models to perform specific tasks out of all the generative capabilities, like summarizing some content. Beyond simply summarizing text, GPT models offer a wide range of creative and analytical capabilities. In the world of content creation and social media marketing, these models act as tireless assistants, helping marketers and writers overcome creative blocks by generating everything from catchy ad copy and social media posts to full-length articles and even poetry. For developers and quality assurance engineers, tools like GitHub Copilot have become indispensable partners, using GPT to suggest and complete code as they type, debug complex programs, and even write documentation. In other big industries like healthcare, GPT

© Codrina Merigo 2026
C. Merigo, *AI-Enabled Apps with .NET MAUI*, https://doi.org/10.1007/979-8-8688-1817-2_10

is being used to streamline administrative tasks, generate patient summaries, and assist with medical research by analyzing and summarizing vast amounts of data. In the legal and finance fields, these models can quickly review legal documents for compliance, analyze market trends, and even generate financial forecasts, providing professionals with powerful insights and saving companies' time.

OpenAI Models

Like the Azure AI models, OpenAI models are generally classified based on their capabilities or the type of data the model has been designed to interact with. Most models belong to a model family, they also have different versions, and they offer different levels of power, and of course, based on the power, the cost may differ. You can check out the pricing for each model available at `https://platform.openai.com/docs/pricing`.

The GPT family models are language models and are designed to understand and generate text, then extended to generate audio, images, and various content. Some of them, like GPT-4 and GPT-5, are multimodal models that can process text and images as input, but they primarily will give a text as output.

DALL-E models are specialized in text-to-image generation, so based on the prompt, they will generate an image. We can see once again the importance of the prompt, always be specific and never take anything for granted. This model can also be found in ChatGPT, so users can generate images inside the conversation.

The Whisper model deals with audio and helps you generate audio to text. It can be used for transcribing audio or to translate spoken language.

OpenAI offers models that are built for specific tasks, like the o3-deep-research model. You can find a list of the models at `https://platform.openai.com/docs/models`.

Content Summarizer

We all have those chatty friends who send us superlong messages when we are in a rush. Sometimes I wish I could just have a summary of what they are writing to me. A content summarizer can help us save time and improve our understanding of the text as it quickly distills large amounts of information. Not only to my best friends' long messages, but you can also apply this to research, meeting transcripts, lectures, or news. You can also use it in customer service scenarios. When the chat is handed over to a human, you can send a summary of the support chatbot conversation with the user.

It can also be applied to other scenarios. Imagine opening an app and being greeted with a long article, a dozen messages, or a never-ending thread of comments—sometimes it's just too much to read at once. In digital apps, content summarizers can turn long, complex text into bite-sized, easy-to-digest pieces, making life easier for everyone—whether someone has cognitive disabilities, is rushing between tasks, or just wants to get to the key points quickly. Even social media feels lighter when endless posts and threads are distilled into simple highlights you can scan in seconds.

Basically, anywhere there's a long text, a content summarizer will help you understand, act on, and share information without feeling overwhelmed. You can also apply the content summarizer to audio. I personally don't send audio messages, but there are people who constantly rely on them. And, contrary to written text, you can't even quickly skim through sound. So, we can first convert audio to text using a speech-to-text service, such as the Azure Speech-to-Text which we have seen in Chapter 8; and once we have the transcript, we can send it to the content summarizer. Also, if needed, you can even convert the summary back to audio if you want to.

Integrate a Content Summarizer in a .NET MAUI Application

Incorporating a content summarization feature into a .NET MAUI application is really like all the other examples from Azure that we have seen so far.

The heart of this functionality lies in communication with OpenAI's GPT series of models, such as GPT-5-nano or the more advanced GPT-5. These models are accessed via a RESTful API.

The process begins on the client side, your .NET MAUI app, where a user provides a large block of text. This text is then packaged into a structured request, specifically a `ChatCompletionCreateRequest`. This request is not a simple data transfer; it's a carefully crafted instruction set that tells the AI precisely what to do. It includes a `system message`, which provides context and defines the model's role, for example, "You are my assistant who summarizes text."

Following this, a `user message` contains the actual text to be summarized. The request also includes parameters to define the model to be used and to control the generated output, such as `MaxTokens` to limit the summary's length and `Temperature` to adjust the creativity and randomness of the response.

Once the request is sent over a secure HTTP connection to OpenAI's servers, the specified language model, already trained, processes the input. It applies its vast learned knowledge of language to understand the key ideas and condense them into a coherent summary. The API then returns a JSON response containing the generated summary. Your .NET MAUI app receives this response, parses the JSON to extract the summary text, and finally displays it to the user inside the application.

Let's start by creating a new .NET MAUI application, clean out the `MainPage.xaml.cs` page, and replace it with the following content. We will have labels for the title and description of the page, an `Editor` element where the user can paste the text, a summarize button, and another label where we would place the summarized content. You can find the MainPage.xaml implementation in Listing 10-1.

Listing 10-1. MainPage.xaml updates

```xml
<ContentPage xmlns="http://schemas.microsoft.com/dotnet/2021/maui"
             xmlns:x="http://schemas.microsoft.com/winfx/2009/xaml"
             x:Class="Chapter10.MainPage">

    <ScrollView>
        <VerticalStackLayout
            Padding="30,0"
            Spacing="25">

            <Label Text="Try content summarizer"
                    FontSize="18"
                    TextColor="Purple"
                    />
            <Label Text="Paste some text below to generate a concise
            summary."
                    FontSize="16" />

            <Editor x:Name="InputEditor"
                    Placeholder="Paste your text here..."
                    HeightRequest="200"
                    AutoSize="TextChanges"
                    FontSize="14" />
```

```
<Button x:Name="SummarizeButton"
    Text="Summarize"
    Clicked="SummarizeButton_Clicked"/>

<Label x:Name="OutputLabel"
        Text="Your summary will appear here..."
        FontSize="14"
        TextColor="DarkRed" />

    </VerticalStackLayout>
  </ScrollView>

</ContentPage>
```

Next, we will need to get our OpenAI API key from the portal. Go to https://platform.openai.com/api-keys, log in, and click Create new secret key. If you already used OpenAI in Chapter 3, you already have a project, and you could use the same key. Otherwise, you can create a new project and a new key. After you have your secret key, create a new class OpenAIParameters.cs and save your key. You can find the implementation in Listing 10-2, just repalce YOUR_APIKEY_HERE wuth your key.

Listing 10-2. Save your key string

```
using System;
using System.Collections.Generic;
using System.Linq;
using System.Text;
using System.Threading.Tasks;

namespace Chapter10
{
    public static class OpenAIParameters
    {
        public const string APIKey = "YOUR_APIKEY_HERE";
    }
}
```

Now, it is time to call the OpenAI API. Let's create a new folder called Services and inside this folder, a new class OpenAISummarizerService.cs.

In our service, we will be calling the `https://api.openai.com/v1/chat/` `completions`. Apart from setting the API key in the header, we will need to send specific info in the request body to the model in the following JSON format, that you can see in Listin 10-3.

Listing 10-3. Input JSON

```json
'{
    "model": "gpt-4o-mini",
    "messages": [
      {
        "role": "system",
        "content": "You are a helpful assistant."
      },
      {
        "role": "user",
        "content": "Hello!"
      }
    ]
  }'
```

After we call the service, we will need to interpret the result JSON. It might look similar to the one in Listing 10-4.

Listing 10-4. `API response JSON`

```json
{
  "id": " chatcmpl-B9MBs8CjcvOU2jLn4n57OS5qMJKn",
  "object": "chat.completion",
  "created": 1758714404,
  "model": "gpt-3.5-turbo-0125",
  "choices": [
    {
      "index": 0,
      "message": {
        "role": "assistant",
        "content": "your response - the summarized content",
        "refusal": null,
```

```json
      "annotations": []
    },
    "logprobs": null,
    "finish_reason": "stop"
  }
],
"usage": {
  "prompt_tokens": 7938,
  "completion_tokens": 97,
  "total_tokens": 8035,
  "prompt_tokens_details": {
    "cached_tokens": 0,
    "audio_tokens": 0
  },
  "completion_tokens_details": {
    "reasoning_tokens": 0,
    "audio_tokens": 0,
    "accepted_prediction_tokens": 0,
    "rejected_prediction_tokens": 0
  }
},
"service_tier": "default",
"system_fingerprint": null
}
```

To get our summarized text, we will focus on just a part of the JSON, finding the
message JSON and then the content key, where we will find our summarized text.
You can always check the reference API at https://platform.openai.com/docs/
api-reference/chat/create?lang=csharp. You can find the full implementation in
Listing 10-5.

Listing 10-5. OpenAISummarizerService.cs class

```
using System;
using System.Collections.Generic;
using System.Linq;
using System.Net.Http;
```

```csharp
using System.Net.Http.Headers;
using System.Text;
using System.Text.Json;
using System.Threading.Tasks;

namespace Chapter10.Services
{
    public class OpenAISummarizerService
    {
        private readonly HttpClient _httpClient;
        private readonly string _apiKey;

        public OpenAISummarizerService(HttpClient httpClient,
        string apiKey)
        {
            _httpClient = httpClient;
            _apiKey = apiKey;
        }

        public async Task<string> SummarizeTextAsync(string text)
        {
            if (string.IsNullOrWhiteSpace(text))
                return "Please enter some text to summarize.";

            _httpClient.DefaultRequestHeaders.Authorization = new Authentic
            ationHeaderValue("Bearer", _apiKey);

            var requestBody = new
            {
                model = "gpt-3.5-turbo",
                messages = new[]
                {
                new { role = "system", content = "You are my assistant that
                summarizes text concisely." },
                new { role = "user", content = $"Summarize the following
                text: {text}" }
                }
            };
```

```
var jsonContent = JsonSerializer.Serialize(requestBody);
var content = new StringContent(jsonContent, Encoding.UTF8,
"application/json");

try
{
    var response = await _httpClient.PostAsync("https://api.
    openai.com/v1/chat/completions", content);
    response.EnsureSuccessStatusCode();

    string responseString = await response.Content.
    ReadAsStringAsync();

    using var document = JsonDocument.Parse(responseString);
    var root = document.RootElement;

    if (root.TryGetProperty("choices", out JsonElement
    choicesElement) &&
        choicesElement.ValueKind == JsonValueKind.Array &&
        choicesElement.EnumerateArray().Any())
    {
        var messageElement = choicesElement.EnumerateArray().
        First().GetProperty("message");
        if (messageElement.TryGetProperty("content", out
        JsonElement contentElement) &&
            contentElement.ValueKind == JsonValueKind.String)
        {
            return contentElement.GetString();
        }
        else
        {
            return "Unexpected content format in API
            response.";
        }
    }
    else
    {
```

```
                    return "No summary generated. Please try again.";
                }
            }
            catch (Exception ex)
            {
                return $"An unexpected error occurred: {ex.Message}";
            }
        }
    }
}
```

Once we have our OpenAISummarizerService.cs implemented, we can go to
our MainPage.xaml.cs and call the API from the SummarizeButton_Clicked(object
sender, EventArgs e) method when the Button is clicked. You can find the full
implementation of MainPage.xaml.cs in Listing 10-6.

Listing 10-6. MainPage.xaml.cs

```
using Chapter10.Services;
using System.Net.Http.Headers;
using System.Text.Json;

namespace Chapter10
{
    public partial class MainPage : ContentPage
    {
        private readonly HttpClient _httpClient;
        private readonly OpenAISummarizerService _summarizerService;
        public MainPage()
        {
            InitializeComponent();
            _httpClient = new HttpClient();
            _summarizerService = new OpenAISummarizerService(_httpClient,
            OpenAIParameters.APIKey);
        }

        private async void SummarizeButton_Clicked(object sender, EventArgs e)
        {
```

```
if (string.IsNullOrWhiteSpace(InputEditor.Text))
{
    OutputLabel.Text = "Please enter some text to summarize.";
    return;
}
else
{
    OutputLabel.Text = "Summarizing...";
    string summary = await _summarizerService.
    SummarizeTextAsync(InputEditor.Text);
    OutputLabel.Text = summary;
}

    }
  }

}
```

Now, it's time to build and test our application! As I am using Visual Studio, I just deployed a Windows application. You can always leverage all the targeted platforms following this example.

Next, we need some text, preferably a long one. I was thinking about which text to use, and I remembered that in Italy, in the first two years of high school, everyone must read the first recognized Italian novel, called *The Betrothed* (in Italian, it is *I promessi sposi),* written by the Italian poet, novelist, and philosopher Alessandro Manzoni. So, as I had to learn that too for my first novel as soon as I arrived in Italy, I just looked for the first chapter online and used it to test our application.

And now, if you are curious, I can tell you a little bit more about this novel. Or better yet, we can ask the content summarizer service to summarize it all for us. I can assure you that studying chapter by chapter, understanding all the subplots and their cultural references, is way more fun, but we'll use this example to see the service in action:

I Promessi Sposi by Alessandro Manzoni tells the story of Renzo and Lucia, two young lovers in 17th-century Lombardy whose marriage is obstructed by the cruel nobleman Don Rodrigo. Forced to flee and endure hardships, Lucia is protected by a convent and experiences the moral power of figures like Fra Cristoforo and the reformed criminal Innominato (the unnamed), while Renzo faces social unrest and famine in Milan.

The novel explores themes of love, justice, faith, and redemption, blending fictional characters with historical events like the plague of 1630. Through detailed storytelling and moral reflection, Manzoni highlights the struggle of ordinary people against oppression, the influence of providence, and the potential for human transformation, all while shaping modern Italian prose and the Italian language.

And back to our summarizer app, you can see the summary of the first chapter of the novel in Figure 10-1. You can use the summary as input to a Text-to-Speech API like the OpenAI's Audio API.

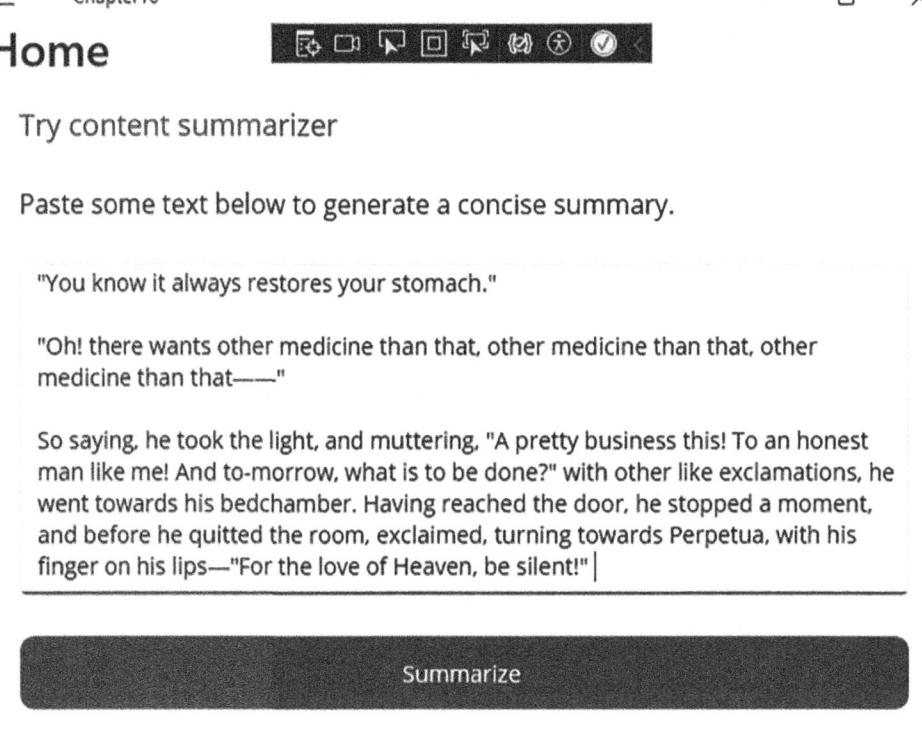

Figure 10-1. *Output of the content summarizer application*

You can find more info about Text-to-Speech API and how to structure it at `https://platform.openai.com/docs/guides/text-to-speech`.

Summary

In this chapter, we have explored OpenAI models and capabilities. We have used a content summarizer in a .NET MAUI application to summarize a long text; and, on the way, we encountered what is generally considered to be the first modern Italian novel.

In the next chapter, we will move to Google AI models and Google Gemini capabilities. We will learn more about search and search engines. We will also create an application that uses Google Gemini to search based on predefined information.

CHAPTER 11

Let Google Gemini Search into Your .NET MAUI App

Introduction

In this chapter, we will get an overview of Google Gemini and how Google Search works. We will explore Google Gemini APIs and implement a search example in a .NET MAUI application. We will also learn more about retrieval-augmented generation (RAG), a powerful AI pattern that we can use when we interact with local files.

Google Search

For lots of people, when you say "*Google,*" they associate it with the search engine. It also became a new way of saying: "*let me Google that.*" There are other search engines around the world, but I think Google is the most famous one. The first search engine was created back in 1990, but the web search era began around 1993–1994, when web pages have become increasingly more. A search engine is a software system that helps a user find information within specific collection of data or on the Internet. The first search engine, called Archie and created by a student at McGill University in Canada, indexed filenames of a File Transfer Protocol (FTP) archive. Then other text search tools were created, but the first to index full pages was WebCrawler in 1994. Others, like AltaVista from 1995, were famous due to its speed and big index. Google search engine just perfected the models that were around.

Nowadays, we mainly refer to web search as the process of finding information on the World Wide Web. To do that, a search engine crawls the web by using automated bots, also known as spiders or web crawlers. These bots browse the Internet, follow all

© Codrina Merigo 2026
C. Merigo, *AI-Enabled Apps with .NET MAUI*, https://doi.org/10.1007/979-8-8688-1817-2_11

the hyperlinks from all the pages, and collect all the useful information to create an index of the web content. They usually have a starting point, a list of known URLs where they start the discovery. During discovery, they not only visit the page but also download the content and parse all the HTML to find all the connected links. If new links are found, they are added to the queue or URL to be visited next, and the process continues, by following all the links. All the collected data, including text, images, videos, and other metadata, is organized and stored in a huge database called an index.

When we, as web users, perform a web search by typing a query to this search engine, the engine looks inside the index and a prepared ranking system to give us the result. The goal of ranking the results is to show the user the most relevant and useful result. During ranking, different factors play an important part such as relevance, authority, how new the info is, if the user clicks the result, and how quickly the page is displayed. Google's innovation in the search engine world was the PageRank, an algorithm that assigns a number to a web page based on the quantity and quality of the incoming links; you can see them as "votes" of confidence. In this AI era, also search engines adopted AI that uses modern AI-based ranking with the help of machine learning and neural networks (like Google's RankBrain, BERT, Gemini, OpenAI embeddings) to understand meaning, not just words.

Ranking a web page is directly tied to Search Engine Optimization (SEO) and Search Engine Advertising (SEA). These are great web marketing tools. SEO is a technique to improve a website's visibility, in an organic way and without paying, in a search engine ranking. The goal of SEO is to appear as high as possible in the result of the search engine. We can achieve SEO easily by using relevant keywords in the title and the content, getting backlinks from known and trusted websites, using a good user experience, and having updated content. SEA, on the other hand, buys visibility by paying for ads in search engines, for example, using *Google Ads*. In this way, the results will appear at the top part of the results page, usually in a sponsored results section. Ranking still matters to these paid website links too, since poor-quality ads won't show if they are not relevant, even if you pay more. If you have your website, you can use Google Search Console (GSC) to check how Google sees, indexes, and interacts with your website, before the user actually visits your pages.

Google Gemini

While traditional search engines crawl, index, and rank pages, AI-powered search chatbots like Google Gemini can understand the query, summarize the best results to you from multiple sources, and even act conversationally refining step by step. While Google Search only ranks links, Gemini ranks the meaning thanks to AI. You might have noticed that when you perform a search now on Google, you might have an AI overview as the first result as now Google Gemini is now grounded in Google Search. Gemini is your *"everyday assistant from Google"* and uses generative AI too, like ChatGPT that we have seen in previous chapters. You can also think of Gemini as an ecosystem of different AI models optimized for various tasks and platforms. This ecosystem is now an essential part of Google products and services, from the AI assistant that can interact with Google Workspace and even Android parts. It is a multimodal system built to process multiple data formats at the same time. It uses advanced reasoning to navigate through complex information, like dealing with mathematics, physics, or coding.

There are different models available that are tailored to specific needs:

- **Gemini Ultra**: The biggest and most advanced model, built for tough challenges that need deep reasoning, like complex coding or scientific research.

- **Gemini Pro**: The all-rounder. It's powerful, flexible, and efficient, making it the engine behind the main Gemini chatbot and many of Google's AI tools.

- **Gemini Flash**: Superfast and budget-friendly. Perfect for tasks that need speed, like real-time chat, quick answers, or text summaries.

- **Gemini Nano**: The tiniest but super handy model, designed to run right on your device (like Google Pixel phones). This means you get AI help without even needing an Internet connection.

Retrieval-Augmented Generation

While thinking about the example app for this chapter, I didn't just want to use Google Gemini APIs into .NET MAUI, but also wanted to search inside our app. We can use the retrieval-augmented generation (RAG) pattern by integrating a local resource search before using AI. Imagine that our user will ask us a question, the app will first search inside the local resources for relevant text, then this text will be combined with the initial ask and sent to AI, Gemini in this case, that will use the context to give us a more accurate answer based on the app data.

The RAG process combines two main phases:

1. Retrieval: The *"Look-Up"* step

   The first part of the process starts with your knowledge base. This is simply the collection of information you want the AI to rely on. It could be your company's internal wiki, a library of legal contracts, product manuals, recent news, or even the embedded resources inside a .NET MAUI app. Think of it as the pool of knowledge the AI will dip into when answering questions.

   Next comes indexing, where that information is prepared in a way that makes it easy to search. Instead of storing raw text, the system transforms each piece into vector embeddings—essentially numbers that capture the meaning of the text. This allows the AI to look for related concepts and ideas, not just exact keyword matches, which makes search results much smarter.

   Finally, there's the search step. When you ask a question, the system uses the indexed data to find the most relevant snippets. These pieces of information act as the factual backbone of the process, ensuring that the AI doesn't just guess but instead pulls from real, reliable sources.

2. Generation: The *"Formulation"* step

   Once the right information is retrieved, it's time to combine it into an augmented prompt. Your original question is enriched with the snippets of knowledge found in the first step, giving the AI a detailed context to work with. This makes the request more specific and helps guide the model toward a meaningful answer.

   This augmented prompt is then sent to the large language model (LLM), such as Google Gemini. With the extra context in hand, the model doesn't just rely on its general training but tailors its response to your specific data. This is what bridges the gap between generic AI and personalized, data-aware answers.

The final stage is the response. The model produces an answer that's grounded in your actual knowledge base, reducing the chance of hallucinations (AI "making things up") and improving accuracy. The result is a response that feels natural and conversational but is also reliable and fact-checked against your own data.

Imagine a standard LLM as a legendary metal guitarist. They've practiced for decades, memorized every riff, and can shred like crazy. But sometimes, when you ask them to play a new song, they just improvise. It *sounds* awesome, but… it's not always the song you asked for. That's the problem: hallucinations.

Now, with RAG—it's like handing that guitarist a setlist and the sheet music right before the show. Suddenly, they don't just play something that "feels right," they play *your exact song*, note for note.

- **Reduces Hallucinations**: No more random solos in the middle of "Master of Puppets." With RAG, the AI sticks to the actual track list (the retrieved documents).

- **Access to Current Information**: Bands release new albums all the time. Without RAG, your guitarist is stuck in 2019. With RAG, you just drop the new songs into the library, and boom—they can play the latest hits tonight, no retraining tour needed.

- **Domain-Specific Knowledge**: Every band has its own style, weird time signatures, and custom gear. With RAG, the AI can specialize in your band's sound (your company's data) without rewriting all the music theory from scratch.

- **Transparency and Trust**: Fans love when the band calls out, *"This one's from Ride the Lightning!"* RAG does the same—citing sources so you know exactly which "album" (document) the answer came from.

- **Cost-effective**: Retraining a model is like rerecording your entire discography in a new studio—it's expensive and takes forever. Updating a knowledge base? That's just adding new tracks to the setlist—fast, cheap, and ready for the next gig.

So, RAG turns your LLM from a wild soloist into a tight, trustworthy metal band, still heavy, still powerful, but now always on track with the music you want.

Add Gemini to a .NET MAUI App

Now, let's see how we can integrate Gemini into a .NET MAUI app and RAG to perform our specific search. You can already think that this is a great scenario for enterprise applications too as they have lots of data. Not only enterprise search, but we can create a customer support chatbot based on enterprise FAQs. You can apply this combo also to create a research assistant or a documentation bot, just give your app the documents you have and let RAG do the rest. I will be more than happy to learn about your scenario and how you applied this.

To start, go to Google AI Studio at `https://aistudio.google.com/prompts/new_chat`, sign in with your account, or create a new one.

Now, it's time to build, so we need to get an API key. You can create a new one or use the same from Chapter 3.

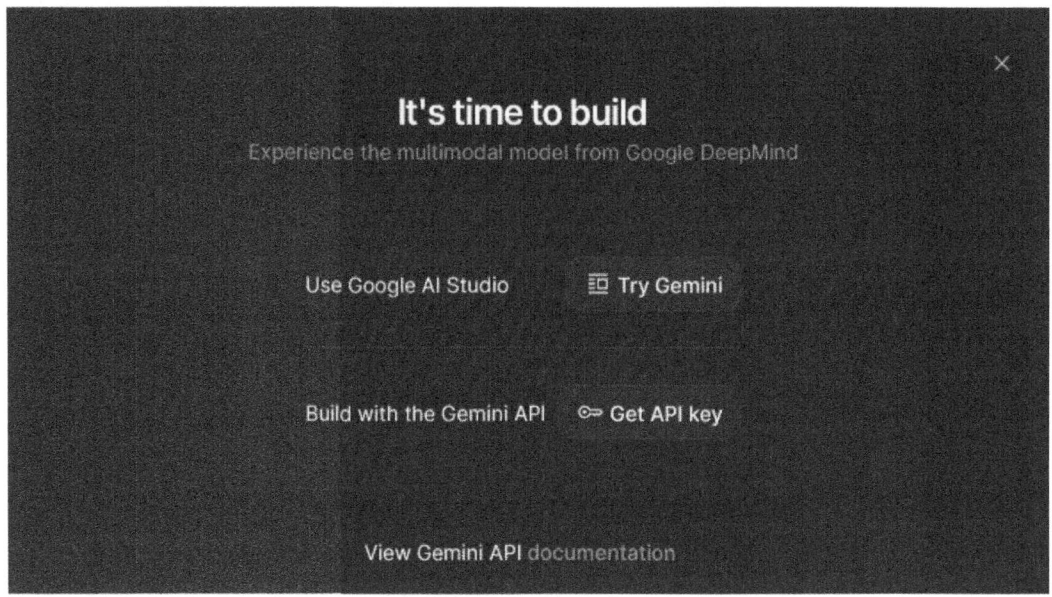

Figure 11-1. *Google AI Studio prompt*

Click *Get API key* or go to `https://aistudio.google.com/apikey` to get your key. Copy your key and store it securely.

Next, create a new .NET MAUI empty project.

Retrieve your copied key and create an APIKeys.cs class and store your key in a new string.

```
public const string GeminiAPIKey = "YOUR_API_KEY_HERE";
```

Modify MainPage.xaml so we can have an Entry where the user types the question, a button to send the query to Gemini, and a WebView to display the result. The result can be easily bind to a WebView so we can render bold tests, line, and breaks. The modified VerticalStackLayout can be found in Listing 11-1.

Listing 11-1. Xaml page

```
<VerticalStackLayout Padding="20" Spacing="10">
    <Entry x:Name="UserQueryEntry" Placeholder="Type your question
    here..." />
    <Button Text="Ask Gemini" Clicked="OnButtonClicked"/>
    < WebView x:Name="ResultWebView " />
</VerticalStackLayout>
```

To create our own data, we can create a simple list of strings and add our data in a List<string> Documents. You can add files, connect to your databases, blob storage, etc.

I just used some metal music samples and created a knowledge base locally inside the KnowledgeBase class. You can find the class with some sample data in Listing 11-2.

Listing 11-2. KnowledgeBase class

```
public static class KnowledgeBase
{
    public static readonly List<string> Documents = new()
    {
        // History
        "Metal music originated in the late 1960s and early 1970s,
        combining elements of blues rock and psychedelic rock.",
        "Black Sabbath, formed in 1968, is often credited as the first
        heavy metal band.",
        "Metallica, Iron Maiden, and Judas Priest helped define the sound
        of metal in the 1980s.",
```

```
// Subgenres
"Heavy metal is the original form of metal, characterized by
distorted guitars, emphatic rhythms, and strong vocals.",
"Thrash metal is fast, aggressive, and features complex guitar
riffs; Metallica and Slayer are key bands.",
"Death metal is extreme, often featuring growled vocals and heavily
distorted guitars; Death and Cannibal Corpse are pioneers.",
"Black metal emphasizes atmosphere and often features shrieked
vocals and blast beats; Mayhem and Darkthrone are influential
bands.",
"Power metal features melodic vocals and epic themes, often with
fantasy-inspired lyrics; Helloween and Blind Guardian are notable
bands.",
"Doom metal is slower, heavier, and more melancholic, with Black
Sabbath being a major influence.",

    };
}
```

Next, we will focus on our services. Create a Service folder and a new
GeminiService.cs c# class. In this class, we will call the Google Gemini API.

You can check the API request and response format at https://ai.google.dev/api/
generate-content. We will be using the gemini-2.5-flash-lite model, and the full URL
will look like this: https://generativelanguage.googleapis.com/v1beta/models/
gemini-2.5-flash-lite:streamGenerateContent. We will generate simple text content
in the example, the generated content might also contain bold strings in the **string**
format or line breaks, and we will bind that inside a WebView. You can find the complete
GeminiService implementation in Listing 11-3.

Listing 11-3. GeminiAPI service class

```
using Chapter11;
using System.Net.Http;
using System.Net.Http.Headers;
using System.Text;
using System.Text.Json;
using System.Threading.Tasks;
```

```csharp
public class GeminiService
{
    private readonly HttpClient _httpClient;

    public GeminiService()
    {
        _httpClient = new HttpClient();

    }

    public async Task<string> GetCompletionJsonAsync(Task<string> prompt)
    {
        var url = $"https://generativelanguage.googleapis.com/v1beta/
        models/gemini-2.5-flash-lite:streamGenerateContent?key={APIKeys.
        GeminiAPIKey}";

        // Build payload to match Gemini JSON structure
        var payload = new
        {
            contents = new[]
                {
                new
                {
                    role = "user",
                    parts = new[]
                    {
                        new { text = prompt.Result }
                    }
                }
            }
        };
        var json = System.Text.Json.JsonSerializer.Serialize(payload);
        var response = await _httpClient.PostAsync(url,
            new StringContent(json, Encoding.UTF8, "application/json"));
        response.EnsureSuccessStatusCode();
        return await response.Content.ReadAsStringAsync();
    }
}
```

As we have a private knowledge base, we will need to create a `Retriever` class that will be used by a RAG service to search for the documents we have. We will be performing a simple search by splitting the query into words and looking for the match in the document, then we will get the top three results. You can find the Retriever class in Listing 11-4.

Listing 11-4. Retriever class

```
public class Retriever
{
    public List<string> Search(string query, int top = 3)
    {
        var results = new List<string>();
        if (string.IsNullOrWhiteSpace(query))
            return results;

        // Split query into words
        string[] queryWords = query.ToLowerInvariant()
        .Split(' ', StringSplitOptions.RemoveEmptyEntries);

        foreach (var doc in KnowledgeBase.Documents)
        {
            string docLower = doc.ToLowerInvariant();

            // Check if any word in the query exists in the document
            if (queryWords.Any(word => docLower.Contains(word)))
            {
                results.Add(doc);
                if (results.Count >= top) //get top 3 results
                    break;
            }
        }

        return results;
    }
}
```

Now, it is time to implement our RAGService.cs. You can find it in Listing 11-5. Retriever.Search(query) returns a list of relevant documents from your knowledge base. The RagService can then send the augmented prompt to Google Gemini to generate answers to questions like:

"Tell me more about metal music."

"Which bands shaped thrash metal?"

"What instruments and techniques are used in metal?"

Listing 11-5. RagService class

```
public class RagService
{
    private readonly GeminiService _geminiService;

    public RagService()
    {
        _geminiService = new GeminiService();
    }

    public async Task<string> AskAsync(string userQuery, List<string>
    retrievedDocs)
    {
        var sb = new StringBuilder();
        sb.AppendLine("Use the following context to answer the question:");
            foreach (var doc in retrievedDocs)
            {
                sb.AppendLine($"- {doc}");
            }

        sb.AppendLine();
        sb.AppendLine($"Question: {userQuery}");

        return sb.ToString();
    }
}
```

Now, let's move to `MainPage.xaml.cs` to handle the user's input. When a user types a question into the `UserQueryEntry` box, our app springs into action. First, `Retriever.Search` scans the local knowledge base to find the most relevant documents. Next, `RagService.AskAsync` combines these documents with the user's question, creating a richer, context-aware prompt. This prompt is then sent to Google Gemini through `GeminiService.GetCompletionAsync`, which generates a thoughtful and informed answer. Finally, the response appears in the `ResultWebView`, giving the user a clear, helpful reply right in the app. You can find the implementation in Listing 11-6.

Listing 11-6. MainPage.xaml.cs class

```
public partial class MainPage : ContentPage
{
    private readonly RagService _ragService;
    private readonly Retriever _retriever;
    private readonly GeminiService _geminiService;

    public MainPage()
    {
        InitializeComponent();
        _ragService = new RagService();
        _retriever = new Retriever();
        _geminiService = new GeminiService();
    }

    private async void OnButtonClicked(object sender, EventArgs e)
    {
        string userQuery = UserQueryEntry.Text?.Trim();
        if (string.IsNullOrEmpty(userQuery))
        {
            await DisplayAlert("Warning", "Please type a question.", "OK");
            return;
        }

        ResultWebView.Source = new HtmlWebViewSource
        {
```

```
        Html = $"<html><body><p style='color:blue;'>Thinking...</p>
        </body></html>"
    };

    try
    {
        // Retrieve context
        var retrievedDocs = _retriever.Search(userQuery);

        //  Build augmented prompt
        var augmentedPrompt = _ragService.AskAsync(userQuery,
        retrievedDocs);

        // Get Gemini response as JSON
        string jsonResponse = await _geminiService.GetCompletionJsonAsy
        nc(augmentedPrompt);

        // Parse JSON and combine all text parts
        string response = ParseGeminiJson(jsonResponse);
        string htmlText = ConvertToHtml(response);
        ResultWebView.Source = new HtmlWebViewSource
        { Html = htmlText };

    }
    catch (Exception ex)
    {
        ResultWebView.Source = new HtmlWebViewSource
        {
            Html = $"<html><body><p style='color:red;'>Error:
            {ex.Message}</p></body></html>"
        };
    }
}

private string ParseGeminiJson(string json)
{
    using var doc = JsonDocument.Parse(json);
    var root = doc.RootElement;
    var sb = new StringBuilder();
```

```
        foreach (var chunk in root.EnumerateArray())
        {
            var candidates = chunk.GetProperty("candidates");
            if (candidates.GetArrayLength() == 0) continue;

            var content = candidates[0].GetProperty("content");
            if (!content.TryGetProperty("parts", out var parts)) continue;

            foreach (var part in parts.EnumerateArray())
            {
                string text = part.GetProperty("text").GetString();
                if (!string.IsNullOrEmpty(text))
                    sb.Append(text);
            }
        }

        return sb.ToString();
    }
    public string ConvertToHtml(string text)
    {
        if (string.IsNullOrWhiteSpace(text))
            return string.Empty;

        // Replace **bold** with <b>bold</b>
        string html = System.Text.RegularExpressions.Regex.Replace(
            text,
            @"\*\*(.+?)\*\*",
            "<b>$1</b>");

        // Replace line breaks with <br>
        html = html.Replace("\n", "<br>");

        return html;
    }
}
```

After building and deploying our app, we can ask everything we want to Gemini about metal music. I have created a windows app this time, as with .NET MAUI you can target any platform. After performing a simple query *"Tell me more about metal music,"* you can see the results on the screen.

The API will generate content to you based on the input text; you can see that highlights in bold the important information for you. You can see the result in Figure 11-2.

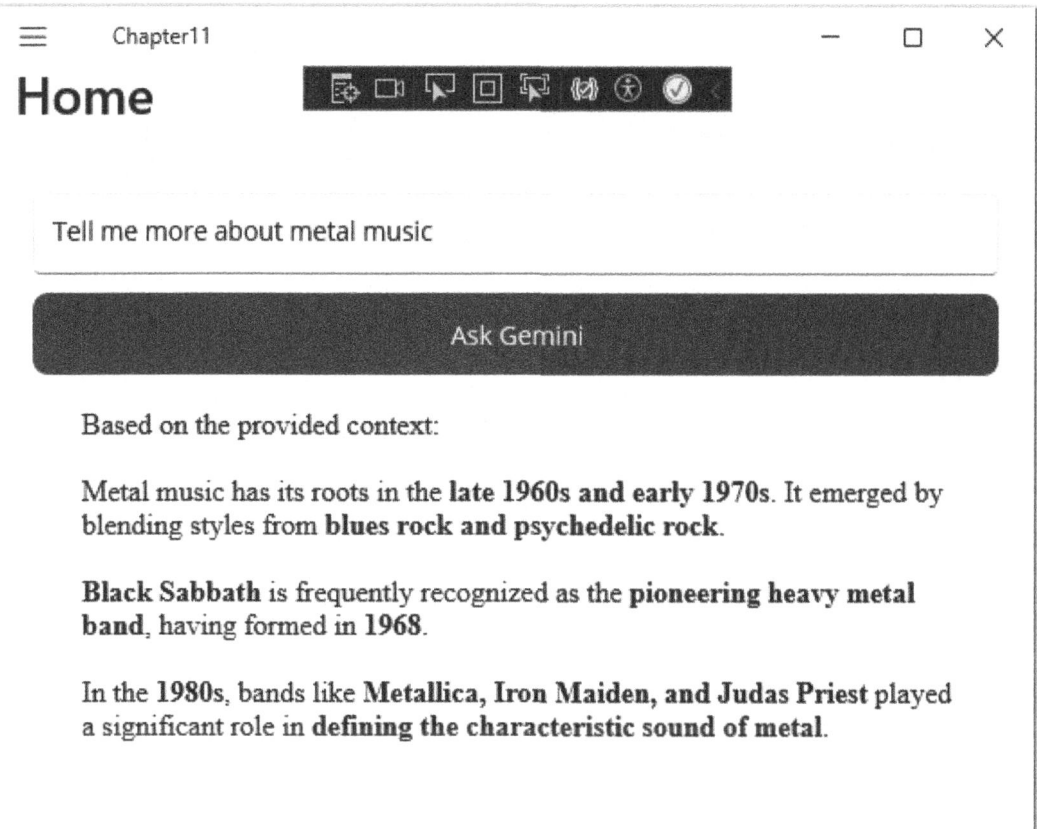

Figure 11-2. *Result of the app–metal music*

If you ask another query, outside of the knowledge base that has been ingested, for example, *"classic pizza recipe,"* we will have another response. You can see the result in Figure 11-3. In the example, we have grounded the response to use only the documents that have been provided. As you can see, from the provided text, we cannot get a classic pizza recipe.

Giving a knowledge base, an internal dataset, or files can be great for internal applications or scenarios like a chatbot or customer service bot that relies only on custom files, documentation, or procedures.

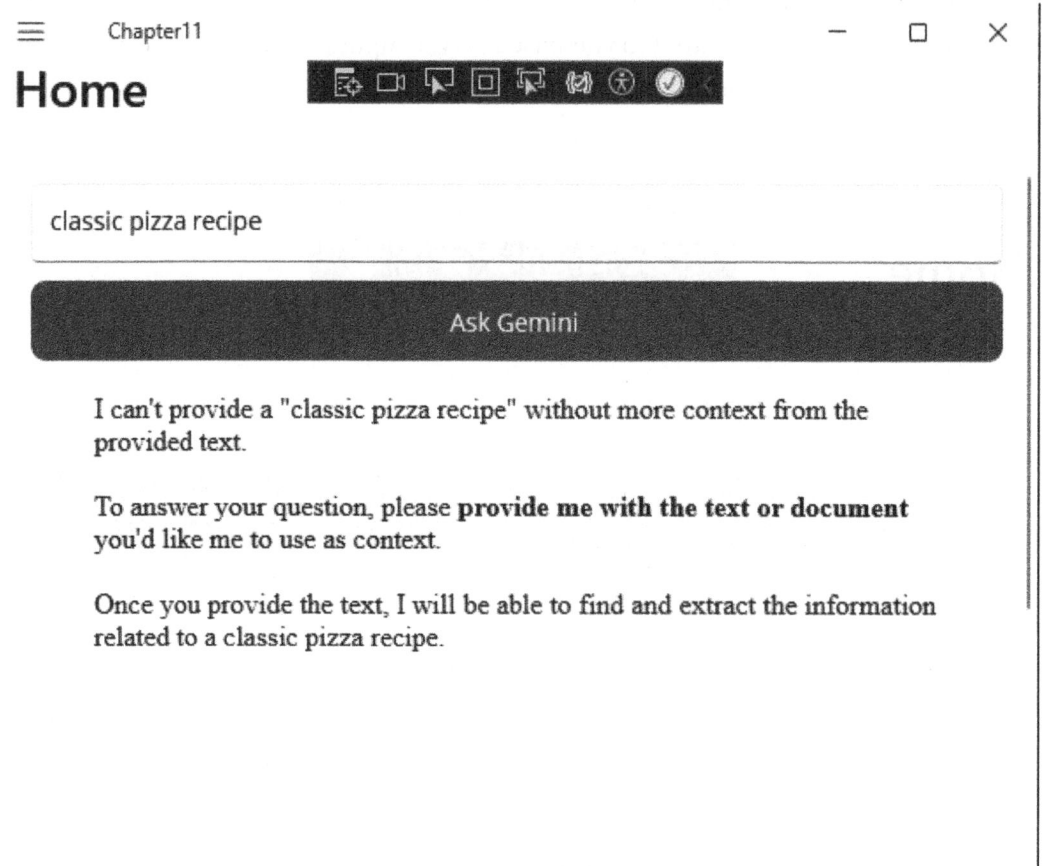

Figure 11-3. *Results based on knowledge base–classic pizza recipe query*

We can modify our logic to search outside the knowledge base and use full functionality of Google Gemini Search. We can add an if statement in the AskAsync method inside the RagService.cs. You can find the new implementation in Listing 11-7. If we don't have any information inside the text provided, we will use Gemini general knowledge to provide an answer to the user.

Listing 11-7. Modified RagService.cs class

```
public async Task<string> AskAsync(string userQuery, List<string>
retrievedDocs)
{
    var sb = new StringBuilder();
    if (retrievedDocs != null && retrievedDocs.Any())
    {
        sb.AppendLine("Use the following context to answer the question:");

        foreach (var doc in retrievedDocs)
        {
            sb.AppendLine($"- {doc}");
        }
    }
    else
    {
        sb.AppendLine("No relevant documents found. Answer based on
        general knowledge:");
        sb.AppendLine(); // extra line before the question
    }

    sb.AppendLine();
    sb.AppendLine($"Question: {userQuery}");

    return sb.ToString();
}
```

And the final result will be an actual recipe, based on general knowledge. You can see the result in Figure 11-4.

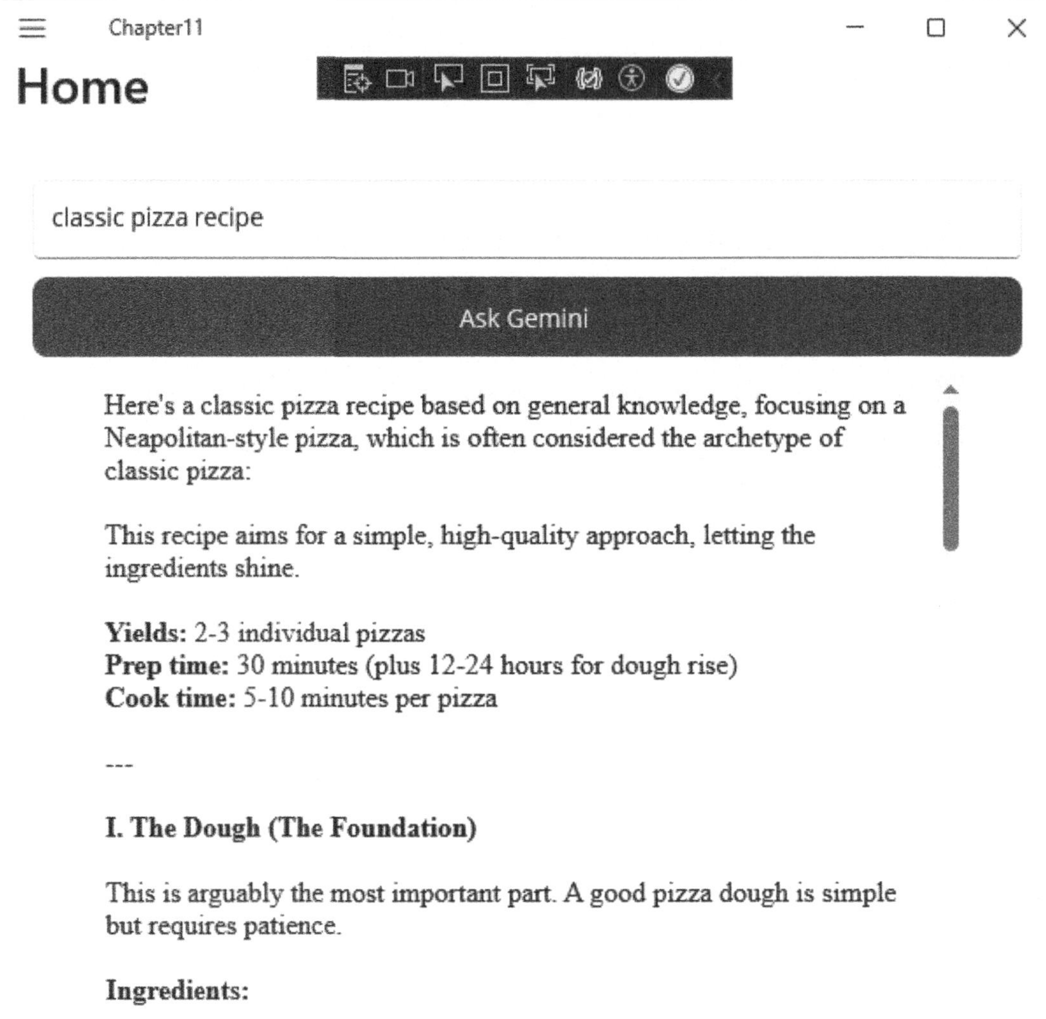

Figure 11-4. *Result with general knowledge–classic pizza recipe query*

As always, examples are simple just to show the power of the AI and .NET MAUI. I advise creating a back-end service (e.g., an *ASP.NET Core Web API*) that hosts the RAG pipeline. This service will handle all the heavy lifting: data ingestion, chunking, embedding, and interacting with the vector store and the Gemini API.

For enterprise apps, you can also check Semantic Kernel, a lightweight, open source development kit that lets you easily build AI agents and integrate the latest AI models into your C#, Python, or Java codebase. It serves as efficient middleware that enables rapid delivery of enterprise-grade solutions.

You can learn more about Semantic Kernel at `https://learn.microsoft.com/semantic-kernel/overview/`.

We have used the Google AI API and the `generateContent` method to generate our response. We have generated simple text, but this API can receive and generate images, audio, and many more formats.

You can learn more at `https://ai.google.dev/api/generate-content`.

You can also play around with different models that better suit your needs and also your credit. You can check the costs, details, and latest models at `https://ai.google.dev/gemini-api/docs/model`. In the example above, I have used a lite version that does not support image or audio generation and live APIs. There are specific models, trained for audio, images, or text to speech. Also, check the AI models based on your needs.

Summary

In this chapter, we have looked more closely at Google AI and Google Gemini. We also review search engines and how they work. Then, we met retrieval-augmented generation (RAG) and learned how to use it in a .NET MAUI app. The app has an internal knowledge base and uses the Google Gemini API to generate responses based on a user query.

In the next chapter, we will see how AI can also work offline, directly on your device, thanks to Edge AI. We will also create an AI model that we will use in a .NET MAUI app. The app will not need any Internet connection; it will take a picture and classify it based on the model logic.

CHAPTER 12

Edge AI and Offline AI Models

Introduction

In this chapter, we will get an overview of how we can create and run AI directly on devices, thanks to Edge AI. We will see how Edge AI is used and how we can implement it in our .NET MAUI app. We will see also main advantages of using Edge AI and some real-life use cases.

Edge AI

So far, all the models we have used are somewhere on the cloud and receive data from our application. That is why we need to make sure our applications that use Azure AI services, Google Gemini, or OpenAI services are connected to the Internet. Thanks to Edge AI, we can run AI models directly on the devices where we generate the data. We will be using the so-called *local edge devices* that are computing hardware located near the source where data is generated, rather than centralized in a cloud or data center. We might forget sometimes that the cloud is also hardware, somewhere, so with the models we have seen so far, we will send data to a computer somewhere that will run the AI model and send us a response. With Edge AI devices, data is processed locally and reduces latency, also saves on bandwidth, and enables faster decision-making for some applications. We can think of smart sensors or Internet of Things (IoT) deployments or smart cameras.

© Codrina Merigo 2026
C. Merigo, *AI-Enabled Apps with .NET MAUI*, https://doi.org/10.1007/979-8-8688-1817-2_12

Local AI Devices

Edge devices—such as sensors, cameras, or smart machines—begin their work by gathering data directly from the environment around them. Instead of transmitting all this raw information to a remote cloud service for processing, they handle much of the analysis locally, right on the device itself.

This shift is powerful for several reasons. First, it dramatically reduces latency: because the data doesn't need to make a round trip to a server and back, the system can react almost instantly, which is critical for time-sensitive scenarios like autonomous driving, health monitoring, or industrial safety. Second, local processing improves efficiency by trimming down the amount of data that must be sent across networks, lowering bandwidth consumption and helping organizations save on infrastructure and cloud costs. Beyond speed and efficiency, Edge AI also offers important security advantages. Since sensitive information never has to leave the device, it remains safer from interception or misuse, and local threat detection can run in real time without waiting on a central system. Taken together, these benefits make Edge AI a compelling approach for applications where speed, efficiency, privacy, and reliability all matter.

We can think of the Edge ecosystem as being shaped by five main categories of devices, each playing a specific role in how data is captured, processed, and delivered:

- **IoT Sensors**: These are small, specialized devices that gather data directly from the environment, such as temperature, motion, humidity, or pressure. They form the foundation of many edge applications by providing the raw information needed for analysis.

- **Smart Cameras**: More advanced than traditional cameras, these devices don't just record video; they can analyze it in real time using AI models to detect objects, recognize faces, or identify anomalies— perfect for applications like security, traffic monitoring, and industrial automation.

- **Servers**: Edge servers act as local hubs, providing additional processing power and storage closer to where the data is generated. They can handle heavier workloads than sensors or cameras and often serve as the bridge between on-site devices and cloud infrastructure.

- **Processors**: These are the engines that make local AI possible, ranging from CPUs and GPUs to more specialized accelerators like TPUs or NPUs. They're optimized to run machine learning models efficiently on edge devices, enabling quick inference with minimal power usage.

- **uCPE (Universal Customer Premises Equipment)**: This flexible, software-driven networking equipment replaces traditional hardware appliances. At the edge, uCPE helps manage connectivity, security, and virtualization, allowing enterprises to run multiple network functions on a single device while keeping data local.

Edge AI and .NET MAUI

Edge AI is all about bringing the power of AI directly into your devices—like phones, tablets, or IoT sensors—so they can process data right where it's created instead of always sending it to the cloud. In a .NET MAUI app, this means you can take a trained model (e.g., one exported from Azure Custom Vision as ONNX), embed it in your app, and run predictions locally, even without an Internet connection. Imagine using the camera in your MAUI app to check if a pen has its cap on; the app would capture an image, run it through the AI model on the device, and instantly show you the result—all fast, private, and offline. What makes this even more powerful is that .NET MAUI not only gives you access to the device's full capabilities but also provides a cross-platform API—so you can tap into camera, storage, sensors, and processing power in a unified way across iOS, Android, Windows, and macOS.

This combination makes Edge AI in .NET MAUI an awesome approach for scenarios that need quick responses, work in places without reliable connectivity, or handle sensitive data securely.

What I always loved about Xamarin and now on .NET MAUI is that we can also "control" the actual physical devices. Coming from web development, this feature felt like a miracle to me. To run AI locally on a device such as a phone, or tablet, several pieces need to come together.

First, you need a pretrained AI model, often exported in formats like TensorFlow Lite or ONNX, which can be deployed across platforms. Since edge devices typically have limited resources compared to cloud servers, these models are often optimized to be smaller and more efficient, for example, by using quantization techniques.

To speed up inference, devices take advantage of different types of hardware acceleration:

- **CPU (Central Processing Unit)**: The general-purpose processor found in every device. CPUs are flexible and can handle AI tasks, though they are not always the most efficient for heavy neural network computations.

- **GPU (Graphics Processing Unit)**: Originally designed for rendering graphics, GPUs excel at parallel processing, making them ideal for tasks like image recognition and deep learning. Many mobile devices now include **mobile GPUs** optimized for performance with lower power consumption.

- **NPU (Neural Processing Unit)**: A specialized chip designed specifically for running neural networks and AI workloads. NPUs deliver high performance for tasks such as natural language processing or computer vision, while using much less energy than CPUs or GPUs. Modern smartphones (like some Android and iOS devices) often include NPUs for on-device AI.

- **TPU (Tensor Processing Unit)**: A custom accelerator created by Google to efficiently handle tensor operations, which are at the heart of deep learning models. The **Google Coral TPU** is a version designed for edge applications, available as USB devices, PCIe cards, or integrated modules that allow developers to run advanced AI models locally at high speed with very low power usage.

To tie all this together, runtime libraries provide the software layer needed to execute these models efficiently. Common options include **ONNX Runtime Mobile** (ideal for .NET applications), **TensorFlow Lite** (popular in Android and iOS ecosystems), and **ML. NET** (well-suited for Windows and Linux edge devices). This combination of optimized models, specialized hardware, and lightweight runtimes makes it possible to bring advanced AI experiences directly onto edge devices.

The flow of Edge AI in a .NET MAUI app starts with training your AI model, which can be done using Python frameworks or Azure AI/ML services. Once the model is trained, it is exported in a format suitable for edge deployment, such as ONNX or TensorFlow Lite. This model is then embedded directly into your MAUI application, allowing it to run inference locally on the device—for example, performing image recognition, natural language processing, or anomaly detection—without relying on a cloud connection. Finally, the app processes the results and displays them through the MAUI user interface, giving users fast, responsive, and private AI-powered functionality across all supported platforms.

Create Your AI Model

To implement Edge AI in a .NET MAUI app, we will need a model, more specifically a trained model. For this example, I will be using ONNX models and Azure Custom Vision. We have seen in previous chapter the power of Azure and that it enables us to create our custom models.

To start, we will go to `https://www.customvision.ai/`, log in with your Azure account, and create a new project by clicking "New Project" as in Figure 12-1.

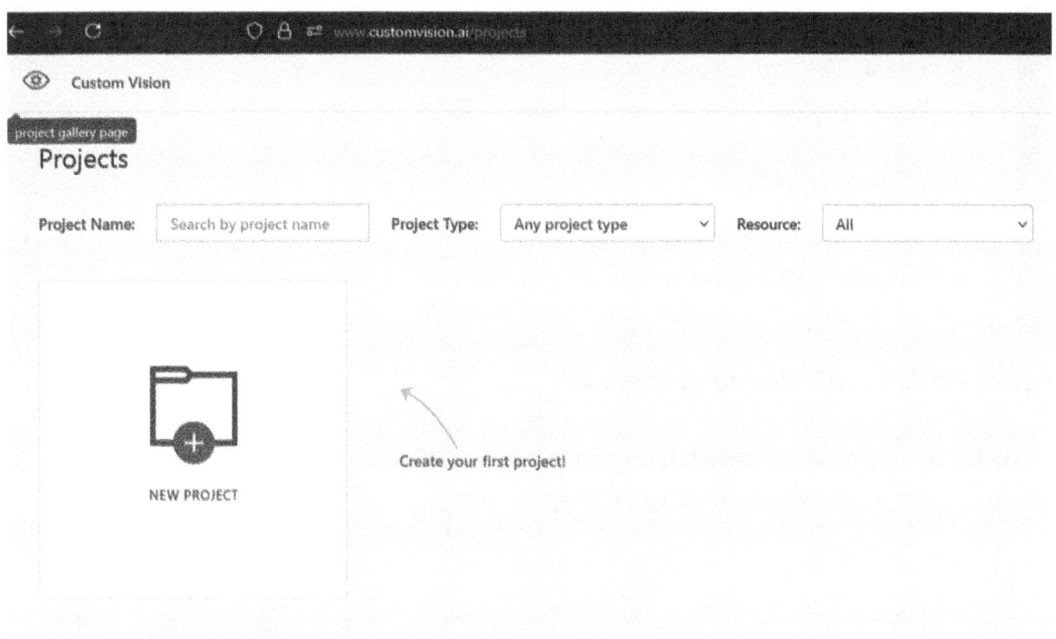

Figure 12-1. *Create new project in Custom Vision*

Then, inside the new window that opned, as shown in Figure 12-2, we will give our project a name and a description. We can use an existing Azure resource or create a new one. We will choose Classification in the Project Types and then choose Classification Types Multiclass; in this way, each image has one label.

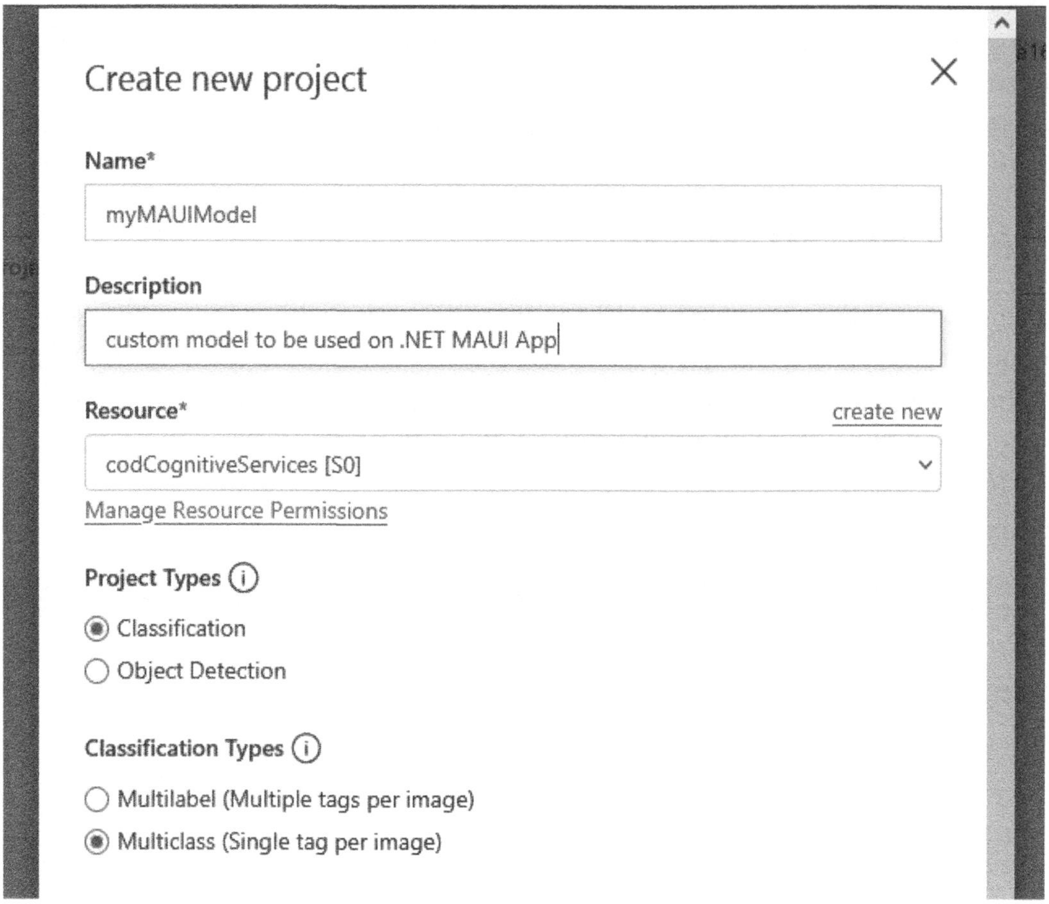

Figure 12-2. *Create new project model*

As for the domain, as shown in Figure 12-3, we will need a compact one as we will have to export it, and then click Create project.

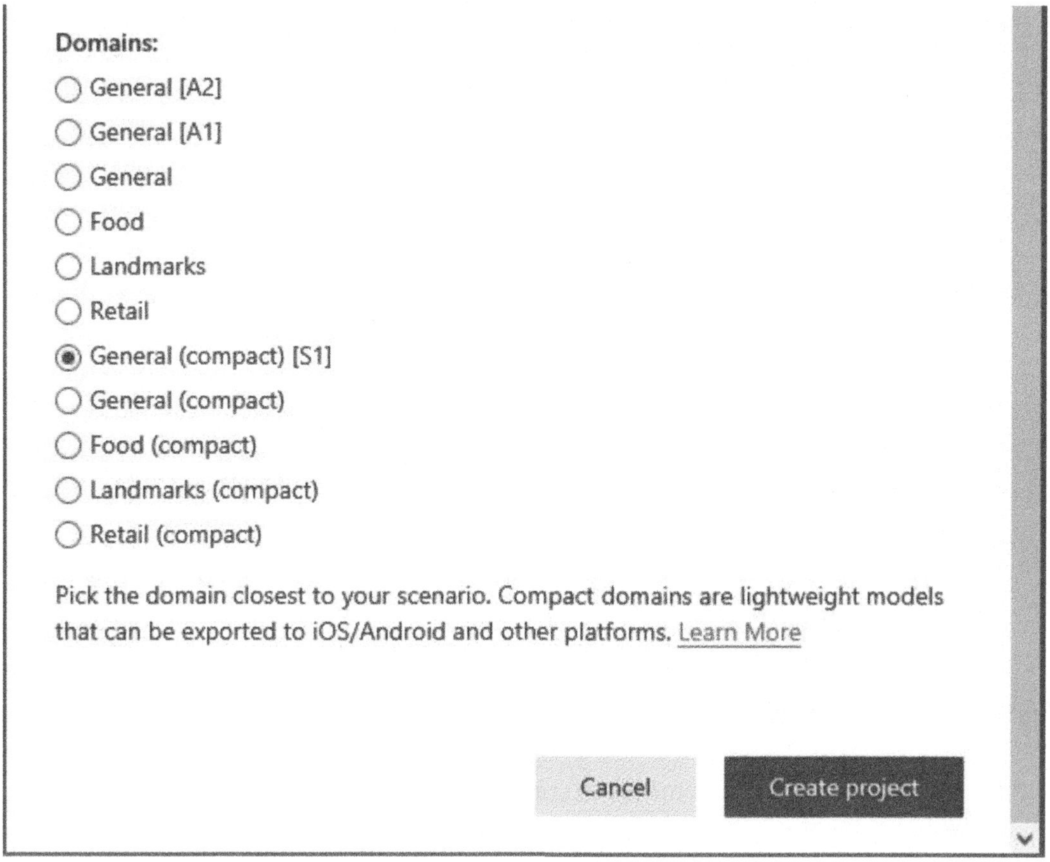

Domains:

○ General [A2]

○ General [A1]

○ General

○ Food

○ Landmarks

○ Retail

● General (compact) [S1]

○ General (compact)

○ Food (compact)

○ Landmarks (compact)

○ Retail (compact)

Pick the domain closest to your scenario. Compact domains are lightweight models that can be exported to iOS/Android and other platforms. Learn More

Cancel   Create project

Figure 12-3. *Domain selection*

Once our project has been created, we will be redirected to the project space as shown in Figure 12-4.

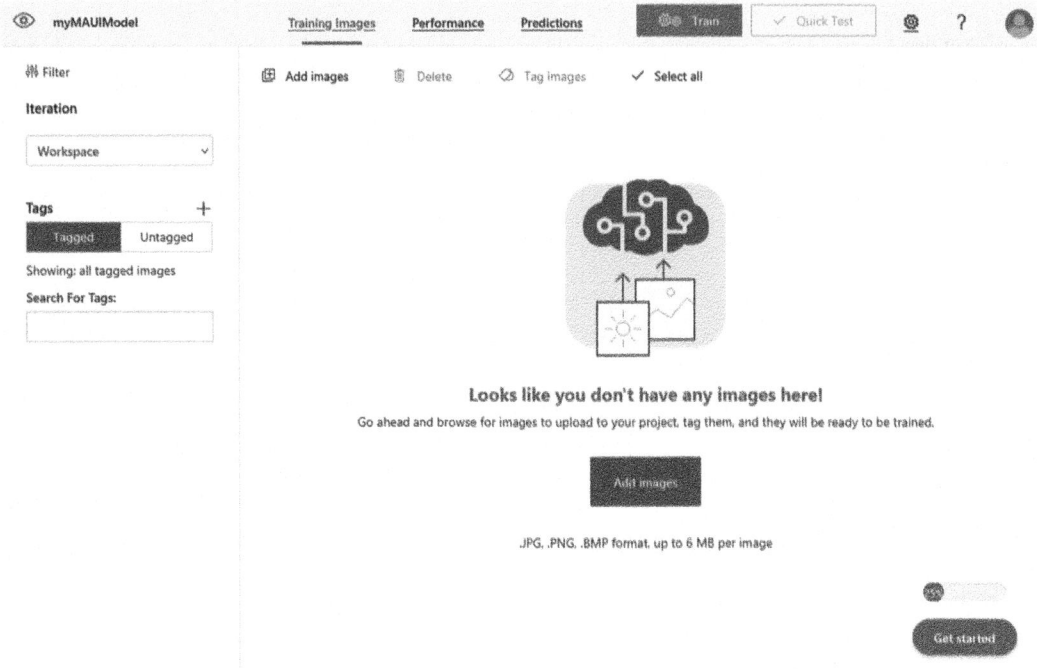

Figure 12-4. *New project space*

I was thinking about which model to create, using image classification. You might already get a feeling that I am not the most creative person, but something that you don't know is that this book has been ideated and created on paper, and my desk always has pens on it. Lots of pens: a black one that never has its cap on, but the blue one is a fountain pen, and it needs its cap on. The red one is a little random and then some highlighters that should have the cap on.

So, I thought about a model that identifies if the pen has the cap or not. We will take a picture of a pen and run the model that identifies if the pan has the cap on or not. I bet you can create a similar model with whatever classification you might need. To train the model, we will need images. We can gather images of pens with and without caps. We will upload our images by clicking Add images as shown in Figure 12-5.

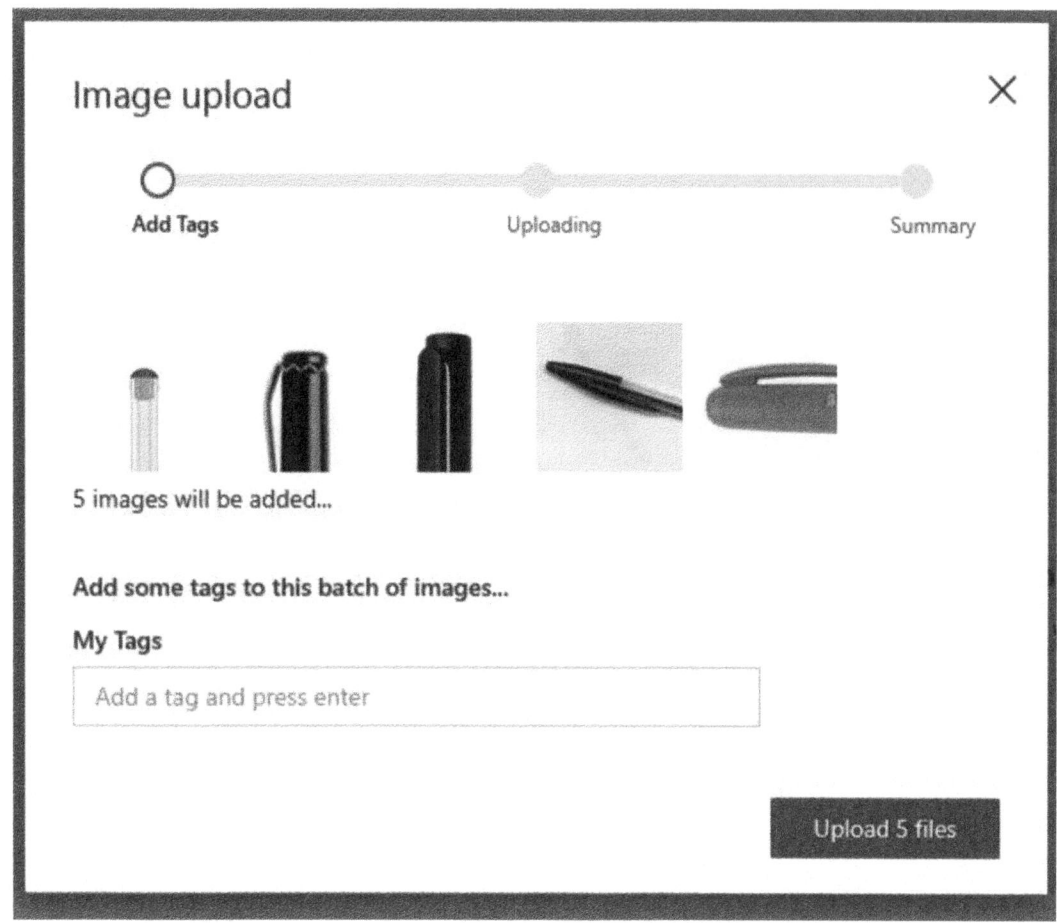

Figure 12-5. *Upload images of model*

Same for pens without cap as shown in Figure 12-6.

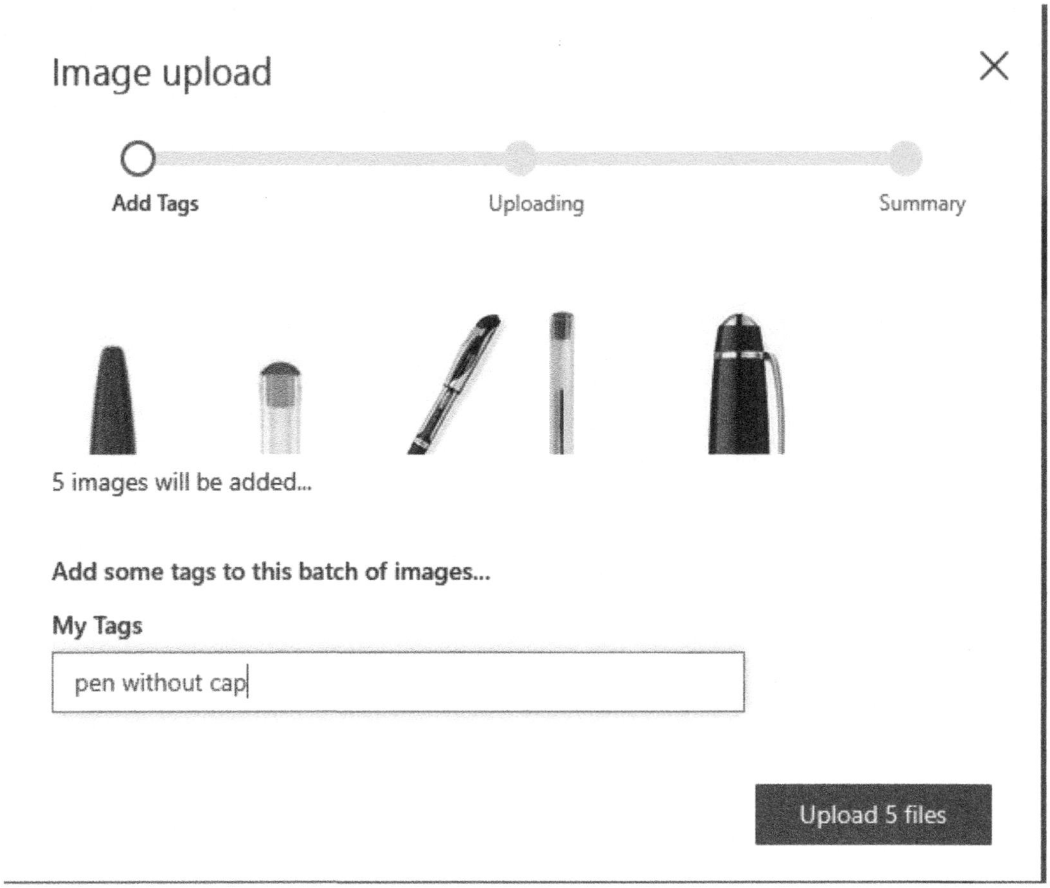

Image upload
Add Tags
Uploading
Summary
5 images will be added...
Add some tags to this batch of images...
My Tags
pen without cap
Upload 5 files

***Figure 12-6.** Upload image model with tags*

After we have uploaded our images and tagged them all, we will click Train from the top bar as shown in Figure 12-7.

myMAUIModel
Training Images
Performance
Predictions
Train
Quick Test
?

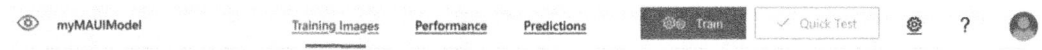

***Figure 12-7.** Train button*

We will then choose the training type on the modal dialog window that will open—Quick training can work for us. Then click Train as shown in Figure 12-8. We will need to use at least 50 images to have an accurate model.

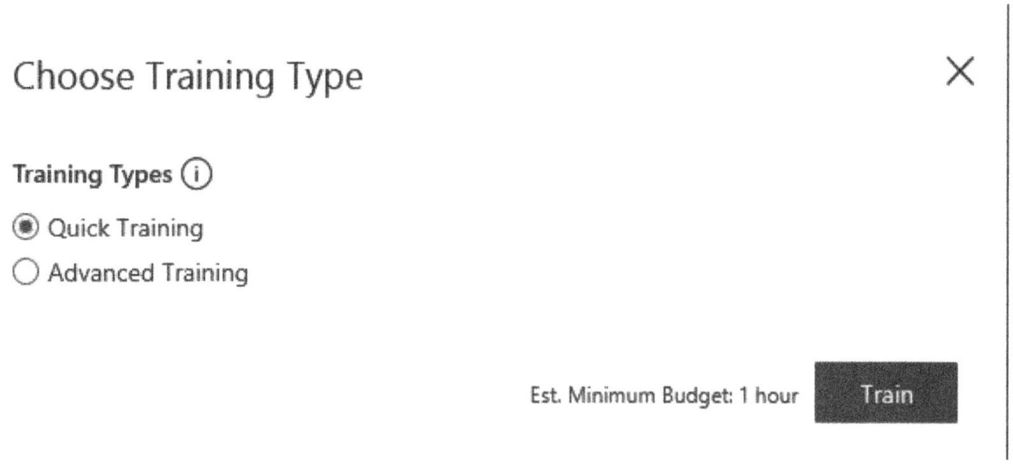

Choose Training Type   ✕

Training Types ⓘ

⦿ Quick Training

◯ Advanced Training

Est. Minimum Budget: 1 hour   Train

Figure 12-8. *Train model*

Now let's give our model some time for the training, and we can focus on our .NET MAUI application. You can see in Figure 12-9 that your model is undergoing different iterations.

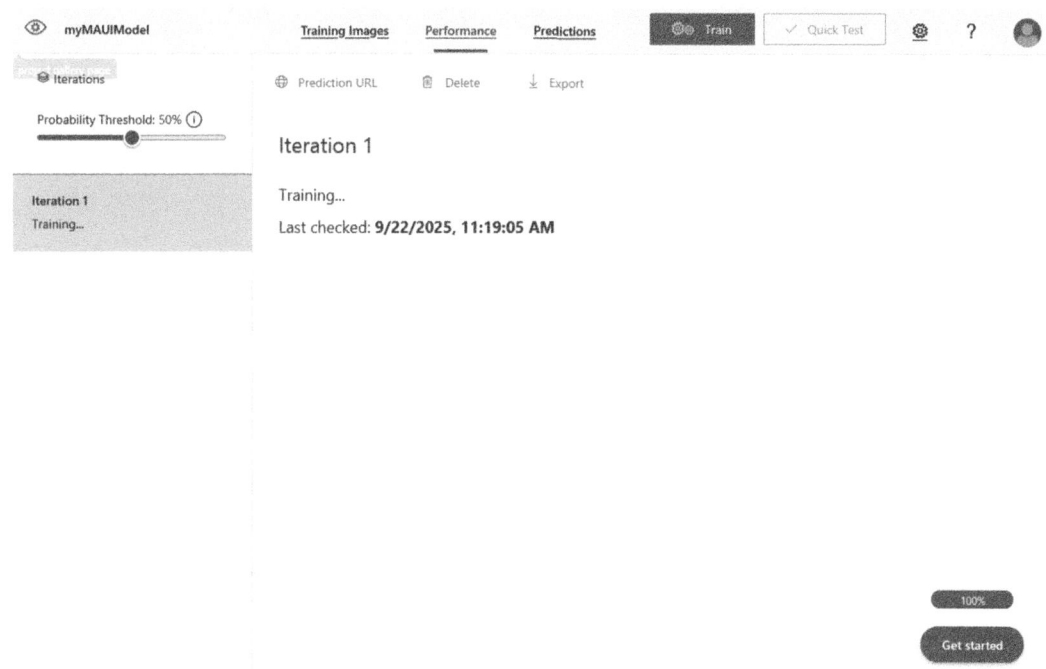

Figure 12-9. *Model iterations training*

If you are already familiar with custom models and Python language, you can use other tools to train your model like PyTorch or TensorFlow.

We can test our model by clicking *Quick Test* on the top bar. We can use an image URL or browse a local file, and once the image has been uploaded, we can see in the prediction part the tag with the probability as in Figure 12-10. It is important to use lots of images for training; I recommend more than 50, so the model can be really accurate.

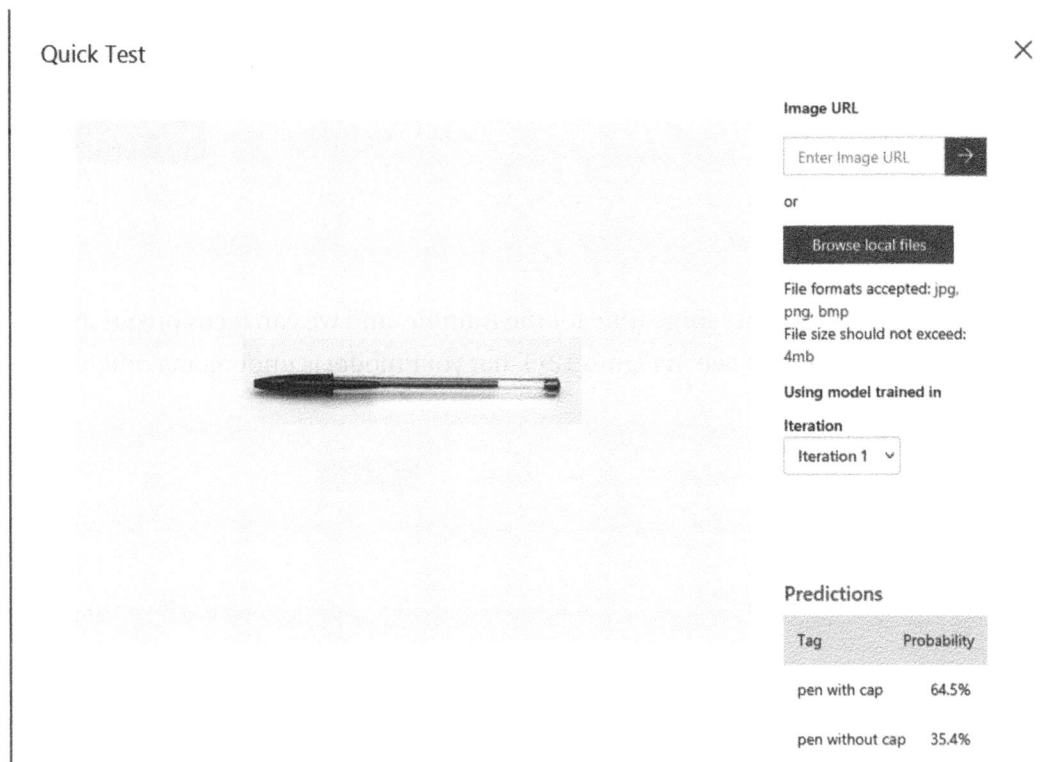

Figure 12-10. Quick test model window

Once our model is trained, we can export it to ONNX. ONNX works great with .NET so we can embed it in our .NET MAUI application. We will copy the file inside the app's resources folder and run the model inference locally using ONNX Runtime mobile.

We will click Export and in the new window, shown in Figure 12-11, choose ONNX.

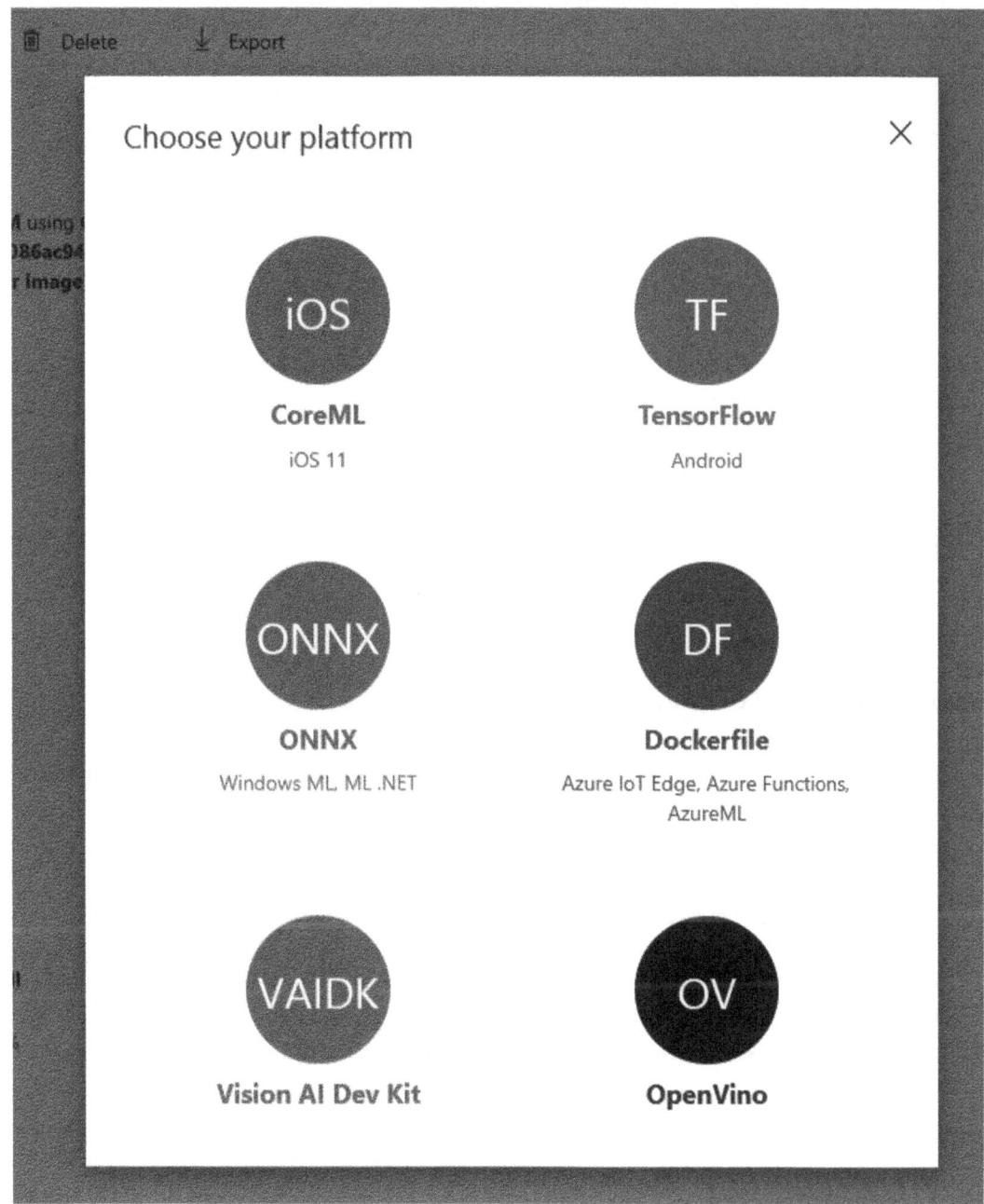

Figure 12-11. *Export model*

And once again ONNX in the dialog box as in Figure 12-12.

Figure 12-12. *ONNX export model*

So, let's create a new .NET MAUI empty project. To use ONNX, we will need to add two NuGet packages to our .NET MAUI project.

- Microsoft.ML.OnnxRuntime

- Microsoft.ML.OnnxRuntime.MLModel

We will also need SkiaSharp to work with our image.

Once we have exported and downloaded our model, we will need to unzip the folder. Inside the solution, upload the .onnx file from the unzipped folder inside Resources/Raw. Set the file as an `Maui asset` by right-clicking on the file, set `Build action` property, and make sure you select `Maui asset` as Build Action. Also check that `Copy to Output Directory` is set to `Copy if newer`.

In the unzipped folder, we have also a file `metadata_properties.json` that we can open to check all the properties. The content of the file is shown in Listing 12-1.

Listing 12-1. `metadata_properties.json` content

```
{
    "CustomVision.Metadata.AdditionalModelInfo": "",
    "CustomVision.Metadata.Version": "1.2",
    "CustomVision.Postprocess.Method": "ClassificationMultiClass",
    "CustomVision.Postprocess.Yolo.Biases": "[]",
    "CustomVision.Postprocess.Yolo.NmsThreshold": "0.0",
    "CustomVision.Preprocess.CropHeight": "0",
    "CustomVision.Preprocess.CropMethod": "FullImageShorterSide",
    "CustomVision.Preprocess.CropWidth": "0",
    "CustomVision.Preprocess.MaxDimension": "0",
    "CustomVision.Preprocess.MaxScale": "0.0",
    "CustomVision.Preprocess.MinDimension": "0",
    "CustomVision.Preprocess.MinScale": "0.0",
    "CustomVision.Preprocess.NormalizeMean": "[0.0, 0.0, 0.0]",
    "CustomVision.Preprocess.NormalizeStd": "[1.0, 1.0, 1.0]",
    "CustomVision.Preprocess.ResizeMethod": "Stretch",
    "CustomVision.Preprocess.TargetHeight": "300",
    "CustomVision.Preprocess.TargetWidth": "300",
    "Image.BitmapPixelFormat": "Rgb8",
    "Image.ColorSpaceGamma": "SRGB",
    "Image.NominalPixelRange": "Normalized_0_1"
}
```

Our UI will be simple. We will take a picture from the app, so we will need a button with *Take photo* test, an image to display the image, and a label where we will see our result, after the model has used the taken image and identified if the pen inside the image has the cap on or not. To start, we will modify `MainPage.xaml` with the following xaml code that can be found in Listing 12-2.

Listing 12-2. MainPage.xaml code

```
<ContentPage xmlns="http://schemas.microsoft.com/dotnet/2021/maui"
             xmlns:x="http://schemas.microsoft.com/winfx/2009/xaml"
             x:Class="Chapter12.MainPage">

    <ScrollView>
        <VerticalStackLayout
            Padding="30,0"
            Spacing="25">
            <Label x:Name="WelcomeLabel" FontSize="18" TextColor="Purple"
            Text="Let's try our offline AI Model"></Label>
            <Button Text="Take Photo" Clicked="Button_Clicked"/>
            <Image x:Name="CapturedImage" HeightRequest="300"/>
            <Label x:Name="ResultLabel" FontSize="18" Text="Your
            catalogation result will appear here"/>
        </VerticalStackLayout>
    </ScrollView>
</ContentPage>
```

In the code behind, all the magic will happen. Before we see the code, I can anticipate that we will be using a tensor. A tensor can be seen as a multidimensional array where we can store data, especially for AI models and machine learning. AI models, like the one we have created so far, don't actually work with images, text, they work with numbers. Tensors will have input data (you can see them like the pixels of the images), model parameters, and output predictions. In our model, if we have a 30×300 RGB image, that will translate to a tensor that will have the shape (1, 3, 300, 300), where 1 indicates it is one image, 3 indicates how many color channels we use (RGB—Red, Green, Blue), 300 indicates the height, and the last 300 indicates the width of the image. So, the magic happens on tensors, same as for machine learning or deep learning.

We can check width and height in the `metadata_properties.json` file. You can see the width and height metadata in Listing 12-3.

Listing 12-3. Metadata_properties.json detail information

```
"CustomVision.Preprocess.TargetHeight": "300",
"CustomVision.Preprocess.TargetWidth": "300",
```

To process our captured image, we will need to process the stream, and we will be using SkiaSharp. Just add the method from Listing 12-4 into your MainPage.xaml.cs.

Listing 12-4. PreprocessImage method

```
private async Task<Tensor<float>> PreprocessImage(Stream stream)
{
    // Resize image to 300x300 and normalize to 0-1 range
    using var bitmap = new SkiaSharp.SKBitmap(300, 300);
    using var original = SkiaSharp.SKBitmap.Decode(stream);

    using var canvas = new SkiaSharp.SKCanvas(bitmap);
    canvas.DrawBitmap(original, new SkiaSharp.SKRect(0, 0, 300, 300));

    // Convert to float tensor (1, 3, 300, 300)
    var tensor = new DenseTensor<float>(new[] { 1, 3, 300, 300 });
    for (int y = 0; y < 300; y++)
    {
        for (int x = 0; x < 300; x++)
        {
            var color = bitmap.GetPixel(x, y);
            tensor[0, 0, y, x] = color.Red / 255f;
            tensor[0, 1, y, x] = color.Green / 255f;
            tensor[0, 2, y, x] = color.Blue / 255f;
        }
    }
    return tensor;
}
```

The Button_Clicked method, shown in Listing 12-5, will be taking the photo and displaying it on the page. After that, we will be preprocessing the image as we have seen in the code above, so we are ready to run the inference. Running the inference means that the AI model will be ready to make a prediction based on the input data. Essentially, inference is the model applying what it learned during training to new data. Unlike training, inference doesn't change the model's weight; it simply evaluates the input and produces a prediction. Running inference locally on the device, as in the app, makes the process fast, private, and offline, allowing the AI to deliver immediate results without relying on the cloud as inference happens on the device. In previous online examples, we don't really see the inference and processing steps as all happens in the cloud, we only get the final output.

Listing 12-5. Button_Clicked method to run the model

```
private async void Button_Clicked(object sender, EventArgs e)
{
    try
    {
        var photo = await MediaPicker.Default.CapturePhotoAsync();
        if (photo == null) return;

        // Display the captured image on the page
        var stream = await photo.OpenReadAsync();

        using var originalStream = await photo.OpenReadAsync();
        var memoryStream = new MemoryStream();
        await originalStream.CopyToAsync(memoryStream);
        memoryStream.Position = 0; // Reset position before using

        CapturedImage.Source = ImageSource.FromStream(() =>
        {
            memoryStream.Position = 0; // Reset again for ImageSource
            return memoryStream;
        });

        // Preprocess image for ONNX model
        stream.Position = 0;
        var tensor = await PreprocessImage(stream);

        // Run inference
        var inputs = new List<NamedOnnxValue>
    {
        NamedOnnxValue.CreateFromTensor("data", tensor)
    };

        // Run the model on the device
        using var results = _session.Run(inputs);
```

```csharp
        //Gets the model prediction information converted to a float array
        var output = results.First().AsEnumerable<float>().ToArray();

        // Interpret result based on the value
        ResultLabel.Text = output[0] > 0.5 ? "Pen has the cap on" : "Pen
        does NOT have the cap on";
    }
    catch (Exception ex)
    {
        await DisplayAlert("Error", ex.Message, "OK");
    }
}
```

As we will need to use the ONNX model and create a InferenceSession, we will need to create one in our MainPage() and load the model. You can find the final Main Page.xaml.cs in Listing 12-6. You can learn more about this class at https://onnxruntime.ai/docs/api/csharp/api/Microsoft.ML.OnnxRuntime. InferenceSession.html.

Listing 12-6. LoadModelFromResources method and create InferenceSession

```csharp
using Microsoft.Maui.Media;
using Microsoft.ML.OnnxRuntime;
using Microsoft.ML.OnnxRuntime.Tensors;
using System.IO;
using System.Reflection;

namespace Chapter12
{
    public partial class MainPage : ContentPage
    {

        private InferenceSession _session;
public MainPage()
{
    InitializeComponent();
    LoadModelFromResources();
}
```

```
private async void LoadModelFromResources()
{
    // Open the ONNX file from Resources/Raw
    using var stream = await FileSystem.
    OpenAppPackageFileAsync("model.onnx");

    // Copy to cache directory to get a real path
    var tempPath = Path.Combine(FileSystem.CacheDirectory,
    "model.onnx");
    using var fileStream = File.Create(tempPath);
    await stream.CopyToAsync(fileStream);

    // Load ONNX runtime session
    _session = new InferenceSession(tempPath);
}
}
```

As we are using the camera to take the photo, we will need to give the app the right permission in the AndroidManifest.xml or equivalent in the iOS Info.plist file. We will also need permission to WRITE_EXTERNAL_STORAGE in the manifest.

Now, we can build, deploy, and test our application. Just take a pen without a cap, take a picture, and wait for the AI model answer. Remember, the output depends on your model, how many images it had to train, and how accurate it is. You can see the result I had in Figure 12-13.

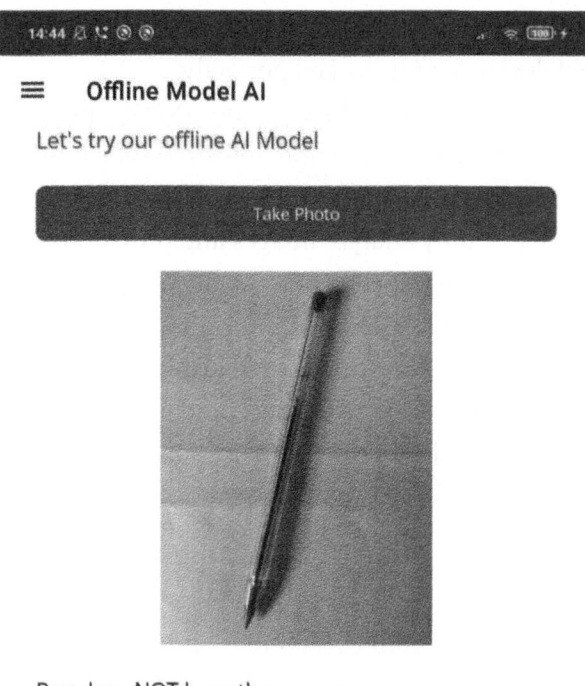

Figure 12-13. Test your offline model output screen

You can also leverage hardware acceleration and ensure that your AI runs efficiently and uses the device's power optimally as we have full control over the device capabilities.

With .NET MAUI, our Edge AI models will work the same on all platforms. I have tested on a pretty old android device, and it worked perfectly.

After implementing all these steps—loading the ONNX model from resources, capturing our images, preprocessing them into tensors, and running inference locally on the device—we have successfully built a fully functional Edge AI application using .NET MAUI. The app can instantly analyze images and provide predictions without relying on the cloud, ensuring fast, secure, and private AI processing. By combining MAUI's cross-platform capabilities with ONNX Runtime, we can deliver seamless user experience across mobile and desktop devices while taking full advantage of the device's hardware. This approach demonstrates the power and flexibility of Edge AI in real-world applications, making AI accessible, efficient, and responsive directly on user devices.

Summary

In this chapter, we have looked at offline AI models and created our first model that uses image classification to determine if a pen has its cap on or not. We then added the model to a .NET MAUI app. From the app, we can take a picture of a pen, run the model offline, and display the result.

In the next chapter, we will see how ethics are applied to AI and how it influences the way we create our AI and our AI-enabled applications moving forward.

CHAPTER 13

Ethical Considerations with AI and AI Applications

Introduction

We have seen in the previous chapters how to technically work with different AI services. In this chapter, we will go through some major ethical considerations related to AI and AI applications.

Ethics

Ethics is the study of what is right and what is wrong and how we, people, should behave. It is a branch of philosophy and helps us decide how to act in different situations and how to treat others. Ethics might differ from laws, morals, or values. Personal beliefs might differ, or our values might guide us in an ethical way; applying ethics when we design, build, and use AI means that we must think carefully about what is right or what is wrong and not be blinded by personal morals or values.

Ethical thinking can help us prevent discrimination or bias like an AI system that might help people with resume scanning that filters out minorities, misinformation like crafting fake news, or information through a chat bot privacy invasion like collecting data without users' permission—we'll see more about privacy in Chapter 14.

© Codrina Merigo 2026
C. Merigo, *AI-Enabled Apps with .NET MAUI*, https://doi.org/10.1007/979-8-8688-1817-2_13

We should also verify that the AI service we are using is treating people equally without favoritism. As AI has grown exponentially over the years, lots of entities and big tech companies around the world have taken some time to think about how to apply ethics to AI.

Ethics and AI

AI might seem like a new field, so you might think that ethics applied to AI is new too. Experimenting and algorithm design related to AI have always been an interesting topic for the academic community. Ethics in research has been always a priority. The Belmont report was released back in April 1979 by the National Commission for the Protection of Human Subjects of Biomedical and Behavioral Research. It outlines ethical principles and guidelines for conducting research involving human subjects. It contains three main principles:

1. **Respect for Persons**: This principle emphasizes treating individuals as autonomous agents capable of making their own decisions, while also protecting those with diminished autonomy. It requires obtaining informed consent by providing clear, understandable information about the research, ensuring voluntary participation, and respecting privacy and confidentiality.

2. **Beneficence**: Researchers must maximize possible benefits and minimize potential harms to participants. This involves carefully assessing risks and benefits to protect subjects from harm while promoting their well-being.

3. **Justice**: This principle ensures the fair distribution of the benefits and burdens of research, meaning that no group of people should bear undue risks or be unfairly excluded from potential benefits. Subject selection must be equitable and just.

You can find the full report at `https://www.hhs.gov/ohrp/sites/default/files/the-belmont-report-508c_FINAL.pdf`.

Together, these principles guide ethical conduct in research involving human subjects by safeguarding their rights and welfare. These principles can be easily adapted to guide responsible AI development. The report's three core principles—respect for persons, beneficence, and justice—map well to contemporary AI ethics concerns.

- Respect for persons means respecting user autonomy and ensuring transparency about how AI systems collect and use personal data. It also involves protecting users with diminished autonomy and preserving privacy.

- Beneficence requires that AI systems maximize benefits and minimize harms, promoting safety and well-being while preventing harm arising from biased or unsafe AI outputs.

- Justice calls for equitable access to AI technologies and fairness in how AI systems impact different groups, avoiding discrimination and exacerbation of societal inequalities.

Researchers at institutions like NIST suggest applying Belmont principles to AI to ensure ethical stewardship in how humans train AI systems and handle data, fostering transparency, fairness, and responsibility in AI applications. IBM used the Belmont Report to frame their AI ethics approach.

UNESCO Ethical Compass

In November 2021, all the 193 UNESCO Member States adopted the UNESCO recommendation on ethics and artificial intelligence.

UNESCO is the acronym for United Nations Educational, Scientific and Cultural Organization founded in 1945.

UNESCO has created the first value-based framework to ensure AI respects human rights, fairness, dignity, and inclusion and promotes sustainability. UNESCO's Recommendation on the Ethics of Artificial Intelligence sets global standards to uphold human dignity, privacy, fairness, and accountability, echoing Belmont's core values. It is composed of four foundational values and ten ethical principles:

The four values are straightforward:

Human rights and human dignity

Living in peaceful, just, and interconnected societies

Ensuring diversity and inclusiveness

Environment and ecosystem flourishing

And the ten principles accentuate the values:

1. Proportionality and Do No Harm

The use of AI systems must not go beyond what is necessary to achieve a legitimate aim. Risk assessment should be used to prevent harms which may result from such uses.

2. Safety and Security

Unwanted harms (safety risks) as well as vulnerabilities to attack (security risks) should be avoided and addressed by AI actors.

3. Right to Privacy and Data Protection

Privacy must be protected and promoted throughout the AI lifecycle. Adequate data protection frameworks should also be established.

4. Multi-stakeholder and Adaptive Governance & Collaboration

International law & national sovereignty must be respected in the use of data. Additionally, participation of diverse stakeholders is necessary for inclusive approaches to AI governance.

5. Responsibility and Accountability

AI systems should be auditable and traceable. There should be oversight, impact assessment, audit and due diligence mechanisms in place to avoid conflicts with human rights norms and threats to environmental wellbeing.

6. Transparency and Explainability

The ethical deployment of AI systems depends on their transparency & explainability (T&E). The level of T&E should be appropriate to the context, as there may be tensions between T&E and other principles such as privacy, safety and security.

7. Human Oversight and Determination

Member States should ensure that AI systems do not displace ultimate human responsibility and accountability.

8. Sustainability

AI technologies should be assessed against their impacts on 'sustainability', understood as a set of constantly evolving goals including those set out in the UN's Sustainable Development Goals.

9. Awareness & Literacy

Public understanding of AI and data should be promoted through open & accessible education, civic engagement, digital skills & AI ethics training, media & information literacy.

10. Fairness and Non-Discrimination

AI actors should promote social justice, fairness, and non-discrimination while taking an inclusive approach to ensure AI's benefits are accessible to all.

UNESCO also provided two implementation roads Readiness Assessment Methodology (RAM) and Ethical Impact Assessment (EIA) that helps turn the principles into actual policies and support on creating the policies. The recommendation does just this by setting out **11 key areas for policy actions**. You can find more on the key areas at `https://unesdoc.unesco.org/ark:/48223/pf0000385082.page=12`.

UNESCO's recommendations are considered as a soft law that is intended to inform and inspire national legislation worldwide, not all the countries around the world have strong legislation.

AI Regulations Around the World

In 2024, the European Union implemented the world's first comprehensive regulations on AI known as the AI Act. It has a risk-based structure, it even bans some AI while tightly regulating other systems, and it's inspiring and influencing many emerging and developing countries. It requires a high level of transparency, human oversight, data quality standards and CE marking. The letters "*CE*" appear on many products traded on the extended Single Market in the European Economic Area (EEA). They signify that products sold in the EEA have been assessed to meet high safety, health, and environmental protection requirements. As I currently work in a medical company, you can imagine that working with AI in this field is highly regulated, especially in the European Union, and software that uses AI for medical purposes must have the CE mark and medical device mark.

Some countries like South Korea have the so-called AI basic act very similar to the in European Union Act. Canada has also a very similar act. While some other countries like Japan or Singapore adopt a soft law and deferred voluntary AI governance, China has a strict top-down control on AI with strong regulation on generative AI or content watermarking.

Other states like the United States don't have yet federal laws, but some executive orders must be applied or some acts like the Algorithmic Accountability Act. There are also many state-level laws related to bias or facial recognition that can be applied. The focus on these laws is on innovation and self-regulation.

As of now, more laws are still forming. Based on where your application will be available, I suggest you look for local and regional AI laws.

Big Tech Companies and Responsible AI

Maybe you might have noticed when working with the AI APIs that in the documentation, there is usually a mention on ethics related to AI. Big tech companies like Microsoft, Google, or OpenAI have their own frameworks and principles when describing their AI. Microsoft has partnered with UNESCO to advance responsible AI together with seven other global companies.

Microsoft's six core principles are straightforward and are applied to all their Azure AI services that we have seen in the previous chapters. Microsoft has identified these principles that shall guide AI development and use.

Fairness

Reliability and safety

Privacy and security

Transparency

Accountability

Inclusiveness

You can find more about these principles and see them in action at `https://www.microsoft.com/ai/principles-and-approach#ai-principles`.

Google's AI core principles stick to three important concepts that guide the development and deployment of their systems.

1. Bold innovation

2. Responsible development and deployment

3. Collaborative progress, together

You can learn more on how Google apply these principles at `https://ai.google/principles/`.

As an AI-first company, OpenAI's mission is to *"ensure that artificial general intelligence—AI systems that are generally smarter than humans—benefits all of humanity."*

To apply this, they have developed the OpenAI Charter that describes everything they do in the AI field. You can read more at `https://openai.com/charter/`.

AI Pope Act

Not only have states or tech companies spent their time investing in regulating and creating policies related to AI. The Catholic Church wants to ensure that AI applications align with the religious word and values and focus on avoiding discrimination, harm, or undermining human dignity. In 2020, there was the Rome Call for AI ethics created from Pope Francis's vision of ethical AI. New implementation might come in 2025.

The latest version of the act "Antiqua et Nova: Note on the Relationship Between Artificial Intelligence and Human Intelligence" can be found at `https://press.vatican.va/content/salastampa/it/bollettino/pubblico/2025/01/28/0083/01166.html#ing`.

"Antiqua et Nova: Note on the Relationship Between Artificial Intelligence and Human Intelligence" is a doctrinal document from the Vatican, issued in January 2025 by the Dicastery for the Doctrine of the Faith and the Dicastery for Culture and Education, and approved by Pope Francis. The Vatican's 2025 note on artificial intelligence reminds us that while AI is a powerful tool, it's not the same as human intelligence. Human thought is rooted in dignity, freedom, and moral responsibility, while AI simply processes data. The document highlights the many good things AI can bring—like advances in education, healthcare, and scientific discovery—but it also warns of risks such as deepfakes, manipulation, privacy concerns, and growing inequality. Its main message is clear: AI should always serve people, never replace what makes us human. By using AI responsibly—with transparency, accountability, and care—we can make sure technology contributes to the common good and helps build a more just and humane world. This doctrinal document was mainly intended for Church leaders and people who transmit faith, but also for others: developers, users, and institutions who use AI and play a moral role.

Considerations

We might not be there yet at a global AI ethical law, but regulations are not here to scare you or to slow you down—they are here to guide us all toward building smarter and more respectable technology. Whether it's the UNESCO compass, European Union's AI regulation, or your local laws, the message is consistent—build AI with intention, fairness, and transparency. As a .NET MAUI developer, you can easily create cross-platform applications that not only look great and work on different devices but also respect the user rights and dignity. As you proceed with your amazing ideas, it is great to know the rules and design your app align with ethical AI so you can get a competitive advantage. Think of these frameworks as road maps and compasses that help you navigate the decision around user data in fairness. These frameworks remind us that we build AI apps for our users and that at the heart of every AI system it's a person that needs attention, protection, and care. So, let's build AI-enabled applications that make people empowered, that helps people and never create harm. We should always be proud of our applications, not only of the UI or the performance, but also in terms of AI principles.

Summary

In this chapter, we have seen some ethical considerations to be applied when working with AI and AI-enabled applications. From UNESCO's ethical compass to different AI regulations around the world, we have seen how ethics is at the core of what AI does. We then focused on responsible AI and how big tech companies applies it. We then review together the call from AI from the Pope's Act that enforces the use of AI all over the industries and all over the world.

In the next chapter, we will see together how to apply common security standards and recommendations. By the end of the chapter, we will have a dev-friendly checklist focused on security to be used for your AI-enabled .NET MAUI application.

CHAPTER 14

Security Standards and AI

Introduction

In this chapter, you will get an overview of how to apply common security standards and recommendations when working with AI and AI-enabled applications.

Maybe it is thanks to my university studies in IT security that always makes me think about protecting my app before I complete it. In this world of mobile applications, the features of your app might get all the spotlight, but think of the security of your app as a backstage crew that makes sure the show can actually happen.

As I love metal music, I often think of the app as the powerful guitar: you can have the most beautiful solo or the heaviest riff, but if your amplifier does not work, something will go terribly wrong. Security in your .NET MAUI app is the same. You sure have the most beautiful written code, but if you leave the backdoor open (literally, in your API calls), something might go wrong. You have to remember that your app is not just code, it is data. And when adding AI, there might be lots of data, including biometric or sensitive data. It is important to double-check everything before going live, and even if you don't have a full backstage crew, we can use some common habits that I will also summarize in a developer friendly checklist at the end of the chapter. If we go back to the music show analogy, security is part of the show, not an afterthought.

When we build a .NET MAUI mobile app that hooks into powerful AI platforms, we're not just writing code—we're carrying the weight of user trust. Every request, every token, and every response from an AI model deserves to be handled with care. In the world of mobile apps, the environment can be unpredictable—so it's always better to code like someone's trying to break in.

© Codrina Merigo 2026
C. Merigo, *AI-Enabled Apps with .NET MAUI*, https://doi.org/10.1007/979-8-8688-1817-2_14

API Calls

By now, we have worked with different API calls. It is important to remember to never use HTTP but use HTTPS. We have seen in Chapter 3 how to use the API calls in our code and the URLs always have an "https://" endpoint. Make sure they use the TLS (Transport Layer Security) version 1.2 or higher. As with .NET MAUI, we are using .NET Framework; it supports the use of the latest Transport Layer Security (TLS) protocol to secure network communications by default.

A common attack that might happen in this scenario is man in the middle (MITM) even if we are using the HTTPS-encrypted channel with TLS. In this scenario, the attacker can identify the URL of your API call and position himself in the middle of the communication and make it appear like normal communication is happening. To avoid these attacks, it is important to always verify the server certificate. To reduce MITM attacks in our .NET MAUI application, we can implement certificate pinning. Normally, your app just checks if the server has a valid SSL/TLS certificate from a trusted authority, and that's usually enough for most cases. But with certificate pinning, you take it one step further. You "pin" a specific certificate—or its public key or hash—directly inside your app. Then, every time your app talks to the API, it asks, *"Hey, does this certificate match the one I already know and trust?"* If the answer is no, the connection is blocked right away, even if the certificate itself is technically valid but has been swapped out by someone with bad intentions.

If you are working in a company, you can ask your IT department for the valid certificate's public key. If you just want to test or just understand the implementation, you can create a self-signed certificate and use its public key for your app. Just head over to `https://learn.microsoft.com/dotnet/framework/wcf/feature-details/how-to-create-temporary-certificates-for-use-during-development` and follow the steps to create the certificate.

Once you have the public key, you can implement the actual certificate pinning. We will still use the `HttpClient` class and create a new instance of the `HttpClientHandler` to validate the server's certificate at every request. To test this, let's create a simple .NET MAUI application and add the crtificate pinning logic as shown in Listing 14-1.

Listing 14-1. Certificate pinning example

```
using System.Net;
using System.Net.Security;
using System.Security.Cryptography.X509Certificates;
```

```csharp
namespace CertificatePinning
{
    public class ServiceClient
    {
        private HttpClient Client { get; set; }

        private HttpClientHandler clientHandler;

        public ServiceClient()
        {
            clientHandler = new HttpClientHandler();
            clientHandler.ServerCertificateCustomValidationCallback =
                ValidateServerCertificate;
            Client = new HttpClient(clientHandler);
        }

        public async Task MakeCallAsync(string url)
        {
            HttpResponseMessage response;
            try
            {
                response = await Client.
                    GetAsync(url);
            }
            catch (HttpRequestException ex)
            {
                if (ex.InnerException is WebException e && e.Status ==
                    WebExceptionStatus.TrustFailure)
                {
                    response = new
                        HttpResponseMessage(
                        HttpStatusCode.MethodNotAllowed);
                }
                else
                    response = new
```

```
                        HttpResponseMessage(
                        HttpStatusCode.ServiceUnavailable);
        }
        catch (Exception ex)
        {
            response = new
                HttpResponseMessage(
                HttpStatusCode.InternalServerError);
        }
    }

static async Task Main()
{
    // Create an HttpClientHandler object and set to use default
       credentials
    HttpClientHandler handler = new HttpClientHandler();

    // Set custom server validation callback
    handler.ServerCertificateCustomValidationCallback =
    ServerCertificateCustomValidation;

    // Create an HttpClient object
    HttpClient client = new HttpClient(handler);

    // Call asynchronous network methods in a try/catch block to handle
       exceptions
    try
    {
        HttpResponseMessage response = await client.GetAsync(url);

        response.EnsureSuccessStatusCode();

        string responseBody = await response.Content.ReadAsStringAsync();
        Console.WriteLine($"Read {responseBody.Length} characters");
    }
    catch (HttpRequestException e)
    {
        Console.WriteLine("\nException Caught!");
```

```
        Console.WriteLine($"Message: {e.Message} ");
    }

    // Need to call dispose on the HttpClient and HttpClientHandler objects
    // when done using them, so the app doesn't leak resources
    handler.Dispose();
    client.Dispose();
}

private static bool ServerCertificateCustomValidation(HttpRequestMess
age requestMessage, X509Certificate2? certificate, X509Chain? chain,
SslPolicyErrors sslErrors)
{
    // It is possible to see the information of the certificate provided by
    the server.
    Console.WriteLine($"Requested URI: {requestMessage.RequestUri}");
    Console.WriteLine($"Effective date: {certificate?.
    GetEffectiveDateString()}");
    Console.WriteLine($"Exp date: {certificate?.
    GetExpirationDateString()}");
    Console.WriteLine($"Issuer: {certificate?.Issuer}");
    Console.WriteLine($"Subject: {certificate?.Subject}");

string certificateKey= certificate?.GetPublicKeyString().
                                ToUpper();
string publicKey="OUR PUBLIC KET";

 // verify the public key with the public key that we have
         return publicKey.ToUpper() == certificateKey;

}
}
}
```

If the public key from the server's certificate matches the one you have,
the connection is good to go. But if they don't match, validation fails, and an
HttpRequestException is thrown.

The tricky part? That same exception can pop up for lots of reasons—not just because of a certificate mismatch. The good news is that you can dig deeper by checking its `InnerException`. If it's a `WebException` with a status of `TrustFailure`, then you know for sure the issue is with the certificate validation, making it easy to handle in your implementation.

Secure Storage

In the implementation above, we have the public key as a string just for testing purposes. You can imagine that in a real-world scenario, this is not the best implementation. Secure storage is your best friend to protect information on your .NET MAUI app. As the word says, it is a secure storage for you. We have the `SecureStorage` class in `Microsoft.Maui.Storage` namespace that we can use to store in a secure way key/value pairs.

To save a value, it only needs to be done once with just a line of code–how simple it is with .NET MAUI:

```
await SecureStorage.Default.SetAsync("publicKey", "MYPUBLICKEY");
```

To read a value from the `SecureStorage`, we can call the `GetSync` method and pass the key we are looking for as shown in Listing 14-2.

Listing 14-2. Read key from SecureStorage

```
string publicKey = await SecureStorage.Default.GetAsync("publicKey ");
//check if null
if (publicKey == null)
{
    // No value is associated with the key " oauth_ publicKey "
}
```

To remove a value, we can call the `Remove` method as shown in Listing 14-3.

Listing 14-3. Remove key from SecureStorage

```
bool success = SecureStorage.Default.Remove("publicKey ");
```

We can also decide to remove all the values by using `SecureStorage.Default.RemoveAll();`.

The built-in SecureStorage class in .NET MAUI provides encrypted storage by leveraging Keystore (Android) and Keychain (iOS/Mac Catalyst).

To use this feature in your Android app, you must edit your manifest file to disable the `allowBackup` feature to be applied to your SecureStorage.

Set the `android:fullBackupContent` attribute in your *AndroidManifest.xml* as shown in Listing 14-4.

Listing 14-4. AndroidManifest.xml flag

```
<application ...
  android:fullBackupContent="@xml/ auto_backup_noSecureStorage ">
</application>
```

Create a new XML file named *auto_backup_noSecureStorage.xml* in the *Platforms/Android/Resources/xml* directory with the build action of *AndroidResource*. Set the content as shown in Listing 14-5 that includes all shared preferences except for SecureStorage.

Listing 14-5. New xml resource file

```
<?xml version="1.0" encoding="utf-8"?>
<full-backup-content>
    <include domain="sharedpref" path="."/>
    <exclude domain="sharedpref" path="${applicationId}.microsoft.maui.
    essentials.preferences.xml"/>
</full-backup-content>
```

For iOS or Mac Catalyst, create an *Entitlements.plist* file within the iOS folder and define keychain access groups to allow secure data storage as shown in Listing 14-6.

Listing 14-6. Entitlements.plist file

```
<?xml version="1.0" encoding="UTF-8"?>
<!DOCTYPE plist PUBLIC "-//Apple//DTD PLIST 1.0//EN" "http://www.apple.com/
DTDs/PropertyList-1.0.dtd">
<plist version="1.0">
<dict>
 <key>keychain-access-groups</key>
```

```
<array>
 <string>"Your App Bundle Id"</string>
 </array>
</dict>
</plist>
```

In the project properties, under iOS Bundle Signing, set the Custom Entitlements to *Entitlements.plist*, the file you just created.

You can also use secure cloud storage like Microsoft Azure Key Vault, Google Cloud Key Management, or AWS Key Management Service (KMS) to store your keys, but these services might come with additional costs.

Data Encryption

Secure Storage provides an encrypted storage mechanism, ensuring that sensitive data remains protected. It uses platform-specific encryption, and you can store confidential information like API keys.

Even with *Secure Storage*, you may need to encrypt local files, SQLite databases, or cached AI results.

To encrypt your data, you can use the latest Advanced Encryption Standard AES-256 for custom encryption. The `System.Security.Cryptography` namespace contains the Aes.cs class that we can use to encrypt our data. To learn more about encrypting data, you can go to `https://learn.microsoft.com/dotnet/standard/security/encrypting-data`.

We have seen some examples in the previous chapter, but maybe you will structure your AI assistant to use a local database by adding SQLite engine and use the database from you shared code. Consider using SQLCipher to encrypt your SQLite database. `SQLCipher` is provided by a company called `Zetetic` and you can find more on their website at `https://www.zetetic.net/sqlcipher/`. You can add the *sqllite-net-sqlcipher* NuGet package to your solution and use the community license for your app or check the other license they offer.

In .NET MAUI, the operating system handles cryptography operations so remember that not all the .NET cryptographic features can be used. If you want to learn more, check `https://learn.microsoft.com/dotnet/standard/security/cross-platform-cryptography`.

Authentication and Authorization

In a production scenario, our app will provide username and password, after registration to authenticate itself against an authority. In this way, they will be authorized to the app, based on their user rights.

If our app communicates with ASP.NET web application, we can use ASP.NET Core identity or use external authentication providers such as Microsoft or Google or use modern authentication methods like OAuth 2.0 or Auth0. We can also implement multifactor authentication (MFA) where possible or use biometric authentication.

We can also implement `IdentityServer` to authenticate a user or to give the user access to a resource and must include an access token to every API request.

Input Validation

As our assistant uses different input to use the different AI services we are integrating, to enhance the security of our app, we can also validate the input to defend malicious input and avoid attacks such as SQL injection, cross-site scripting (XSS), or command-and-control attack. Validation is also common practice if your app captures user's input.

If you are used to the Model-View-ViewModel (MVVM) pattern, you might have already used the `ValidatableObject` and the `Validate` method to verify input like email formats of password that must comply with a predefined rule. You can find more about validation at `https://learn.microsoft.com/dotnet/architecture/maui/validation`.

For a more general input validation, we can create a Sanitize class as shown in Listing 14-7 to make sure we filter the input.

Listing 14-7. Sanitize class

```
public static class MySanitize
{
    // Basic allowlist approach (whitelist allowed characters/patterns)
       using regular expression
    private static readonly Regex Allowed = new(@"^[\p{L}\
    p{N}\s\.,;:!?()'\-]{1,2000}$", RegexOptions.Compiled);
```

```
public static string Sanitize(string input)
{
    if (string.IsNullOrWhiteSpace(input)) return string.Empty;
    input = input.Trim();

    // reject if contains control sequences, system tokens, or URL-
        looking inputs
    if (input.Contains("```") || input.Contains("--") || input.
    Contains("system:") || input.Contains("http://") || input.
    Contains("https://"))
        throw new InvalidOperationException("Input not allowed.");

    if (!Allowed.IsMatch(input))
        return Regex.Replace(input, @"[^\p{L}\p{N}\s\.,;:!?()'\-]",
        string.Empty);

    return input;
    }
}
```

Check Your Logs

Checking your input is important, but you must check your logs too as you might carelessly logged as output some sensitive data, or your debugging logged strings have reached production. Remember to never log usernames, passwords, keys, or personal data. Keep your logs clean and log only nonsensitive data and metadata.

Check for Updates

As old libraries or packages can become vulnerable to attacks, it is important to always keep them up-to-date.

For your nugget packages, in your Visual Studio, open *"Manage NuGet packages,"* and click on *Updates* as shown in Figure 14-1. After that, *Select all packages,* and click on *Update that should now be enabled.*

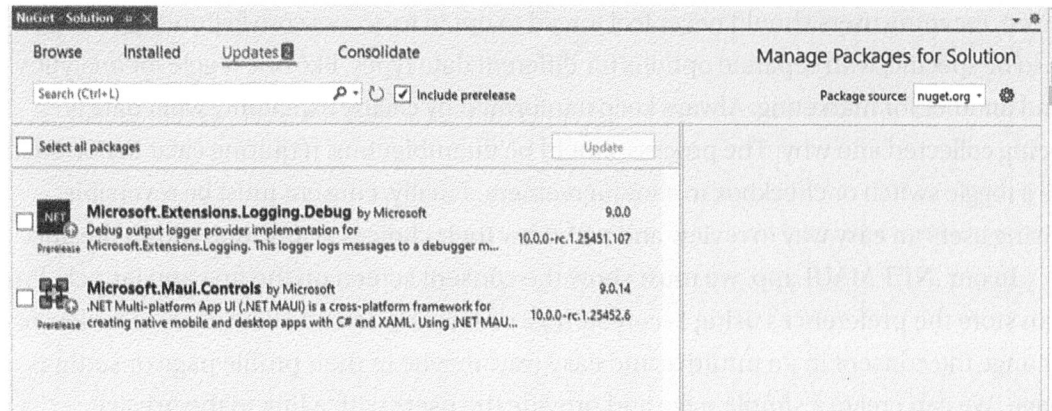

Figure 14-1. *NuGet update window*

If you are using *GitHub*, you can use Dependabot—*automated dependency updates built into GitHub.*

Privacy and Compliance

I am sure that you have heard of privacy, and I feel its definition is not so straightforward in the digital world. We can define privacy as the right to keep all personal matters private. As we use different apps, products, and services, we shall always be the ones that decide which information about us is collected, used, or saved. We have seen in the previous chapter, on ethics, that ethics differs from laws, but privacy invasion can be unethical if we, for example, collect data without user's consent.

If you live in the European Union (EU), like I do, or you work with EU countries, you might also hear about the General Data Protection Regulation (GDPR). GDPR is the strongest privacy and security law that aims to protect personal data of EU citizens and its residents, even if the company or the services used are not part of the EU area. Around the world, there are other similar laws like California Consumer Privacy Act (CCPA) in the United States, Personal Information Protection Law (PIPL) in China, or Brazil's LGDP (*Lei Geral de Proteção de Dados*). I suggest you search for any local or regional privacy laws when defining the geographical scope of your apps.

As developers, while writing our .NET MAUI app, we must make sure we comply with the regulations and laws our users live by and localize our compliance laws. If your user is in the EU, prompt them to the GDPR consent screens. When building a GDPR-compliant consent flow, it's important to follow five key principles. Consent must be freely given, meaning users should never feel forced to opt in to access core features. It should also be specific, with separate options for different data types, like one toggle for analytics and another for marketing. Always keep it informed by clearly explaining what data is being collected and why. The process should be unambiguous, requiring clear action such as a toggle switch or checkbox to show agreement. Finally, consent must be reversible, giving users an easy way to review and withdraw their choices at any time within the app.

In our .NET MAUI app, we must show the consent screen on the first app launch. We can store the preferences using *SecureStorage* or server side and allow users to review or change the consent in an intuitive and easy way, maybe in their profile page or settings page. We can create a simple page and provide the users with a link to the privacy policy document to be accepted by the user, as mandatory action. A clear privacy policy builds trust and keeps your app compliant. Start maybe from a free template, like the ones from `https://www.freeprivacypolicy.com/free-privacy-policy-generator/`, then customize it for your .NET MAUI app. Cover what data you collect, how it's used and protected, and user rights. Make it easy to find, like in your app's settings or a dedicated legal section. We can also invite the user to opt in for additional features like analytics (use anonymous data to understand behaviors) or marketing preferences (like subscribing to newsletters or marketing mails). The toggles shall be off by default.

We can have a simple *ContentPage* with its logic to save the values inside the SecureStorage as shown in Listing 14-8 and the code behind for this page is shown in Listing 14-9.

Listing 14-8. ConsentPage.xaml example

```xml
<ContentPage xmlns="http://schemas.microsoft.com/dotnet/2021/maui"
             x:Class="MyApp.Views.ConsentPage"
             Title="Privacy & Consent">
    <ScrollView Padding="20">
        <VerticalStackLayout Spacing="20">
            <Label Text="We care about your privacy "
                   FontSize="24"
                   FontAttributes="Bold"
                   HorizontalOptions="Center" />

            <Label Text="To give you the best experience, we need your
            consent for some data usage."
                   FontSize="16"
```

```
                    HorizontalOptions="Center" />
<!-- Privacy Policy acceptance -->
            <StackLayout Orientation="Horizontal" Spacing="10">
                <CheckBox x:Name="PrivacyPolicyCheckBox"
                IsChecked="False" />
                <Label VerticalOptions="Center">
                    <Label.FormattedText>
                        <FormattedString>
                            <Span Text="I have read and accept the " />
                            <Span Text="Privacy Policy"
                                TextColor="Blue"
                                TextDecorations="Underline">
                                <Span.GestureRecognizers>
                                    <TapGestureRecognizer Command="{Binding
                                    OpenPrivacyPolicyCommand}" />
                                </Span.GestureRecognizers>
                            </Span>
                        </FormattedString>
                    </Label.FormattedText>
                </Label>
            </StackLayout>
<!-- Analytics toggle -->
            <StackLayout Orientation="Horizontal" Spacing="10">
                <Switch x:Name="AnalyticsSwitch" IsToggled="False" />
                <Label Text="Allow anonymous analytics"
                VerticalOptions="Center" />
            </StackLayout>

            <!-- Marketing toggle -->
            <StackLayout Orientation="Horizontal" Spacing="10">
                <Switch x:Name="MarketingSwitch" IsToggled="False" />
                <Label Text="Receive personalized offers"
                VerticalOptions="Center" />
            </StackLayout>
```

```
            <Button Text="Save Preferences"
                    TextColor="White"
                    Clicked="OnSaveConsentClicked"
                    CornerRadius="10"
                    Padding="10,5" />
        </VerticalStackLayout>
    </ScrollView>
</ContentPage>
```

Listing 14-9. ConsentPage.xaml.cs example

```
public partial class ConsentPage : ContentPage
{
    public ConsentPage()
    {
        InitializeComponent();
        BindingContext = this;
    }

    public Command OpenPrivacyPolicyCommand => new Command(async () =>
    {
        var url = "https:my-privacy-policy";
        await Launcher.Default.OpenAsync(new Uri(url));
    });

    private async void OnSaveConsentClicked(object sender, EventArgs e)
    {
        if (!PrivacyPolicyCheckBox.IsChecked)
        {
            await DisplayAlert("Consent Required", "Please accept the
            Privacy Policy before saving.", "OK");
            return;
        }

        // Save preferences
        bool analytics = AnalyticsSwitch.IsToggled;
        bool marketing = MarketingSwitch.IsToggled;
```

```
    // TODO: Save consent state to secure storage or your backend
    await DisplayAlert("Saved", "Your preferences have been saved
    successfully.", "OK");
    }
}
```

Once we have the values from the user, we can check if we can track analytics or send the marketing info to them by checking the flags inside *SecureStorage*.

We can then check the consent values in `App.xaml.cs` or your main page's `OnAppearing` as shown in Listing 14-10.

Listing 14-10. App.xaml.cs integration with ConsentPage.xaml

```
protected override async void OnAppearing()
{
    base.OnAppearing();
    bool analyticsConsent = (await SecureStorage.GetAsync("consent_
    analytics")) == "True";

    if (analyticsConsent)
    {
        // Initialize analytics SDK an start tracking
    }
    else
    {
        Console.WriteLine("Analytics disabled by user.");
    }
}
```

While privacy policy acceptance is mandatory to use the app, other preferences might change, so make sure you check the flag before performing any related action.

Obfuscation

As developers, we usually think of compiling our code, but the final *dlls* can also be decompiled. An obfuscator can be used to prevent these actions. An obfuscator is a program that takes your code and performs some transformations to make it unreadable from a human or a computer. I know you worked your best to create the perfect variable names and class names, not like me, but sometimes obfuscators can be requested by companies to prevent intruders getting access to some proprietary logic and protect their intellectual property. There are different .NET obfuscators you can use in your .NET MAUI application to really slow down reverse engineering.

Dev-Friendly App Security Checklist

I know all this might be too much, so I want to give you a simple security checklist to apply to your great app once you start coding it. In this way, you can start integrating security from the beginning and save time during coding.

N	Task	Development	Integration	Validation	Production
1	Check your API calls and ensure the use of HTTPS				
2	Use Secure Storage to store your keys				
3	Encrypt your data				
4	Use authentication and authorization				
5	Validate your input				
6	Check your logs				
7	Check for updates				
8	Check for privacy and compliance standards				
9	(Optional) Use an obfuscator for your code				

Summary

In this chapter, we have seen common security standards and how to apply them in our .NET MAUI application that uses AI services. We have seen some common attacks and how to avoid them, together with encryption practices. We reviewed best practices around authentication, authorization, and input validation. We also looked into logs or updates to make our app always up-to-date. We reviewed some privacy and compliance tokens and viewed some obfuscation practices. By the end of the chapter, a security checklist is ready for you to start checking your app.

In the next chapter, we will see how to get our app to the stores. From deployment best practices, assets, and permissions, we will see all we need to have the application in the hands of our users.

Deploying AI-Powered .NET MAUI Apps

Introduction

In this chapter, you will get an overview of how to easily deploy your .NET MAUI application and prepare it for the stores. We will review the deployment steps for .NET MAUI apps and some of the best practices. I bet you have your development environment set up based on the platforms you need to target. If you might be pretty new to .NET MAUI or need a refresh, go to `https://learn.microsoft.com/en-us/ dotnet/maui/get-started/first-app?tabs=vswin&pivots=devices-android`.

Now that we have our beautiful .NET MAUI app that is rich in AI features, we are ready to make it available to our users. We will focus on our app, but I recommend you apply best practices for your back end, too, to have the full ecosystem ready. I have recently used ASP.NET Core as a back end to rely on all .NET features, which I love and prefer. You can find more on ASP.NET Core at `https://learn.microsoft.com/en-us/ aspnet/core/host-and-deploy/`. Feel free to use your existing back end too or create it in your preferred framework and host it on your production environment.

Don't Forget to Test Your Application

Testing your .NET MAUI application that uses AI is crucial as we want to make sure our API AI calls, UIs, and all the cross-platform behaviors work correctly.

We might start with manual testing to ensure that our app runs on our Windows machine, Android emulators, and physical devices, along with macOS and iOS simulators, iPhones, and iPads. We will also verify that all our AI requests work correctly and UI responds to them.

© Codrina Merigo 2026
C. Merigo, *AI-Enabled Apps with .NET MAUI*, https://doi.org/10.1007/979-8-8688-1817-2_15

It is important to check that our devices have Internet access, as mainly our AI APIs are online services from different providers. We need to ensure that the requests to the AI API won't cause errors that can stuck our UI or make it crash. We don't want our features to seem broken without properly handling all the offline scenarios. We can also save battery life and data usage by avoiding unnecessary API calls. It is important to provide clear feedback to the user if they are offline so they can try again later.

We can verify and test during debugging too, use lots of breakpoints, and watch variables to inspect our data and responses from the APIs. Something I use a lot is the Hot Reload feature, I think is my preferred feature while working on UIs that changes and adapt based on API responses.

Unit test helps us test all our API calls and the logic we have added in our methods and classes. We can use xUnit and create a separate Unit Test Project in our solution. We can also use device runners to run our tests. Running tests on a device does more than just verify your logic—it also lets you see how your code performs in a real environment. However, this comes at a cost: tests take longer to execute, and you always have to wait for the device or emulator to start before interacting with it.

For this reason, it's best to reserve device runners for situations where your code specifically depends on the device SDK or when you want to confirm that your code runs correctly on a particular test device. For most other tests, running them locally without a device is faster and more efficient. To learn more about unit testing, you can go to `https://learn.microsoft.com/dotnet/maui/deployment/unit-testing?view=net-maui-9.0`.

UI testing is what brought me into conferences and speaking during Xamarin.Forms era and of course is also very important in .NET MAUI. It allows you to test your UI flows, components, and behaviors cross-platform. You can use Appium, a UI test framework that provides us with the tools to interact with our UI. It is important that all your UI elements have the `AutomationId` property set with a unique value. This property will become your best friend while writing UI tests. You can learn more about UI testing in .NET MAUI at `https://learn.microsoft.com/samples/dotnet/maui-samples/uitest-appium-nunit/`.

Last, but maybe our most important test while working with AI services are the integration tests. We will need to make sure that our AI APIs work together with our UI all the time, that we have the expected results, and that our UI displays the AI API's response as we want. For testing, we can always use dependency injection to mock our AI data.

We have seen in the previous chapter that security is very important, and vulnerabilities might be around the corner. For this reason, it's important to perform also penetration testing (pen tests) for our .NET MAUI app that will scan the app and perform security checks. In enterprise setup, regular pen tests are required and can be performed by specialized companies.

AI-Specific Checks

Now that we have tested our AI API calls and the app on all the platforms, it is important to check that our API keys are not in our codebase, but correctly stored in the Secure Storage, Key Vault, or similar structures. As we are using AI and user data, it is important to check that we have our privacy policy and all the personal data handling information, not just for local compliance purposes, but also the app stores require them if your app uses AI. For Google Play and iOS App Store, we can check the data safety section for developers and the privacy requirements. For example, Apple has strict guidelines and may reject applications that make overblown, exaggerated, or unverifiable AI promises. Similarly, Google Play will not accept apps that contain false or misleading claims about AI capabilities. This is why it's essential to use AI services responsibly: focus on creating features that are truthful, transparent, and genuinely useful to your users. Make sure any AI-powered functionality clearly communicates what it can and cannot do, avoid overpromising results, and always design your app with user benefit, safety, and reliability in mind. Responsible use of AI not only helps your app get approved on app stores but also builds trust and credibility with your audience.

After running our tests, we can start monitoring usage on platforms like Azure, OpenAI, or Google. This helps us track how the app is performing in real-world conditions and gives a clear understanding of the associated running costs, allowing us to manage resources efficiently and plan for scaling if needed.

Check Your App Accessibility

Accessibility in .NET MAUI is all about making sure your apps can be enjoyed by everyone, no matter their abilities or the situations they find themselves in. Think of it as designing your app so that people who rely on screen readers, high-contrast themes, keyboard navigation, voice commands, or even gestures can all have a smooth experience.

It's not just about following the law, though complying with accessibility standards like Web Content Accessibility Guidelines or Americans with Disabilities Act is important—it's also about reaching the widest possible audience and creating a better user experience for everyone.

As we saw briefly in Chapter 6, semantic properties in .NET MAUI, like `SemanticProperties.Description`, are a key part of this, helping screen readers understand your UI controls. This is where AI can be a real game-changer.

Imagine your app automatically generating meaningful descriptions for images so that visually impaired users can understand the content without any extra work from you, or AI-powered text-to-speech reading out app content, while speech recognition allows users to interact with your app using their voice.

AI can even analyze your UI to detect low-contrast text, missing labels, or small touch targets and suggest improvements, making accessibility much easier to implement. Beyond that, AI can personalize the app experience dynamically, adjusting font sizes, simplifying content, or offering hints and guidance based on how users interact with your app.

In .NET MAUI, you can take advantage of semantic properties, add meaningful labels and automation IDs for clarity, and use AI tools to check contrast and accessibility across your UI. In this way, you can create apps that are inclusive, intuitive, and delightful for every single user, helping your app reach its full potential while truly making a difference in people's lives.

You can find out more on accessibility in your .NET MAUI app and also an accessibility checklist at `https://learn.microsoft.com/dotnet/maui/fundamentals/accessibility?view=net-maui-9.0`.

Check App Permissions

Since our app uses different AI services and interacts with device features, it's essential to enable the necessary permissions in each platform's manifest. At a minimum, Internet access must be granted so the app can communicate with AI services for processing data, generating responses, or fetching results. Additionally, depending on the functionality of your app, you may need to request access to device cameras (for taking pictures or scanning), microphone (for recording voice or audio commands), and storage or media library (for saving photos, videos, or other content). Properly declaring these permissions ensures that the app can fully utilize AI features while complying with platform security and privacy policies, and it also helps avoid runtime errors or store rejections. For windows apps, capabilities must be declared in the app manifest and the system will prompt the user when the feature is first accessed. In Android, you can set your permissions in the `AndroidManifest.xml`, while on iOS, you can set the description in `Info.plist` file; otherwise, your app will crash when accessing the feature. For macOS, you can set the permission in the `Entitlements.plist` file. You can learn more about permissions at `https://learn.microsoft.com/en-us/dotnet/maui/platform-integration/appmodel/permissions?view=net-maui-9.0&tabs=android`.

Remember to request only the permissions your application actually needs in order to maintain compliance and avoid store rejections.

If you are implementing offline AI in a .NET MAUI app, there are several important considerations to ensure your app runs smoothly and efficiently across devices:

1. **Mind the Model Size**: Mobile devices and low-end hardware may struggle with very large models, so optimize or compress them to reduce memory usage and load times.

2. **Optimize Performance**: Leverage hardware acceleration (e.g., GPU delegates on Android, CoreML on iOS) to significantly speed up inference.

3. **Plan for Model Updates**: Even when AI runs locally, provide a mechanism to download new model versions when the device is online, so the app can improve without a full reinstall.

4. **Test Across All Platforms**: Differences in CPU architecture, memory, and supported libraries mean behavior may vary between Windows, Android, and iOS. Test broadly to ensure consistency.

5. **Consider a Hybrid Approach**: Use offline AI for fast, real-time predictions and cloud AI for compute-heavy tasks, giving users the best of both worlds.

6. **Protect Privacy and Device Storage**: Keep sensitive data on the device and avoid storing unnecessary large datasets that could affect storage or performance.

By carefully addressing these aspects, you can deliver robust, reliable, and efficient offline AI experience in your MAUI applications.

Get Your Assets Ready

Our app is visual first–icons, logos, and visual assets will greet your user as soon as they will download and install your application. When we prepare the app for deployment, all the visual assets are also important for the store's approval. Each platform we target has a specific requirement and specific store guidelines.

Our app icon is the first thing our users see, both on the stores page and on the device home screen. We need to make sure our image files are high-resolution, while we keep our design recognizable. Our app icon will have multiple sizes, and we can use vector graphics (SVG) for our icons and all over our .NET MAUI app. .NET MAUI automatically converts SVG files to PNG when building your app. This means that when you add an SVG to your MAUI project, you should reference it in XAML or C# using a .png extension, not .svg. The original SVG file itself only needs to be included in your project file; you don't need to reference it anywhere else.

The second graphic our users see, while we load our magic in the background, is the splash screen. While it is important to keep our loading time minimal, we can keep the user entertainment with a simple branding screen or some sneak-peak text information of our application.

Other assets for the stores include screenshots, store graphics, or store listing images. Make sure you check the right format and resolution for your assets to ensure compliance with the store requirements and that your application looks awesome on every screen and every device.

Your Apps Metadata Is Who You Are

Before moving to the code preparation itself, it is important to prepare all your metadata carefully. Metadata includes everything that describes your app to users and app stores: the app name, description, screenshots, icons, category, keywords, privacy policy, support URLs, and release notes. Each platform—Android, iOS, macOS, Windows, and Tizen—has specific requirements and recommended sizes for these assets. Well-prepared metadata ensures that your app is discoverable, professional-looking, and compliant with store guidelines. It also helps users understand your app's features, encourages downloads, and reduces the likelihood of rejections during review. Maintaining consistency in app name, versioning, and branding across platforms is critical to provide a seamless multiplatform experience and build trust with your users.

Remember to be consistent across platforms and provide accurate descriptions to convey the value of your app clearly. Make sure you update your metadata as the app evolves or each time important features are added.

Get Your Certificates

We have seen in the previous chapters the importance of security and certificates. When deploying a .NET MAUI app, certificates and signing keys are essential to ensure your app is trusted, secure, and accepted by app stores and devices. Each platform has specific requirements: on Android, a keystore (.jks) signs your app to verify your identity and allow future updates; on iOS and macOS, Apple requires development and distribution certificates along with provisioning profiles to bind your app ID and devices; for Windows, a code-signing certificate (.pfx) is needed to verify authenticity and generate the MSIX package; and on Tizen, a Tizen certificate profile signs your .tpk package for device and store recognition. Proper certificate management ensures that your app can be installed on real devices, submitted to stores, and updated in the future. It's important to keep certificates secure, back them up, and differentiate between development and distribution certificates to avoid mistakes.

Prepare Your Accounts and Packages

Your app is beautiful, tested, and checked, and your privacy documents are all set. Now is the time to have your developer accounts ready for app stores' publishing. You already have your Azure, OpenAI, or Google Gemini account to handle your API and API keys.

Based on your application or if you want to target all platforms, you will need an Apple developer account, Google Play developer account, Microsoft Partner Center account, or Samsung developer account if you target also the Tizen devices.

You can also generate certificates from the developer portals that you will use to sign your app packages before the submission.

Now you are ready to begin the deployment process. For each platform, you must ensure that your app is properly configured, including manifest files, permissions, icons, splash screens, and store metadata such as descriptions and screenshots. On Android, you will generate a signed **.aab** file and upload it to the Google Play Console, specifying app details, pricing, and distribution regions. On iOS, you must archive the app as an **.ipa** file and upload it through App Store Connect or Transporter, ensuring that provisioning profiles, certificates, and bundle identifiers are correctly set up and optionally using TestFlight for beta testing before final release. For macOS, you create a signed **.pkg** or **.app** archive and submit it via the Mac App Store using App Store Connect, following Apple's guidelines for notarization and distribution. For Tizen, you generate a signed **.tpk** package and submit it via the Samsung Galaxy Store Seller Portal, ensuring compliance with Samsung's platform requirements. On Windows, you will create a **.msixupload** package and submit it to the Microsoft Partner Center, configuring store details, capabilities, and versioning. For Tizen, you generate a signed **.tpk** package and submit it via the **Samsung Galaxy Store Seller Portal**, ensuring compliance with Samsung's platform requirements. Throughout the process, it's important to verify that all platform-specific requirements are met, such as privacy policies, AI or device permissions, and app functionality, so that the app passes review and becomes available to users on the respective stores efficiently and without delays.

Keeping your app's version consistent across all platforms is a simple but important practice when deploying a .NET MAUI app to multiple stores. Since your app shares the same core code but runs on iOS, macOS, Android, Windows, and Tizen, it's helpful for users to clearly see which version they're using and know it matches the latest updates. Consistent versioning also makes bug tracking, support, release notes, and user communication much easier.

For instance, if you release version **1.1.0** (first digit is usually the major version, second digit indicates a minor version, and third digit is usually used for patches) on Android, it's a good idea to use the same version on iOS, macOS, Windows, and Tizen. This includes both the version number and the build number, which some platforms, like iOS, use internally. Keeping these aligned prevents confusion, avoids support burden from mismatched features, and ensures that analytics, crash reports, and user feedback correspond to the correct release across all devices.

A practical way to do this is by maintaining a central versioning file or configuration in your MAUI project that automatically updates the version and builds number for each platform during the build. This makes sure that every app store shows the same release and keeps multiplatform management smooth, simple, and reliable.

Conquer the World with Your App

Your app is ready now to be submitted to the stores. After submitting a .NET MAUI app, each platform conducts its own review process before making the app available to users. On Google Play, the review usually takes a few hours to a couple of days, focusing on compliance with content policies, functionality, and security; once approved, the app can be published immediately or scheduled for a later release. Apple's App Store and macOS App Store tend to have a longer review cycle, often ranging from one to three days (and sometimes longer for first submissions), as Apple carefully checks performance, user experience, privacy, and compliance; once approved, you can either release right away, set a specific date, or use phased release to gradually roll out the app. On Windows, Microsoft typically reviews apps within a day, validating security, packaging, and store requirements before publishing in the Microsoft Store. Samsung's Tizen Store also requires review of the signed TPK package, which can take a few days, ensuring compatibility and guideline compliance before publishing in the Galaxy Store.

These review times vary depending on factors such as account reputation, app complexity, or the store's current workload, so it's always a good idea to plan for some buffer time before major release dates. Don't panic if your app gets rejected; review the comments and send it again. On some stores, you can also book time with the team to review the submission.

And once your app has passed all these steps—complete with testing, certificates, icons, metadata, and store reviews—it's finally out there. Your AI-enabled .NET MAUI app is now ready to conquer the world, reaching users across platforms and devices with a single codebase. By combining cross-platform reach with the power of AI, it can deliver smarter, more personalized, and engaging experiences. With this, your app is not only fulfilling its mission to deliver value but also leveraging intelligent capabilities to stand out, adapt, and truly make an impact as it begins its journey in the hands of real people.

Summary

In this chapter, we have seen how to bring our AI-enabled .NET MAUI app to production. We have seen the importance of testing the application, how to check on some specific AI settings, and ensuring our app has the right permissions set. We then reviewed how to prepare our assets and metadata, together with their importance. Lastly, we have reviewed the accounts and store details necessary to get the app live on the stores.

In the next chapter, we will bring together everything we have seen across the different chapters. We will reflect on how AI can empower and enrich your application. I promise you it won't be a boring summary, but more a look ahead of this technology and an invitation to continue your AI journey beyond the examples of this book.

CHAPTER 16

Conclusion

If you reached this last chapter, I first want to thank you so much for coming with me along this journey. Then, I also hope that you had fun and curiosity reading this book. Even if this book was scribbled in a notebook, now it is finally ready for you. The aim was to give you insights on AI and how you can use it with .NET MAUI, my and maybe your favorite framework.

At this point you might ask: *Codrina where is my AI assistant?*

It is just hidden inside all the previous chapters. When I was signing the structure of the contents, I thought about an app that would look like Figure 16-1.

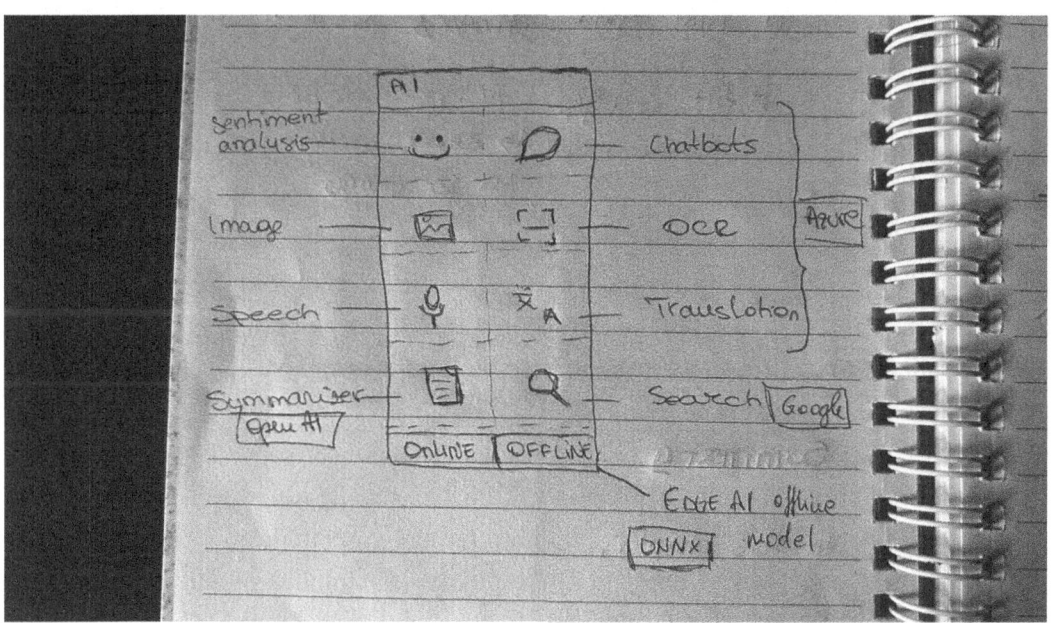

Figure 16-1. *Concept UI assistant app*

© Codrina Merigo 2026
C. Merigo, *AI-Enabled Apps with .NET MAUI*, https://doi.org/10.1007/979-8-8688-1817-2_16

This is the UI I had in mind for our assistant. So, if we just get all the examples and put them in a big .NET MAUI project, we have our AI assistant. An assistant that can *feel* as we have seen in Chapter 4. An assistant that contains different chatbots as in Chapter5. An assistant that can *see* through the device camera as in Chapters 6 and 7. It can also *hear* and *speak* thanks to speech recognition from Chapter 8. An assistant that has powerful *translation* capabilities described in Chapter 9. Also, an assistant that can *summarize* long text as we have seen in Chapter 10. It also has powerful *search* features and can search inside our knowledge base as demonstrated in Chapter 11. And maybe, one of my favorite features: it can also *work offline* and use *our* own models as we showed in Chapter 12.

If you take these examples, put them together and use the information available in Chapter 13, Chapter 14, and Chapter 15, your assistant is ready to be distributed on your preferred app store. You have all you need to write your app. I could have created a full one, but I preferred to keep the focus on AI and how to integrate it into a .NET MAUI app.

Another great feature that I love about AI is that you can mix and match all the services to tailor them to your needs. For example, a smart meeting assistant can transcribe audio using Speech-to-Text, analyze sentiment, and extract key phrases with Text Analytics, summarize discussions and generate action items via Azure OpenAI, translate content for multilingual teams using Translator, and index transcripts for easy retrieval with Cognitive Search. Similarly, customer support bots leverage OpenAI for natural responses, Text Analytics to detect sentiment, Computer Vision to analyze images sent by customers, and Form Recognizer to extract structured data from documents, while Speech Services enable voice interactions. It is important that you frame your problem that you want to solve with AI, then you can search through all the models available for the ones that fit your scenario and your needs. You can also adapt an existing model or create your own, as we have seen in Chapter 11.

.NET MAUI and AI are continuously evolving and might converge at some time to define modern app development. In Visual Studio, we can already experience that with GitHub Copilot or different extensions available. I really think that soon we will see more applications that not only work cross-platform but are also intelligent and capable of amazing things. AI models are also evolving their power, while shrinking in size, so they can run smoothly on the user's devices.

I also want to invite you to reach out if you have ideas or just for a chat about .NET MAUI and AI and how you have used the examples in this book or how you have mixed the AI services in your application.

Last, I want to share with you my favorite quote from Seneca:

Every new beginning comes from some other beginning's end.

In the same way, every project, application, and chapter we complete opens the door to new opportunities and discoveries. I hope that this book has not only provided you with practical knowledge and tools but also inspired you to continue exploring, building, and learning. Every ending is just the start of your next adventure in AI and .NET MAUI.

Index

A

.aab, 5, 277
ActivityIndicator, 29
Advanced Encryption Standard, 260
AES-256, 260
AI agents, 220
AI-generated content, 22, 29–34
AI + machine learning, 20, 74
AI models, 18–19, 201, 205, 220, 221,
      223–244, 253, 282
AI pattern, 203
AI Pope Act, 251–252
AI-powered content summarizer, 189–201
AI-powered translations, 171–187
AI services, 13, 15, 19–23, 28–31, 34, 35,
      37–39, 61, 71, 120, 159, 173, 223,
      245, 246, 250, 261, 268,
      272–274, 282
AI translation, 171–187
Alternate text, 107, 109, 110
Android, 3–8, 11, 13, 70, 120, 159, 165, 205,
      225, 226, 244, 259, 271, 275,
      277, 278
Android JDK, 8
AndroidManifest.xml, 123, 146, 159, 242,
      259, 275
Android phone, 123, 147
Android SDK, 8, 9, 70
API responses, 24, 59, 194, 272
APIs, 4, 19, 23, 64, 89, 111, 137, 151, 173,
      189, 203, 225, 250, 253, 271
.app, 278

Appium, 272
App permissions, 274–275
Artificial intelligence (AI), 13, 15, 23, 55,
      73, 109, 138, 151, 171, 190, 203,
      223, 245, 253, 271
Artificial neural networks (ANNs), 18, 172
ASP.NET Core identity, 261
ASP.NET Core Web API, 220
async, 29, 41, 46, 50
AudioManager, 163, 169
Authentication, 28–53, 261, 268
Azure, 9, 20, 21, 30, 34, 36, 61, 62, 73, 74,
      79, 83–85, 91, 113, 154, 159, 161,
      163, 174, 190, 223, 227, 273, 277
Azure AI, 13, 15, 19–21, 28, 34–46, 53, 124,
      133, 135, 138, 147, 150, 151, 153,
      190, 227
Azure AI Bot Service, 73
Azure AI Foundry, 20, 84, 85
Azure AI Language, 55, 57–58, 71, 174
Azure AI Speech Service, 151, 152, 170
Azure AI Studio, 84
Azure AI translation service, 170, 171
Azure AI Translator, 173, 187
Azure AI Vision Image Analysis, 148
Azure AI Vision optical character
      recognition, 137
Azure AI Vision Studio, 110, 111, 138
Azure bot, 74, 75, 77
Azure chatbot, 74–79
Azure Custom Vision, 141, 225, 227
Azure endpoint, 30

285

© Codrina Merigo 2026
C. Merigo, *AI-Enabled Apps with .NET MAUI*, https://doi.org/10.1007/979-8-8688-1817-2

The manufacturer's authorised representative in the EU is Springer
Nature Customer Service Centre GmbH, Europaplatz 3, 69115 Heidelberg,
Germany. If you have any concerns regarding our products, please
contact ProductSafety@springernature.com

Printed and bound by CPI Group (UK) Ltd, Croydon, CR0 4YY
23/04/2026
02095592-0019